BRANDS IN THE BALANCE

Meeting the challenges to commercial identity

KEVIN DRAWBAUGH

REUTERS

Published by **Pearson Education**
London / New York / San Francisco / Toronto / Sydney / Tokyo / Singapore
Hong Kong / Cape Town / Madrid / Paris / Milan / Munich / Amsterdam

PEARSON EDUCATION LIMITED

Head Office:
Edinburgh Gate
Harlow CM20 2JE
Tel: +44 (0)1279 623623
Fax: +44 (0)1279 431059

London Office:
128 Long Acre
London WC2E 9AN
Tel: +44 (0)20 7447 2000
Fax: +44 (0)20 7240 5771
Website: www.business-minds.com
....

First published in Great Britain in 2001

The right of Kevin Drawbaugh to be identified as author
of this work has been asserted by him in accordance
with the Copyright, Designs and Patents Act 1988.

ISBN 0 273 65035 1

British Library Cataloguing in Publication Data
A CIP catalogue record for this book can be obtained from the British Library

10 9 8 7 6 5 4 3 2 1

Typeset by Pantek Arts Ltd, Maidstone, Kent
Printed and bound in Great Britain by Biddles Ltd, Guildford, Surrey.

The Publishers' policy is to use paper manufactured from sustainable forests.

ABOUT THE AUTHOR

Kevin Drawbaugh has written about business for seven years as a correspondent for Reuters in New York, Chicago and London. His work has appeared in newspapers worldwide, including *The New York Times*, *The Washington Post* and *The Wall Street Journal*. He was formerly an editor and reporter covering business and government for daily newspapers in Indiana, Maryland and Virginia. He holds degrees in US history from Indiana University and in economics and communication from American University in Washington, DC. He lives near London with his wife and two sons.

For my dear Margaret, with love and thanks

CONTENTS

FOREWORD

THERE'S NOT MUCH PRODUCT DIFFERENTIATION among colas or beers or computers. The same can be said for services such as health care or airlines or long-distance telephones. Yet the makers and providers of these products and services would be fools not to claim that their products – or the companies themselves – are truly special. Otherwise, a company's product or service is dismissed as a commodity, which is typically bought at the lowest price.

Branding, or imbuing a product, service or entire company with special qualities, helps to insulate a company from the downward spiral of price competition. But as Kevin Drawbaugh so insightfully notes in this book, brands have to do much more than protect the price of a product.

Brands must deftly transcend international borders, they must help consumers navigate the consumption landscape and they must convey a sense of prestige, power, sex appeal or friendliness. It's an enormously expensive, complex process. And as Drawbaugh writes, branding is not without its risks. Successful brands must be ready to accept the socio-cultural consequences and obligations that go with that enormous power. Beware the backlash.

The case histories in this book, drawn from the experiences of 20 of the world's leading brands, underscore how vital a well-managed brand is to success in the 21st century. *Brands in the Balance* is a book written by a journalist who's reported from both side of the Atlantic and will well serve marketers anywhere in the world faced with the daunting challenge of nurturing a brand.

Edmund Lawler
Advertising columnist, Advertising Age's Business-to-Business *magazine*
and author of Underdog Marketing

ACKNOWLEDGEMENTS

Thank you to Reuters for giving me the opportunity to tackle this project. I am indebted to Alexander Smith, Hester Abrams and everyone on the European equities desk for their support. Special thanks to Julie Steenhuysen, my colleague in Chicago, and Joe Ortiz, my colleague in London, for their assistance. I am grateful for the support and guidance of Izabel Grindal, Elaine Herlihy, Mary-Ellen Barker, Keith Stafford, and Michael Stott at Reuters, as well as Martin Drewe, Linda Dhondy, Jason Bennett, and Josephine Bryan at Pearson. Paul Scruton and Corrie Parsonson deserve applause for their work on the graphics.

This book could not have been written without the assistance and co-operation of the people at the companies involved, including those executives named in the text and those unnamed: Tomaso Galli in Florence; Alain-Serge Delaitte, Lorrain Kressman and Hugh Morrison in Paris; Michiel Berssenbrugge in Amsterdam; Jeff Prescott in Nashville; Mary Auvin in St Paul; John Dreyer in Los Angeles; Nissa Anklesaria in Santa Clara; and Dominic Shales, Emma Baptist, Alison Crombie, Dora McCabe, Shirley-Anne Mcandrew, Mike Haines, Clare Dimond, Sarah Longhorn, James Rothnie and Paul Pendergrass in London.

Finally, my love and thanks go to my wife and sons for their patience.

JUMPING ON THE BRAND WAGON

'Brand! Brand!! Brand!!! That's the message ... for the late '90s and beyond'

Tom Peters, in *The Circle of Innovation*, 1997

I DROVE OUR RENTED MINIVAN out of Malaga airport and pointed it towards Granada, anticipating a long-awaited family rendezvous with Spanish history. I wanted to share with my wife and two sons a cherished fascination with the Alhambra.

Cruising down the highway under a bright Mediterranean sun, I told them about the Moors and the Christians, about Ferdinand and Isabella, about Washington Irving and his timeless story of the mighty hilltop fortress. There was no sound from the safety seats in the back. Finally, one of the boys gleefully exclaimed, 'Hey, look Dad, there's a Toys R Us! Cool!'

Sure enough, there it was – the familiar gawking grin of Geoffrey the Giraffe. Down the road were billboards for Ford, Volkswagen, Fanta Orange, Pizza Hut. Soon appeared the inevitable Golden Arches and I was fending off desperate pleas for Happy Meals. This was exotic Spain? Indeed it was. But, in some ways, it could have been Illinois or Italy or Mexico or Japan.

Brands are everywhere today, in distant lands you might not expect and in familiar places. Stickers on the soccer goals at my sons' school chirpily proclaim, 'Coca-Cola, Enjoy!' Brands are plastered all over clothing, household items, buildings, buses, taxis, train carriages. On the internet they pop up out of nowhere trying to sell you something. The world is under brand bombardment.

Why? Because brands – the ideas, words, graphic designs and sounds that symbolize products, services and the companies behind them – are *the* hot idea in business today.

The world is speeding into the information age. Style is taking a seat next to substance and the language of commerce is shifting to images and perceptions from nuts and bolts. As a result, everyone is jumping on the brand wagon. Not just the usual consumer goods companies, but banks, brokers, insurers, utilities, publishers, athletes, accountants, lawyers, artists, musicians, governments, charities – all see a strong brand as vital to success in the post-industrial economy.

Brands are bigger than ever, but as a result it is also true that more than ever is expected of them. From the boardroom and the supermarket to the internet and the city streets, new challenges are confronting brands and pushing the booming field of brand management toward a critical juncture. Consumers and citizens want brands that are more helpful and trustworthy. Businesses want brands to be more accountable and coherent, while the web presents an entirely new array of demands.

As a business journalist in Europe and the United States I have written about brands for many years. In interview after interview with brand managers I have noticed patterns in situations remembered, strategies and tactics described, outcomes explained. *Brands in the Balance* is about those patterns and what they mean to brand marketing. The book is meant for anyone interested in brands, but primarily for those who study and manage them. In a journalistic style, *Brands in the Balance* takes the pulse of branding at the beginning of a new century and presents 20 case studies based on interviews with leaders on both sides of the Atlantic, including:

- Michael Eisner, CEO of US entertainment and media legend Walt Disney Co.;
- Bernard Arnault, CEO of French luxury goods conglomerate LVMH;
- Domenico De Sole, CEO of Italian design and fashion powerhouse Gucci Group;
- Patrick Ricard, CEO of venerable French spirits group Pernod Ricard;
- Jack Keenan, deputy CEO of the world's largest spirits business, Britain's Diageo;
- Stelios Haji-Ioannou, CEO of upstart UK budget airline easyJet;

- Charlie Frenette, president of the European unit of US soft drinks leader Coca-Cola Co.;
- Alan Harris, president of the European unit of US food group Kellogg Co.;
- Clive Butler, corporate development director at Anglo-Dutch consumer goods group Unilever;
- Karen Edwards, vice-president of marketing at US internet powerhouse Yahoo!;
- David Powell, vice-president of marketing at US diversified manufacturer 3M;
- Daniel Gestetner, CEO of UK-based start-up internet shopping portal ShopSmart;
- Rita Clifton, CEO of UK-based brand consulting firm Interbrand;
- Linda Wolf, CEO of advertising agency Leo Burnett USA.

These branding masters spoke at length with me about how they deal with the demands put on the commercial identities under their supervision. The kinds of stories they had to tell cannot be found in how-to management manuals or academic treatises on theory. There are many such books, some of them valuable and written by eminent experts. But, unlike them, *Brands in the Balance* paints a portrait of the most urgent issues in branding with stories of real brands and real people struggling to come to grips with real challenges.

Brands in the Balance is divided into four sections. Each one begins with a brief analysis surveying opinions and trends in brand marketing, targeting four main problem areas:

1 **In the company**. Inside the firms they serve, brands are increasingly seen as important and measurable assets involved in real economic growth. As a result, performance targets are ratcheting upwards. Marketing departments are being held more accountable. Corporate structures are shifting to make brands more central, with direct responsibility for them held all the way up the chain of command.

In some firms, brands are coming to be seen as organizational ideals that embody the best of the business, demanding careful handling and rigorous protection. The days when the brand was just a catchy slogan and a clever logo cooked up by some suede-shoe creatives in marketing are over. CEOs are in on the act. So are accountants and bankers. Quantitative systems for measuring brand value are emerging and brand managers are having to meet stricter standards.

2 **In the marketplace.** In consumer markets, brands face unprecedented difficulty in winning and keeping public attention. Amid a rising flood of media and messages, brands have to work harder than ever to stand out with meaningful messages that are unique and appealing.

Within this context, an urgent question about globalization is being asked. It is clear to many in brand marketing that the American moment of the 1990s is over. A reaction against US power brands is setting in. European and Asian cultures are reasserting their individuality after a decade of post-Cold-War enthusiasm for all things Uncle Sam, causing governments and consumers to question and resist the swaggering ways of US global brand owners.

> **66** Brands have to work harder than ever to stand out with meaningful messages that are unique and appealing. **99**

Yet, at the same time, the formerly paper-thin veneer of one-world culture is thickening. As transportation, communication and entertainment continue to unify the planet, international brand owners are struggling to balance global efficiencies with respect for local tastes and habits.

Underlying these challenges, of course, is the constant imperative of keeping focused on the basics. In trying to deal with new problems, brand managers too often lose sight of the fundamental keys to branding. A company that can keep the basic tenets in mind, while balancing the global–local issue, and breaking through the ever-growing brand clutter with a unique, useful and trustworthy message, is the company that can succeed in today's branding marketplace.

3 **On the internet.** The e-brand revolution is accelerating the speed with which brands can be introduced and brought to the awareness of the consuming public. For a time, it looked as if e-brands would destroy other old notions about branding. But such revolutionary talk has eased as some high-flying e-brands have crashed to Earth, vindicating time-honoured notions about brand perception. For the e-brands, the new challenge is to differentiate and make themselves better understood.

4 In society. With traditional institutions such as church, family and community in decline in some parts of the world, growing numbers of people look to commercial brands to help them define their personal identities. Some consumers – especially in the USA, Western Europe and Japan – unconsciously gauge their worth by the branded material goods they are able to amass. The right brands bespeak wealth and wealth bespeaks success. Economist Thorstein Veblen's conspicuous consumption theory is alive and well and thriving.

At the same time, some young people in developed societies are rejecting major brands as emblematic of established power. Some brands are being targeted for rebellion and violence, as seen in 1999 and 2000. McDonald's restaurants were bombed by terrorists in Athens and attacked by farmers in France, 'anti-capitalists' in Prague and animal activists in Belgium. Rioters in London and Seattle ransacked outlets of Nike, The Gap, Starbucks and Mercedes.

At either end of these two extremes – from the materialistic status-seeker with a Gold Card, to the idealistic vandal with a baseball bat – the picture is one of individuals reacting to commercial identities with strong emotions and seeking to define themselves through them.

A further consequence of the social brand backlash is that some brands are being targeted by a new class of social and environmental activists. Web-savvy and brand-smart, these gadflies cunningly promote their own agendas by piggy-backing on the notoriety of top brands through boycotts, pickets and physical attacks. These activists know they can gain maximum publicity by targeting brands because big brands win big headlines. The most effective   strategy for dealing with the growing social challenge in front of branding is not an easy one and involves nothing less than changing the culture of business.

Taken together, these four fundamental challenges are sorely testing the vision and skill of brand managers. But they are also having the indirectly beneficial impact of forcing brand owners and managers to step back and reassess what their brands, and their companies, really stand for.

MEDIATING ON NEW LEVELS

The overarching trend in all of this is that brands now mediate between consumers and businesses on more than one level. In the information society, brands still serve their traditional role as symbolic proxies for goods and services, conveying information about them to the market-place and relaying consumers' responses back to companies through sales and market data.

But brands do rather more than that today. They have come to represent not only particular goods and services, but also discrete sets of consumer awareness and understanding of corporate ethics, politics, behaviour and image, environmental responsibility, employee relations, even the personalities of top executives, whether it is Bill Gates at Microsoft or Richard Branson at Virgin. All these issues and perceptions, embodied in the brand, now stand in the dock for public judgement.

Brands act as the conduits through which better-educated consumers communicate back to businesses their raised expectations of what business should be and should do. As a result, brands hold the companies that own them more accountable than ever before to broader social and cultural standards. In a world in which people know more about business, and in which a business *is* its brand, any company seeking the competitive advantage conferred by a strong brand must be ready to accept the socio-cultural consequences and obligations that go with that economic power.

Branding's champions and critics alike are waking up to this reality and realizing that brands matter, not just to the bottom line, but to every-one. 'Although people pretend this is not the case, business runs the world ... So, if the world needs changing and business runs the world, then we need to change business', observed Rita Clifton, CEO of the consulting firm Interbrand and one of the field's most incisive thinkers, in an interview. She went on:

❝Brands matter, not just to the bottom line, but to everyone.❞

'The way business connects through its customers is through its brands. Now, I like a world in which every business, every corporation, indeed every organization is accountable for something. And the people they're account-able to are its customers, its observers, its employees. The way to symbolize that contract of trust is through a brand.'

Brand managers that understand and adjust to this emerging environment will prosper, and possibly even help make the world a better place; those that do not could be in trouble.

Linda Wolf, CEO of the advertising agency Leo Burnett USA in Chicago, put it this way in an interview:

'Consumers today, I think, are going to be a lot harder on brands than they ever have been in the past when they don't deliver on their promise because they just know so much more. The internet is making everyone a savvier consumer ... Companies, marketers have to be a lot more diligent and careful about how they're handling their brands.'

BRANDS THEN

To understand where brands are now and where they are headed, it is important to understand where they have been. Brands started out as a simple form of commercial communication. Craftspeople and farmers as far back as the Greek and Roman empires put identifying marks on their goods before sending them to market. It was not until the early 19th century that tobacco, patent medicine and soap makers developed the first true mass-market brands with uniform packages and proper advertising campaigns.

National brands became established in the USA and Europe towards the end of the 19th century. Forces helping them along included better transportation and communication, efficient assembly-line production and packaging systems and changes in trademark law that gave brands new protections.

Advertising spread as literacy rates rose. Mass retailers shouldered aside the general store. The US population exploded with immigration, providing large markets open to mass merchandising. Some of today's top brands were already established in the 1890s, such as American Express, Coca-Cola, Heinz, Ivory soap, Kodak, Lipton's teas, Quaker Oats, Sears Roebuck and Shredded Wheat. Mass-market brands expanded into the new century, but suffered in the Great Depression in the 1930s.

Retailers gained power over national manufacturers and developed the first in-store brands, often dropping manufacturers' rivals. At the same time, many people during the Depression stopped paying attention to advertising, which came to be seen as deceitful and tasteless in a time of widespread disenchantment with capitalism and free enterprise (as noted by Dartmouth College marketing professor Kevin Lane Keller[1]).

During this difficult period brand management was born. In 1931 Neil McElroy, a junior marketing manager at Cincinnati consumer goods giant Procter & Gamble Co. (P&G), wrote a memorandum proposing a brand-focused management system for Camay soap (as described by University of California-Berkeley marketing professor David Aaker[2]). Camay was then P&G's leading product. McElroy was dissatisfied with the haphazard way that it was marketed. He proposed hiring a full-time 'brand man', an 'assistant brand man' and field employees. Their duties would be to monitor Camay sales and shipments, assess and improve advertising effectiveness, manage an advertising budget, and communicate market data and branding programmes and priorities to personnel throughout the company from production to administration.

The now famous McElroy memo became the model for the classic brand management system – also sometimes known as the P&G system – that was the benchmark for decades after the Second World War. Thousands of firms imitated P&G and prospered. Brands led the way in a vast expansion of the post-war consumer economy. McElroy became CEO of P&G, and later US secretary of defence.

By 1970 many of the brands that would appear 30 years later in Interbrand's 2000 annual ranking of the world's top 75 brands were going strong. Most were American, such as Coca-Cola, McDonald's, General Electric, Ford, Disney and Gillette. But European and Japanese brands were also established, including Mercedes, Heineken, Sony, Toyota and Volkswagen.

Companies like these straddled the globe by the 1980s, but many had become too large and unwieldy. While they possessed and profited from powerful brands, they had no clear idea of those brands' true worth, with many brands seen as under-exploited and under-valued. Such views helped fuel an explosion of merger and acquisition activity in the 1980s that swept up famous names such as RJR Nabisco, Philip Morris, Kraft, Grand Metropolitan, Pillsbury, Nestlé and Rowntree. Boardroom battles involving these firms led to record-setting buyout prices pegged in part to brand values.

The new attractiveness of brands to deal-makers stemmed from some fundamental changes in the economies of the developed world. Managing a business through most of the 19th and 20th centuries had been chiefly about efficient expansion of productive capacity. But by the 1980s economic growth had shifted largely to information and service-based industries. Many traditional markets, especially for consumer goods, had matured. While meaningful technological breakthroughs still occurred in communication, pharmaceuticals and computers, many product areas, and some services like banking and insurance, were bumping up against the limits of innovation and consumer interest. As a result, competitive advantage increasingly hinged on perceptions as consumers faced with many roughly equal product options in given price bands looked to style more than substance. As Disney CEO Michael Eisner said, 'When the choices have become vast, the only thing that will matter are brand names'.

> 66 When the choices have become vast, the only thing that will matter are brand names. 99

The Economist magazine declared 1988 to be 'The Year of the Brand'. Two years later, McDonald's opened a restaurant in Moscow, making its brand as much a political as a commercial symbol. A view even emerged that well-known US brands such as Coca-Cola and Levi's helped topple communism in Russia and Eastern Europe. Brands were in the headlines and major features on the cultural and economic landscape. By the early 1990s the brand wagon was off and running.

BRANDS NOW

Just when brands won recognition and power in the 1980s and 1990s, however, they began to encounter new problems. On the advertising front, fragmentation of media forced an adjustment in communication formulae beyond print and network television. Cable TV, 'below-the-line' communication channels like sports sponsorship, in-store advertising, direct-to-consumer mailings, public relations and the internet gained importance.

In the marketplace brands multiplied in number so fast that observers talked about brand proliferation, as illustrated by the history of Crest. Only once early in its life did Procter & Gamble extend the toothpaste brand – in 1967 with Crest Mint. Then a series of extensions began in

1980 with Advanced Formula Crest, followed by Crest Gel (1981), Crest Tartar Control (1985), Crest for Kids (1987), Crest Neat Squeeze (1991), Crest Baking Soda (1992) and Crest for Sensitive Teeth (1994).[3]

Most brand proliferation stemmed from marketers' desires to exploit successful brands fully by targeting specific market segments more precisely. But the trend was pushed further by deregulation and privatization of key industries, from power utilities and telephones to airlines and banks, and by globalization letting more foreign firms enter new markets with new brands. The proliferation of brands flooded the markets with new identities, increasing choice and competition and straining consumers' attention spans. It has been estimated that the average person is exposed to as many as 10,000 brands in a typical day. In addition, proliferation inflated advertising costs as more and more brands competed for a finite number of major communication channels.

Within the marketing profession, increased demand for accomplished brand managers led to more job hopping. Some brands suffered as a form of careerism took hold in which a new manager would arrive, change a brand beyond all recognition to make a mark and then move on. Many brands lost touch with consumers in this way by being inconsistent. Many marketers also grew more reliant on market research. Sometimes this led to better brands, but often the result was bland, me-too brands.

In the shops, retailers widened their use of private-label, or in-store brands, further complicating the competitive proposition for manufacturer brands, even as pressure for short-term financial performance grew from Wall Street, sometimes at the expense of long-term brand equity.

Business journalism became more aggressive in the 1980s and has improved in sophistication, leading to better and broader public understanding of who owns brands and what they are about. The emergence of the internet accelerated this process, helping create more educated and aware consumers.

Finally, the branding revolution of the past 20 years gave rise to a branch of marketing that produces stacks of books, seminars and consultancies. Theories about brand management and marketing encompass systems for handling 'brand equity', 'identity implementation', 'relationship spectrums', 'brand architecture audits', 'brand knowledge structures' and 'brand-product matrices'. The branding speciality has developed its own language and leadership within major corporations, advertising agencies, business schools and consulting firms. It is possible now to earn a Master's degree in brand management at some US universities.

The ultimate result of these historical forces has been to propel branding to the turning point where it stands today. Brands and the companies that they serve are under pressure – pressure from within businesses to be more profitable yet mindful of the long-term view; from consumers to be simpler and more informative yet not too time-consuming or restrictive; from the web to get online yet also defend the home turf; and from society at large to be more responsible and better behaved yet remain efficient and affordable and unafraid to innovate.

By seeking and winning unprecedented consumer attention in the fast-moving information age, brands help their owners to sell more goods and services. That is their traditional objective and they do a good job at it when properly managed. But that power brings with it risks and obligations. *Brands in the Balance* explores these aspects of branding, beginning with a look at brands in the marketplace.

NOTES

1 Kevin Lane Keller, *Strategic Brand Management: Building, Measuring and Managing Brand Equity*, Upper Saddle River, New Jersey: Prentice Hall, 1998, p. 29.

2 David Aaker and Erich Joachimsthaler, *Brand Leadership*, New York: Free Press, 2000, p. 5.

3 Keller, *Strategic Brand Management*, pp. 31–2.

PART 1

BRANDS IN
THE MARKETPLACE

'An orange is an orange. Unless that orange happens to be a Sunkist, a name 80 per cent of consumers know and trust'

Russell Hanlin, CEO, Sunkist Growers

BRANDS MATTER BECAUSE, FOR BETTER OR FOR WORSE, we are all consumers in the marketplace. Whether the market is a collection of ramshackle food stands at a dusty crossroads in Africa or a supermarket piled high with products in the asphalt suburbs of Western Europe or the USA, everyone goes there.

Consumption is a part – often a big part – of our daily lives. We are constantly sifting and choosing from among a sometimes mind-boggling array of goods and services. On what basis do we make our choices? In many cases, brands – the words, symbols, designs, sounds and ideas that represent particular goods and services – furnish the primary rationale for our decisions as consumers.

For example, one day I went to the cafeteria at work because I was thirsty. I stood in front of the glass door of the cooler cabinet and scanned the beverage cans. I thought to myself, well, I don't really know what I want … I guess I'll just have a Coke. Why did I think that? Have 40 years of exposure to Coca-Cola advertising made me an unthinking captive to the world's top brand? Maybe so, because I bought that Coke, drank it and did not think twice about comparing it to other beverages in the cooler using criteria such as price, nutritional value, volume, style or even taste.

That is what good brands do – they work their way into our lives, becoming familiar and valued signposts helping us to navigate the consumption landscape. We live and move among them almost without thought. Most of the time we disregard them. But when the occasion arises to make a consumption choice, there they are, beckoning and reassuring. They convey whole fabrics of value, attitude, emotion and awareness in a single word, logo or sound. We know them and we rely on them with astonishing regularity.

—

It's no wonder, then, that more and more organizations and individuals want to be in control of brands. But what exactly are they made of and what makes them so powerful? Research over the years has uncovered some basic truths about the ways people buy things, as reported by Harvard University marketing professor David Arnold.[1]

First, consumers approach products with a high level of ignorance about them. They may learn a few facts if the purchase is a costly one, like a car or a computer. But most purchases are made with little or no prior study. Thus consumers never understand a product as well as the company that makes and sells it. Second, consumers, in their ignorance, evaluate and judge goods and services based on attributes that have meaning to themselves. These meanings are often quite difficult to fathom and may focus on attributes that bear little relation to the ones that manufacturers or service providers deem important. Third, the attributes on which consumers focus are frequently intangible.

For example, energy giant Royal Dutch/Shell operates thousands of service stations around the world that it built to sell its primary retail product, petroleum. For decades Shell has promoted its brand as a symbol of quality and technical innovation in petroleum. But recent research has shown one of the top concerns of Shell customers is clean bathrooms. It just so happens that, in addition to being the world's second-largest oil and gas firm, Shell has more public toilets than any other company in the world. 'There's a group of our customers that is more interested in clean toilets than they are in petrol', said Raoul Pinnell, global head of brands and communications at Shell, in an interview. He added that this finding and others are having a major impact on how Shell handles its brand.

Fourth and finally, consumer perceptions are not always rational. They may be emotional and based on factors far removed from the function of the good or service at issue. Memories of experiences with brands, the corporate behaviour of a brand owner, the opinions of friends and experts – all these forces and more shape feelings and attitudes toward brands and the goods and services that they represent.

The upshot of these four truths is that consumers seldom buy things based solely on their functional characteristics as physical goods or distinct services. Much more is involved. This amalgam of feelings, experiences, price sensitivities, convenience, perception and hard fact is wrapped up in the brand.

As Antoine Riboud, former CEO of French food manufacturer Groupe Danone once said, 'It is not yogurts that I make, but Danones'.[2]

BUY ME, TAKE ME, GET ME

If it is true, therefore, that consumers chiefly buy brands, rather than products and services, then what sort of brands do they prefer to buy? One key to answering this important question, the experts say, is to understand two basic aspects of consumer demand: needs and wants.

People obviously need food, clothing and shelter to live. In a post-industrial society they also need transportation, communication, energy, health care, hygiene, education, entertainment, money and informa-tion. Analyzing basic needs such as these helps businesses to define markets and get a view of the competition. For instance, people who need transportation constitute a market. So do people who need entertain-ment. These needs are plentifully met by branded products and services in the developed world.

66 Consumers chiefly buy brands, rather than products and services. 99

But meeting needs is not enough any more. Just try to sell a car based on its ability to carry its occupants from one place to another; a telephone on its ability to allow individuals to converse over a great distance; a shampoo on its ability to cleanse hair; a current account on its useful-ness in paying bills. Consumers take for granted that the goods and services of today will meet basic needs – that a website will provide information; an electric utility, energy; a baseball game, entertainment. Goods and services unable to meet basic needs seldom get to market these days. If they do, they quickly vanish.

If the idea of basic needs is valid, then it is possible to conceive of another set of secondary needs. These are largely intangible require-ments of modern life, but they are no less real. They include the need for security, safety, excitement, fun, status, relaxation, fitness, beauty and convenience. Secondary needs define markets as well. People who need to be fit are a market, as are people who need to feel safe. Combining different types of needs, both basic and secondary, can splin-ter markets into finer categories. People may need, for instance, safe transportation, secure money or prestigious clothing.

However, it is at this juncture that consumer demand in a world of material abundance begins to shade towards a more ephemeral and mysterious motivation – wants. People want their needs to be met in certain ways. Wants are very specific, but change over time, while the needs underlying them do not. For instance, consumers may always need convenient information, but the kind of information that they want, as well as the formats that they want it in, vary remarkably from person to person. The same is true for safe transportation. Some people want a car that looks fast, whether they drive it that way or not; some want a vehicle that looks like it could tackle the Sahara, even if they never leave the city streets.

Wants like these have to do with making statements about personal identity – both to the self and to others. They hinge on style, personality and self-image; on attitudes towards success and fulfilment. Wants involve psychology as much as survival; feelings as much as logic. Brand marketers study consumer wants down to an excruciating level of detail because in them lies the essence of branding. 'A cluster of people who share a want constitute a market segment', stated Arnold.[3]

These, then, are the fundamental keys to branding:

- Locate a market segment.
- Target it with an appealing brand that promises to satisfy the needs and wants involved.
- Position the brand at a reasonable price, in a convenient format, with a consistent underlying value that meets those needs and wants just as well or better than the competition.

People will buy goods and services with appealing brands that meet their needs and satisfy their wants. Sounds straightforward enough – just common sense, really. But given the constantly shifting kaleidoscope of factors involved, it seems remarkable that marketers manage to get it right at all.

MAKING SENSE OF BRAND BUILDING

From a fundamental theory of consumer needs and wants, branding experts develop elaborate systems for uncovering those needs and wants, then matching them up against sets of brand traits that will accomplish the ultimate objective of helping to sell goods and services. This is the exercise of brand building. Labelled variously as brand mapping, brand constitution, brand architecture, brand knowledge structures, brand anatomy, even brand DNA, theories of brand building usually involve a lot of charts with concentric circles, data points scattered across line graphs and heavy jargon that varies in meaning from one book to the next.

In a typical example, Aaker of University of California-Berkeley wrote that brand identity is defined as 'twelve dimensions organized around four perspectives'.[4] His detailed, jargon-filled explanation contains a useful notion, namely that brands are built out of four types of traits. First, the unavoidable ones stemming from the goods and services that they represent, the kinds of people who use them and where those goods and services come from. Second, the company that owns the brand. Third, the personality of the brand, a somewhat vague category. And fourth, the words, pictures and sounds commonly used to symbolize the brand.

Aaker's system is as good as any for ordering brand traits into sensible patterns that can be more easily manipulated. Useful, as well, is the system devised by Jean-Noël Kapferer, who teaches marketing at the HEC School of Management in France. He identifies six facets of brand identity – physique, personality, culture, relationship, reflection and self-image.[5] Such systems can help guide marketers through the process of brand building. But no brand-building system, however comprehensive it may be, can provide the creative spark that – when all is said and done – remains at the core of good branding. 'Branding is not rocket science. It is just as much an art as a science. There is always a creativity and originality component involved with branding', remarked Dartmouth's Keller.[6]

Although they often are arcane and wordy, academic theories of brand building are sometimes valuable, as are related concepts about implementing brand identities through advertising and other communication channels, as well as positioning, tracking and managing brands over time. Theorizing about brands helps managers to understand them better. Good brands are powerful because they combine the right traits with an appealing personality and, in doing so, establish relationships with consumers. These relationships are much like human relationships. Well-managed brands can become like trusted friends to consumers;

> **" Well-managed brands can become like trusted friends to consumers. "**

poorly managed ones can become annoying jerks. If all the academics did was to help minimize the incidence of irritating brands, then they would have accomplished something. But the fact is that brand marketers need all the help they can get, and at no time has this been more true than today.

MARKET REPORTS

Part 1 of *Brands in the Balance* presents eight in-depth case studies that highlight some of the most pressing issues facing brands today in the marketplace. All eight are based on interviews with top brand managers in Europe and the USA:

- Charlie Frenette, president of Coca-Cola Co.'s European operations, discusses the Atlanta soft drinks leader's reassessment of its embrace of globalization in the wake of recent crises, pioneering new perspectives on brands in a world of global commonality and local traditions;

- Patrick Ricard, CEO of French beverages group Pernod Ricard, talks about Ricard, the spirit brand invented by his father that has remained resolutely French, showing that even in a world of apparently rapid globalization, national brands can remain viable and valuable;

- Dick Leinenkugel, vice-president of sales and marketing for Jacob Leinenkugel Brewing Co., a mid-sized Wisconsin brewery owned by the Miller Brewing unit of New-York-based consumer goods giant Philip Morris Cos, tells about his confidence in regional brands;

- Stelios Haji-Ioannou, CEO of UK budget airline easyJet, outlines the advantages of being an underdog brand, displaying a branding sense like that which allows entrepreneurs such as Richard Branson to tap into consumers' naturally rebellious streak;

- Mark Jostes, a marketing manager at Illinois heavy-equipment manufacturer Caterpillar Co., relates an improbable story of brand extension, illustrating the strength of a solid brand even in a market that has almost nothing to do with its core identity;

- René Hooft Graafland, marketing director at Dutch brewery Heineken NV, analyzes the unusually consistent image of the Heineken brand in the ever-changing beer industry, emphasizing the value of keeping a steady hand on the brand tiller over the long term;

- Alan Palmer, international marketing director for confectionery at UK sweets and soft drinks group Cadbury Schweppes, describes the group's approach to brand families, demonstrating a return to a more unified style after decades of divergence;

- Vic Campbell, a marketing manager at US hospital company Columbia/HCA Corp., talks about its failed attempt to impose a single, national brand on its hospital properties, showing the limits of branding within at least one major service industry.

Three of these studies – on Coca-Cola, Ricard and Leinenkugel – focus on the geographical reach of brands in the context of the globalization issue, the most urgent problem now facing branding.

THE END OF THE AMERICAN MOMENT

Since it began about a century ago, the story of commercial brands has moved through phases. The formative years at the outset of the 20th century were about establishing trademark rights, improving distribution methods and testing the new-fangled idea of advertising. The Great Depression saw brands hurt by widespread popular disillusionment with advertising and marketing in general.

The period after the Second World War saw brands in resurgence as demand and consumption soared in the industrialized world. Post-war brand management was chiefly about providing identities for genuinely new goods and services thrown on to the market by recurring waves of technological innovation. By the 1980s, however, innovation rates in many industries – computers, pharmaceuticals and communications being notable exceptions – had slowed. Markets in the developed world for food, household goods, cars and other items had matured. Branding had to shift towards targeting more intangible needs and emotional wants to influence consumer demand. Brands multiplied as market segments were split finer and finer.

> 66 Branding had to shift towards targeting more intangible needs and emotional wants to influence consumer demand. 99

At the same time, the fall of communism and the opening of the less-developed world allowed branding to expand from the developed world into new markets of opportunity. In the growing regions of Latin

America, Southeast Asia and China, India, Eastern Europe and Russia, brand marketing in the 1980s exploded. In these areas branding was once again primarily centred on appealing to basic needs.

Suddenly, brand owners were faced with the prospect of managing brands in one way in the developed world, and in quite another way in the developing world. In addition, they faced the potential costs of supporting brand-management systems not just on one continent or perhaps two, but on five or even six continents populated by consumers with unfamiliar languages, cultures, traditions and values. No self-respecting company was ready to shy away from the exciting promise of growth through globalization in the 1980s, but at the same time the branding challenges looked immense.

The academics rode to the rescue with the theory of globalization, based in part on a 1983 article in the *Harvard Business Review* by marketing professor Theodore Levitt. His compelling thesis was that the world was rapidly unifying, thanks to international trade, transportation, communication and entertainment. So it made sense to market global brands, or ones that could work in all cultures. No longer would it be necessary, Levitt argued, to have separate brands and advertising campaigns for England, Ecuador and Ethiopia. One brand and one campaign, geared at a sufficiently generic level, could serve all these markets with a local adjustment for language.[7]

The cost-savings potential of such an approach was significant, as was the promise of brand 'synergies' – that business catch-all term that so often seems to imply making one plus one equal three. Major corporations seized on the Levitt thesis. US companies, especially, embraced it and released on the world a flood of power brands that soon seemed to sweep all before them. Almost overnight McDonald's was in Moscow; Levi's was in East Berlin; Disney was in Paris; Nike was seemingly everywhere. If you walked across the bridge from Hong Kong into Shenzhen, China, the first thing that caught your eye a few years ago was not the seething panorama of a post-communist Middle Kingdom, but a red-and-white billboard proclaiming 'Welcome to Marlboro Country'.

The theory of globalization coincided with a moment in history when the USA had won the Cold War and suddenly dominated the world as the pre-eminent military and economic superpower. Small wonder then that most of the new global brands of the 1980s and early 1990s were American.

However, the world's love affair with Uncle Sam faded quickly. East Asia and Latin America suffered through economic crises and lost some of their enthusiasm for free markets and the American way. Russia and Eastern Europe sobered up from the heady days of glasnost and perestroika to face the uncertainty of life without cradle-to-grave socialism. Western Europeans found renewed confidence out from under the Russian nuclear threat as they drove towards monetary unification. By the late 1990s a reaction had begun that looked like a backlash against global brands, but was actually just as much a backlash against American economic power and the brands that symbolized it.

'Globalization for a while was like a religion and a lot of companies tried to go it whole hog, but it ran into problems', observed Interbrand CEO Rita Clifton. 'What's happened in the last five or ten years is that the pendulum has ended up somewhere in the middle.' A reassessment of global branding is under way, with top branding academics counselling caution. Aaker wrote: 'Global brand strategy is often misdirected. The priority should be developing not global brands (although such brands might result) but rather global brand leadership'. He and co-author Erich Joachimsthaler cited interviews with 35 firms in reaching the conclusion that global brands are right for some companies, but not all.[8]

Some major US brand owners, faced with the global branding challenge, are now uncertain that American-ness still is an advantage. 'We're yet another global brand that happens to be American', said Karen Edwards, vice-president of marketing at California-based internet giant Yahoo!, in an interview. 'That's not great. It would be a lot easier if we were a global brand from Taiwan … The question is, when people think of Yahoo!, do they think it's American or do they think global? I hope they think global.'

In Part 1 of *Brands in the Balance*, Coca-Cola – the original global brand – addresses the globalization issue at some length. Subsequent chapters on the French spirit Ricard and the Wisconsin beer Leinenkugel provide counterpoints to the globalization thesis, showing that national and regional brands can continue to flourish, even in a world where everyone watches CNN.

The remaining chapters in Part 1 represent a survey of other pressing issues, including brand extension, brand consistency, brand families, underdog brands and the limits of branding.

NOTES

1 David Arnold, *The Handbook of Brand Management*, New York: Economist Books, 1992, pp. 6–9.

2 Jean-Noël Kapferer, *Strategic Brand Management: Creating and Sustaining Brand Equity Long-Term*, London: Kogan Page, 1997, p. 48.

3 Arnold, *The Handbook of Brand Management*, p. 11.

4 David Aaker, *Building Strong Brands*, New York: Free Press, 1996, p. 68.

5 Kapferer, *Strategic Brand Management*, pp. 99–106.

6 Kevin Lane Keller, *Strategic Brand Management: Building, Measuring and Managing Brand Equity*, Upper Saddle River, New Jersey: Prentice Hall, 1998, p. xv.

7 Theodore Levitt, 'The globalization of markets', *Harvard Business Review*, May/June 1983.

8 David Aaker and Erich Joachimsthaler, *Brand Leadership*, New York: Free Press, 2000, pp. 303–30.

1

WORLD OF TROUBLE: COCA-COLA AND THE GLOBAL BRAND

'I'm not sure we understood the world as much as we thought we did'

Douglas Daft, CEO, Coca-Cola Co.

YOU COULDN'T HEAR IT AT THE TIME, but when dozens of Belgian school-children in May 1999 came down with nausea and diarrhoea after sipping contaminated soft drinks made by US beverage giant Coca-Cola Co., a standing eight-count started for the global brand.

The champion of all branding ideas was still on its feet. But it was stunned by a blow that came out of nowhere. What looked like a modest health scare, with no deaths or serious illness resulting, snowballed into the largest product recall in the history of the world's best-known brand.

Thousands of Coca-Cola employees lost their jobs, the CEO resigned amid a flurry of public breast-beating at Atlanta headquarters and, perhaps most importantly, Coca-Cola began openly to question the concept that for decades had been a key driver of its remarkable growth around the world.

'The crisis in Belgium ... struck viciously at the very heart of brand Coca-Cola. In fact, I've been with Coca-Cola for 25 years and I've never seen anything – including New Coke in the United States – have such a deep impact', said Charlie Frenette, president of Coca-Cola Europe and Eurasia. In an interview at Coca-Cola's offices in London, the stocky and voluble Frenette, between swigs from a Diet Coke can, talked at length about his and his company's journey since 1999:

'It changed our mindset.' Now we're saying, there are certain universal truths about Coca-Cola. We're proud of those. It is the character of what makes up this brand. But it's also very local and we'll talk to you in your language, and we would like you to be able to see yourself in these ads.

Exactly what Frenette means when he says things like 'let Coca-Cola be Coca-Cola' or 'we've got to expand from global to local' is still being sorted out. Douglas Daft, named CEO at headquarters after the stormy departure of predecessor Douglas Ivester, is adamant that Coca-Cola must redefine itself. In a speech Daft said:

'1999 was a pretty tough year for Coca-Cola, particularly in Europe. We've said the series of setbacks we suffered ... served as a clear wake-up call for us. In fact, that wake-up call helped us very quickly understand why we must now think local and act local.'

Much of this is doubtless damage control meant to steer attention from the contamination problem itself in Belgium, as well as other difficulties encountered in 1999. But the repeated *mea culpa* speeches, wide-open interviews and intensely local new advertising and promotional campaigns indicate that Coca-Cola is paying more than lip service to addressing its brand problem. As a case study of the changing meanings of commercial identity in a new century, the Coca-Cola episode is invaluable because it directly addresses the social and political challenges faced by major brands. If any brand shows how being famous means also being vulnerable, it has to be Coca-Cola.

The second most widely recognized word on the planet, after 'okay', is Coca-Cola. The brand routinely tops all lists of brand power rankings, far overshadowing other big names such as Microsoft, IBM, General Electric, Ford and Disney. It is worth more than $72.5 billion on its own, according to brand consulting firm Interbrand. That is equal to about half the company's total market capitalization.

Yet the power and presence of the Coca-Cola brand not only could not save the company from its débâcle in 1999, it actually contributed to it. In a novel twist for the 114-year-old organization, its brand had become part of the problem, not part of the solution, as a backlash against global brands hit hard. As Daft said:

'That backlash was a little confusing to us. After all, we had always been the good guys. Frankly we were so successful we did not even see the change coming ... It seemed to some people that the most savvy marketing company in history didn't quite get it. That's probably fair criticism. I'm not sure we understood the world as much as we thought we did.'

FROM COCA LEAF TO FLOWER CHILD

Atlanta pharmacist and Confederate Army veteran John Pemberton concocted a fizzy health tonic in 1886 whose ingredients are still top secret, but were thought to include the following: water, sugar, coca leaf extract, citrate caffeine from cola nuts, caramel, phosphoric acid, vanilla, lime juice, orange and lemon oil, nutmeg, cinnamon and coriander – just the thing to liven up a sleepy Southern afternoon. Pemberton's able bookkeeper Frank Robinson, a Yankee businessman transplanted to the steamy Georgia capital, coined the catchy name and helped set up a company to bring it to market.

Coca-Cola was first sold at a soda fountain in Atlanta for 5 cents a glass, supported by a campaign of free-sample coupons and signs purchased by Pemberton at a cost of about $74. They carried the not-so-imaginative slogan 'Drink Coca-Cola'. The sweet, brown beverage with its stimulating properties caught on and spread gradually across the South, then still recovering from the Civil War.

One-time shop clerk turned druggist Asa Candler, on the look-out for a business opportunity, bought the young Coca-Cola Co. in 1891 for $2,300. He kept Robinson on staff and together the two blazed a branding and advertising path that would become a Coca-Cola legend. They held a design contest that resulted in the now familiar curvaceous bottle being invented by a glass company in Indiana. They associated Coca-Cola with alcohol abolitionism, then a powerful social cause, and dubbed it 'The Great National Temperance Drink'. Amid controversy, they removed the cocaine content from the drink. They bought space for the brand name, in its flowing script, on the sides of buildings, in newspapers and on billboards. They flooded the country with Coca-Cola Girl pin-up calendars and signs, and enlisted Santa Claus as an endorser. By the turn of the century, helped by a network of independent bottlers begun in Tennessee, Coca-Cola was distributed across the USA, Canada and Mexico.

Candler was elected mayor of Atlanta in 1916. Shortly after, Coca-Cola Co. was sold by Candler's family to Atlanta banker and financial dealmaker Ernest Woodruff for what was then the stupendous sum of $25 million. Woodruff named his 33-year-old son Robert president and took the company public at $40 a share. In real terms, each of those initial shares of stock was worth more than $6 million by 1998.

If the hard-selling, high-rolling Candler made Coca-Cola a national brand, then the enduring and reclusive Robert Woodruff over the next 60 years made it one of the first truly global brands in history. He formed a foreign sales office in 1926. He started selling the drink in service stations and out of coolers. He forced bottlers to adhere to quality standards. He dived into radio advertising. He launched two of Coca-Cola's most memorable slogans: 'The pause that refreshes' and 'It's the real thing'. By the outbreak of the Second World War, Coca-Cola was able to say it was being sold in more than 45 countries, but it had still achieved little genuine popularity beyond the USA, Canada and Cuba, then a US protectorate.

Woodruff's finest hour came with the entry of US forces into the war in 1941. Seizing the moment, he announced that every fighting GI would be able to buy a Coca-Cola for 5 cents, no matter where the action was and no matter what the cost. Woodruff convinced the US government that Coca-Cola would be good for morale and Uncle Sam graciously helped the company build dozens of bottling plants that went overseas with the troops. Like chewing gum and nylons, the beverage that the soldiers dubbed simply 'Coke' went global in a big way and became a symbol of America overseas. Huge gains in brand awareness were made as a result and Coca-Cola's growth surged in the years following the war.

Coke became available in cans in 1955, and was a pioneer in advertising on the new medium of television. The company acquired Minute Maid Corp. and introduced Fanta in 1960, Sprite in 1961 and Tab in 1963.

That was also the year of the slogan 'Things go better with Coke'. In 1971 Coca-Cola captured a moment in history with its unforgettable 'I'd like to teach the world to sing' commercial on television. Featuring a circle of fresh-faced, misty-eyed young people from around the world holding hands on an Italian hilltop and singing a flower-child hit by the New Seekers, the spot was a sensation. It cemented the brand's associations with youth and a sunny globalism led by America.

The quirky pop artist Andy Warhol said this about Coca-Cola at the time:

'You can be watching TV and see Coca-Cola, and you know that the president drinks Coke, Liz Taylor drinks Coke, and just think, you can drink Coke, too. A Coke is Coke, and no amount of money can get you a better Coke than the one the bum on the corner is drinking. All the Cokes are the same, and all the Cokes are good. Liz Taylor knows it, the president knows it, the bum knows it, and you know it.'[1]

PEPSI AND THE NEW COKE FLOP

Growth continued through the 1970s, despite an increasingly annoying challenge from Pepsi-Cola of New York City. The perennial number-two, with a sweeter and cheaper cola and a punchy taste-test ad campaign, forced Coca-Cola to face its first real competition, marking the start of the so-called Cola Wars.

In Atlanta, Woodruff, who had dabbled in national politics and ruled the company as a semi-recluse through a series of rubber-stamp presidents for 25 years, finally stepped aside in 1980. He was replaced by Roberto Goizueta, a Cuban-born chemical engineer and long-time Coca-Cola executive.

As one of his first steps at the head of a cadre of younger managers determined to reshape the company, Goizueta introduced Diet Coke. It was the first time the core Coke brand had been extended, and it was a resounding success. He installed 'value-creation' managerial principles within the company. He guided the $700-million purchase in 1982 by Coca-Cola of Columbia Pictures – another radical departure from past practice. Then he sold the movie studio to Sony for a $1 billion profit.

In the meantime, Pepsi continued to claw market share away from Coke. The relentless Pepsi Challenge campaign, begun in Dallas and expanded nationwide, showed blindfolded consumers consistently choosing the sweeter, more lime-flavoured number-two cola over Coke. Nervous executives in Atlanta secretly reproduced the test and, to their horror, got the same results. Goizueta panicked.

Sure that Coke's competitive problem lay in the product and not the brand or the price, he pushed through a reformulation of Coca-Cola to make it sweeter and smoother, or, in short, more like Pepsi. Goizueta convinced Woodruff, then 95 and on his deathbed, of the need for the new recipe. Then he announced to the world in 1985 that Coca-Cola, although it was still selling many millions daily, was being replaced by a better-tasting New Coke. The result was a memorable disaster in branding history.

Consumers were indignant and heaped scorn upon Coca-Cola. Pepsi was delighted and quickly produced advertisements claiming that it was now 'the real thing'. Cases of old Coke flew off the shelves as consumers horded it. The controversial New Coke came out and was an instant flop. Just three months after the launch, Goizueta had to reintroduce the original formula under the name Coca-Cola Classic.

Frenette, now chief of Coke Europe, was working in the US fountain sales division during the New Coke episode. He recalled that time:

'What we learned from that is that we don't own this brand, the consumer does. That the sensory experience of the formulation, and the mind's eye interpretation of it, were inextricably linked. When we changed that equation – even though we had a product that without a doubt on a taste-test basis was superior tasting – the consumer rejected it because they said, that's not my Coke. What we learned is that taste is not just sweetness on the tip of the tongue. But it's the whole sensory experience and what it triggers in the mind's eye … In some people, the sight of the contour bottle alone actually triggers the metabolism to anticipate drinking a Coke. It is the psychology and the flavor chemistry coming together. I believe we know that more clearly today than we did in the past. So the learning of New Coke was this – set your own agenda and be careful of the taste test. This product is not just about that. It's an idea.'

> 66 **What we learned is that we don't own this brand, the consumer does.** 99

The hard-driving Goizueta, unlike his ill-conceived New Coke, did not fade away afterwards. He stayed on and drove Coca-Cola to new heights. He began to view the company's competition as not just Pepsi or other soft-drink makers, but as all beverages, including water. He talked about 'share of throat' and how he hoped to install a third tap on kitchen sinks the world over with a handle marked 'C' for Coke. Ultimately, Goizueta and his company had benefited from the New Coke error because it had showed them the depth of feeling their core brand enjoyed with consumers, especially in the USA.

THE GLOBAL TRUMPET SOUNDS

While Coca-Cola and Pepsi were battling it out for dominance in America, the world around them was changing fast, as were ideas about business and brands.

In 1983, with the Soviet Union on the edge of collapse and free markets set to dominate the world, a *Harvard Business Review* article by marketing professor Theodore Levitt declared the following:

'A powerful new force now drives the world towards a single converging commonality, and that force is technology … The result is a new commercial reality – the emergence of global markets for standardized consumer products on a previously unimagined scale of magnitude. Corporations geared to this new reality benefit from enormous economies of scale in production, distribution, marketing and management. By translating these benefits into reduced world prices, they can decimate competitors that still live in the disabling grip of old assumptions about how the world works. Gone are accustomed differences in national or regional preference … Ancient differences in national tastes and modes of doing business disappear. The commonality of preferences leads inescapably to the standardization of products, manufacturing, and the institutions of trade and commerce.'[2]

Levitt specifically cited Coca-Cola as an example of the new breed of global brand, as he did Sony, Levi's and Revlon. This was not lost on the management of Coca-Cola in Atlanta. Over the decades Coca-Cola had expanded around the world on the back of a network of dozens of independent bottlers. Closely supervised by corporate headquarters, the bottlers nevertheless tended to be owned and managed by local people. They bought Coke syrup from Coca-Cola Co. at fixed rates, mixed it with water and bottled it at their own plants for distribution in their respective markets.

This decentralized distribution model had helped make Coca-Cola a global brand, or one recognized and understood with amazing consistency around the world. It had also allowed the company to expand rapidly without taking on too much overhead and to penetrate new markets without having to learn about them from the ground up. Finally, it had made the bottlers rich and restless. Amidst rising demands by some bottlers for more autonomy and a better financial deal with Atlanta, Goizueta made a crucial decision. He began merging bottlers to bring operations under tighter control and save money through standardization of precisely the sort Levitt had described. The policy had a quick, short-term benefit.

Throughout the late 1980s and early 1990s, with Pepsi management losing its edge, the Coca-Cola stock price soared. When Goizueta took charge, the company's total value was about $4 billion; when he died of lung cancer in 1997, while still at the helm, Coca-Cola was worth $145 billion on the stock market. This amazing gain came partly on a surge in earnings fuelled by cost savings from recentralization.

Instrumental in finding these cost savings by managing the bottler network reform had been Douglas Ivester, a no-nonsense Georgia accountant who had climbed through the financial ranks to become president and chief operating officer under Goizueta. When his boss died, the tough-talking Ivester was named chief executive and chairman. He immediately ran into problems in part brought on by the company's embrace of globalization from the centre.

THE FIZZ GOES FLAT

Coca-Cola had long been a company with a swagger. Self-assured and immensely powerful, it threw its weight around and usually got its way. Under Ivester, as bottler consolidation gradually cut long-standing ties between Atlanta and local markets, the Coca-Cola attitude edged towards arrogance.

At the same time, the company started to disappoint Wall Street. Like many food and beverage manufacturers, Coca-Cola found itself in a difficult position by the mid-1990s. Retailers were merging, gaining market power and demanding discounts from suppliers. Costs were rising rapidly for mass-market advertising, while the general inflation rate stayed low and ate into pricing power.

The select fraternity of 'anchor' bottlers created by Goizueta and Ivester required increasing support from headquarters in the form of marketing contributions, infrastructure investments and other subsidies. Investors in both Coca-Cola and the bottlers were growing restive over this system. Finally, economic crises in Asia, Russia and Latin America knocked the props out from under growth plans.

From 1991 to 1995 Coca-Cola revenues rose annually between 7 and 16 per cent. But they levelled out at about $18.5 billion in 1996 and stayed there for three years. Over the same period annual company profits went flat at about $3.5 billion, after rising annually in mid-teens percentage points (*see* Fig. 1.1 and Fig. 1.2). In search of answers, Ivester turned to a corporate strategy frequently chosen by businesses losing internal growth traction – mergers and acquisitions.

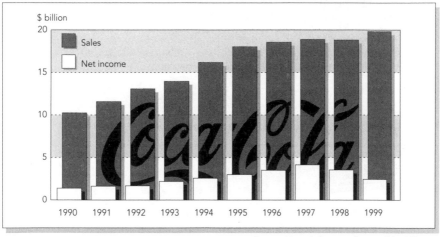

Sources: Hoover's Company Reports, Yahoo! Finance

FIGURE 1.1 Coca-Cola annual figures

First, he targeted the non-US soft drinks unit of Cadbury-Schweppes, the UK sweets and beverages group, with a $1.85-billion offer for its soft-drinks business outside the USA. Second, he made an $844-million bid for Orangina, the peculiar but successful orange-flavoured soft drink owned by French beverages group Pernod Ricard SA. Both proposals would have sharply increased Coca-Cola's strong market position in Western Europe. Pepsico complained loudly and Coca-Cola quickly ran afoul of competition regulators. Eager to flex their European Union muscles, bureaucrats in Brussels and other European capitals had already been geared up to probe what they saw as overly aggressive Coca-Cola business practices. The Cadbury and Orangina proposals met with a chilly official reception.

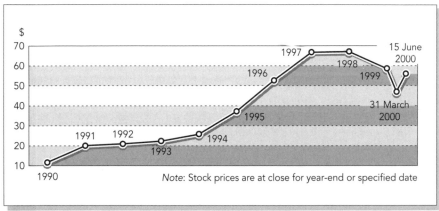

Sources: Hoover's Company Reports, Yahoo! Finance

FIGURE 1.2 Coca-Cola stock price

After months of expensive haggling, Coca-Cola and Pernod Ricard finally dropped the Orangina proposal, which one Coca-Cola executive privately called 'one of the stupidest things we ever tried'. The Cadbury deal went through, but only in a heavily watered-down version that prevented Coca-Cola from gaining control of the Schweppes brands in most key European markets.

The company was further embarrassed by a high-profile and costly racial discrimination lawsuit on its home turf in Atlanta and by weak financial results. The stock price fell through much of 1999, even as the broad market hurtled to record-setting highs.

As these events unfolded, the Belgian contamination crisis hit in May. It started when more than 100 schoolchildren fell ill after drinking Coca-Cola products. Similar reports soon came in from France. The governments of Belgium, France and Luxembourg quickly restricted sales of Coca-Cola products. After a couple of ineffective responses in Brussels the company issued a legalistically worded statement from Atlanta saying it had found no health or safety concerns with its beverages. Consumer advocates and local newspapers in France and the Benelux countries were offended by the company's seemingly cavalier approach.

Further investigation by Coca-Cola resulted in another statement saying that there may have been problems with carbon dioxide injected into some of its products and with fungicide possibly contaminating others. Coca-Cola repeated that it saw no health risk, but agreed to recall millions of containers of soft drinks from store shelves in Belgium, France, the Netherlands and Luxembourg. It was the largest product recall in the history of the company and it cut deeply into quarterly revenues and profits.

Weeks later, agents for the European Commission raided the offices of Coca-Cola bottlers in Germany, Austria, Denmark and the UK, seizing internal documents as part of a probe into alleged bullying of competitors. The company responded that it was in full compliance with European laws. Asked about the raids just hours after they took place, Ivester dismissively remarked: 'It's not something I am very exercised about ... It's not the first time and it won't be the last.'

Four months later, as the damage done to the Coke brand over the preceding summer sank in at headquarters, 52-year-old Ivester resigned after just two-and-a-half years at the helm. He left with a golden parachute valued at $30 million to reward him for 'long and loyal service', regulatory documents showed.

THE REAL THING REPENTANT

In December 1999 Coca-Cola named Daft, a soft-spoken, 56-year-old Australian from the ranks of marketing and operations, to replace Ivester. Moving swiftly to clean house, he restructured the company along more decentralized lines and eliminated 5,400 jobs, or 20 per cent of the globalwork workforce, including 2,500 employees from Atlanta headquarters staff. Taking aim squarely at the smug globalism that had come to pervade the corporate culture, Daft adopted as his motto the phrase 'think local, act local'.

Frenette – point-man on the reintroduction of Coca-Cola products into Belgium after being off the shelves for six weeks due to the recall – was named by Daft to head a new European unit. He recalled later:

'It was a very humbling experience in Belgium, to be sitting there for six weeks and to be having people saying, I want my Coke back and trying to understand why. We made some mistakes, there's no question about it. It was a real wake-up call for us, about where our strengths and weaknesses really were, about how our approach to the marketplace was working and not working. We saw it in living colour. You can do a lot of research, but until you walk into a country the size of Belgium and find that you're not on the shelf ... For me it was, all right, pay attention.'

> **❝ It was a real wake-up call for us, about where our strengths and weaknesses really were. ❞**

The frantic pace of work involved with the reintroduction, and its intensely local style, opened Frenette's eyes to what a big company can do if it strips away the stultifying weight of bureaucracy and politics. He was in Brussels for eight weeks.

'We lived in that office. We took a conference room and emptied it out. We took the brand managers and took their titles away from them. We gave them tasks. We had a meeting every morning at 9 o'clock and every afternoon at 5.30 – what did we learn yesterday from the research, what are we going to do today, what are the learnings for tomorrow?

'We produced eight or ten different television spots within a two-week period of time. Now, that could happen every day. You wouldn't want to run your life like that. But the fact of the matter is you don't need six months to do a commercial, with these hierarchical reviews. Get rid of that stuff and take these 35-year-old and 25-year-old people, who really know what they want to do, and give them a chance to go do something. Find a way to make the decisions quicker. As long as they're within a corridor, let them stumble a little bit, and that's how we're going to learn and we're going to have so much more happening. That was a huge learning for me.'

To bring the brand back in Belgium, the company hit the ground with a wave of sampling campaigns in which young hires personally handed out coupons and greeted consumers at storefronts and elsewhere with various community programmes and with other 'experientially based' efforts.

Within a few months Coca-Cola sales were restored to pre-recall levels in Belgium, but Frenette insisted it was not back to business as usual. Contrary to what Levitt and other global branding enthusiasts may once have preached, Frenette said Coca-Cola rediscovered in Belgium the inherent 'local-ness' of its markets – a finding it must reconcile with equally compelling evidence of emerging 'global-ness'. He went on:

'We can show you lots of research we've done that said there was a global teenager and a global market, and it's right. We did a lot of work on the global consumer study. What we found was there are patterns that exist all over the world. My conclusion at this point is that if you average things up high enough, you can get to commonality, and it's there. But it's about this deep of the total population [holding his thumb and forefinger about a quarter of an inch apart].

'In dress, style, music, lingo, some attitudes, it's there. But the reality is that people live their lives based on the culture they grew up in. For us not to be faddish, and for us to have a global brand that's going to be here 100 years from now, we've got to understand how people live their lives in their communities.'

Similarly, Frenette said, a recent marketing experiment by Coca-Cola in the Harlem area of Manhattan revealed starkly that locale still matters greatly, even in the age of the global village. To address a historically weak record in Harlem, Coca-Cola canvassed the tightly knit, mostly black neighbourhood block-by-block. Research showed people in Harlem tended to live their lives in what the company called a 'five-by-five' block area. Coca-Cola defined a number of these intensely local areas as market zones and hired local people as sales representatives. Frenette claims:

'Our brand preference scores over a two-year period of time doubled. Our volume and profitability in Harlem more than doubled. It was the same brand, Coca-Cola; the same product; the same sensory experience. But we were able to go in and understand what was important to these people and to connect this brand to what was important to them ... So we developed an allegiance. It's just started, but 10 years from now, I believe that we will find we'll have a thousand Harlems around the world.'

BACK TO BASICS

One of Daft's early roll-backs of globalism was to do away with global advertising – a move that flew in the face of prevailing trends in the ad world. The decision reflects a conviction that Coca-Cola, while consistent in some respects around the world, can also mean very different things in different places. In Africa, for instance, Coke frequently competes not only with other beverages, but with a broad range of 'indulgent snack items', such as chocolate, sweets and ice cream. 'The ice cream guys are as big a competitor for us in sub-Saharan Africa as any of the other beverages', Frenette said.

Daft retained a central brand management office in Atlanta called the Strategic Marketing Group, which oversees the company's five international brands: Coke, Sprite, Fanta, Diet Coke and Coke Light. But the bulk of marketing work is now done by country-level brand managers. 'Their job is to find that intersection between the architecture that defines Coca-Cola, its positioning, and the human condition locally or how people live their lives', Frenette said. 'They then have to create communications and programmes that take that intersection and make it come alive.'

A central brand-management database is constantly fed information from consumer surveys and transactions at the retail level. Frenette described the process:

'What we're moving to now is that we can actually track the sales by brand, by package, by day, down to the outlet level. The other thing we're doing is going in and getting causal data from the stores. So we can measure displays, pricing, packaging, competitive environment … Today's brand manager is able to look at attitudes, behaviours, those other causal factors and therefore is able to manage all elements of the marketing mix, not just advertising.'

Coca-Cola knows, for instance, that it should sell Coke in 2-litre bottles next to packages of microwave popcorn in the video section of a typical US supermarket. And that at service stations it needs to sell 20-ounce resealable bottles that fit in a car cup holder. This is all part of fulfilling the company's goal of being within 'arm's reach of desire'. But it is also about creating desire within arm's reach.

Coca-Cola studies carefully what kinds of promotions drive volumes and attitudes. Television advertising accounts for about 25 per cent of Coca-Cola's consumer pressure worldwide. On television the company has moved away from running heavy, short-term bursts of commercials, known as flights, then 'going dark' for a few weeks afterwards. Instead, it now funds a steady stream of ads at a moderate intensity level virtually non-stop.

In-store promotions have greater impact in more sophisticated consumer markets, such as the USA, 'just because of the way the consumer is processing messages', Frenette said. 'There's just so much messaging coming at people … that we know that if we don't activate those point-of-sale displays in the right way, with the right message, we've lost a big opportunity.' In other markets, where Coke is not so familiar, television is more important, while the internet presents an entirely new arena.

With these marketing operations as a backdrop, Frenette said the tricky task now is balancing global branding with local branding. Others in the marketing profession are waking up to this reality, partly by observing Coca-Cola. The global–local balance question plays to Coca-Cola's strengths, Frenette said:

'It's part of the paradox of the product. It is seen as a global brand by a lot of people and it is universal. And yet we have the ability to go in and recognize that people also have values and culture based on the way they live their lives, and to be part of that. That means being at the school and sponsoring the local bike race and being there with the soccer team and doing all of those things ... A business system that can deal with the realities of globalization, and have the sensibilities and sensitivities of dealing with local communities, is the driving force of what makes Coke perhaps the only real global brand that's out there.'

NOTES

1 Ted Friedman, 'The World of *The World of Coca-Cola*', *Communication Research*, Vol. 19, No. 5, October 1992, pp. 642–62.

2 Theodore Levitt, 'The globalization of markets', *Harvard Business Review*, May/June 1983.

2

PRO PATRIA:
RICARD AND THE NATIONAL
BRAND

'More than chic, I would say that the Ricard brand was exotic'

Patrick Ricard, CEO, Pernod Ricard

THE BARTENDRESS STARED AT ME with a puzzled expression as I repeated myself for the third time: 'Ricard on ice, please ... Do you know it?' She shrugged apologetically and admitted she had never heard of it, even though the aperitif that I was after – a pleasant liquorice-tasting drink distilled from aniseed – is the biggest-selling spirit brand in Europe, and even though we were in cosmopolitan Amsterdam. In the end, I settled for a Heineken, which she could pour with her eyes closed.

The lunchtime episode drove home to me a sometimes overlooked reality of branding – it is that however much global brands may be trumpeted as the way of the future, there are important brands that are strong, yet still essentially national in scope. And doing not too badly that way.

Whether it's Ricard and Gitanes cigarettes in France, Hersheys chocolate and Chrysler cars in America, or Carling beer and Tiny computers in Britain, national brands can and do thrive. Of course, most have tested foreign markets. Like Ricard, many are chasing overseas growth even now. Wal-Mart, for example, got to be the world's largest retailer while barely setting foot outside the USA. Today it is rapidly trying to go global. Yet there is something inherently American about Wal-Mart, just as there is something quintessentially French about Ricard. These national traits may never fully translate into another culture's brand language, but they help to define some brands, for better or for worse.

Strongly national brands may be export-handicapped due to differences in taste and style between countries. Harley Davidson, for instance, has trouble selling its brash, burly brand of motorcycles in Britain, where riders favour sleek, sporty bikes. Liquors such as Pirassununga 51 from Brazil, or Jinro Sujo from South Korea have little success away from home due to their unusual tastes, although they sell enough volume domestically to rank among the world's top ten spirits brands (see Fig. 2.1).

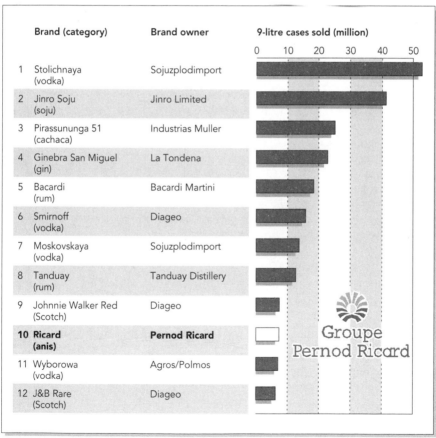

Source: Drinks International Bulletin

FIGURE 2.1 World's 12 top-selling spirits by 1998 volumes

On the other hand, national identities can be an advantage. Marlboro benefits from its 'American-ness', just as Gucci is aided by its origins in Italy or Chanel by its in France. Being German is one of the strongest traits of the Mercedes-Benz car brand. But powerful national traits, for whatever reason, occasionally act as formidable obstacles to globalization – and such has been the case with Ricard.

This limitation has held back Ricard's potential outside France, but it has not hurt it much as a business proposition. Like other national brands, Ricard holds sway over a huge core-customer base in its home market that gives its parent – French beverages group Pernod Ricard – strength and flexibility. Thanks to Ricard's revenues, Pernod Ricard can afford to experiment with other things, confident in the unique domestic relationships it enjoys with its lead brand. As long as those ties are not taken for granted, and even if they cannot be replicated elsewhere, they can form the foundation of a solid business.

> **66** Powerful national traits occasionally act as formidable obstacles to globalization. **99**

'Sales [of Ricard] in France are huge', said Patrick Ricard, the affable second-generation chairman of Pernod Ricard. In an interview, the son of the man who invented it sipped a Ricard on ice. A smoker, he pinched the filters off his Marlboros before lighting up. Friendly and quick to laugh, he told me about the company's efforts to broaden the Ricard brand, the challenges posed therein and the origins of the brand's stubbornly French persona. 'We are not strong everywhere, unfortunately … In southern Europe and Africa, Ricard is strong', he said. 'But you do see the brand in other countries and the idea is to expand.'

Roughly 85 per cent of Ricard's sales are inside France, with much of the remainder in neighbouring Belgium, Luxembourg and ex-colonial Francophone Africa. Beyond the French-speaking world, Ricard is virtually unknown.

Invented in 1932, it is an aniseed-based liqueur classified as a pastis from the Italian word *pasticcio* or trouble, as in troubled water. It was made popular 50 years ago, when its origins in sunny Marseille made it seem exotic in post-war Paris. Packing a punch masked by a liquorice taste that takes some getting used to, Ricard is a favourite midday quaff of working-class French people in the café.

On these strengths, it has become the biggest selling spirits brand in Europe, and one of the largest selling in the world by case volume. Ricard easily outsells more widely known, global spirits such as Gordon's gin, Chivas Regal Scotch or Jim Beam bourbon. Order one of these global brands in just about any bar from Amsterdam to Zürich, and you'll get a drink. But ask for a Ricard and odds are – if you're not in France or one of its nearest neighbours – all you'll get is a blank stare.

CIVILIZING ABSINTHE

The roots of Ricard go back to the turbulent 1780s, when Dr Pierre Ordinaire, a Frenchman exiled in Switzerland, concocted a recipe for an anis drink called absinthe using extract of wormwood and other herbs. The recipe found its way into the hands of young French businessman Henri-Louis Pernod. Convinced of its potential, he built the world's first large absinthe distillery in Switzerland in 1797. Six years later, with demand soaring, he built a larger one in France. There he set up the company Pernod Fils and absinthe took France by storm.

The drink – tasty and mildly hallucinogenic due to the wormwood content – became wildly popular over the next few decades, especially with the artists and poets of Parisian café society. Picasso, Manet and Degas painted people drinking it, and imbibed considerable quantities themselves. Van Gogh reputedly was an absinthe addict, which possibly explains his strange perception of light. The writers Rimbaud, Verlaine, Poe, Wilde and later Hemingway praised absinthe in poetry and prose.

The addictive drink's fame crested oddly with the famous 1905 murder by the unknown Frenchman Jean Lanfray of his wife one night in a drunken absinthe frenzy. The case was seized upon by the growing abolitionist movement. Absinthe came to be blamed for all manner of excess and immorality and was banned in Switzerland in 1907; in France in 1915, and in the USA shortly after.

After the First World War the French government allowed Pernod Fils to resume production with strict limits on the recipe. Wormwood extract was banned and removed from the formula. More anis was substituted and the alcohol content held to a legal limit. The product that resulted was a commercial success, but it was no longer absinthe. Its taste and intoxicating effects were very different and many drinkers rejected it.

Some French families reacted by resurrecting the custom of distilling their own aniseed drinks, using private recipes that they preferred over Pernod. Some contained wormwood; some did not. These clandestine spirits found their way into the cafés of Provence and Marseille, where they were discovered by the enterprising son of an area wine merchant, Paul Ricard.

He liked the taste of some of these bootleg elixirs, but knew their quality, taste and safety were too unreliable to be commercially viable, let alone legal. In secret he began tinkering with his own recipe in the hopes that he might some day bring it to a wider market. As he had foreseen, the government in 1933 eased restrictions on aniseed drinks. Wormwood remained off-limits and still does today, but alcohol and ingredients limits were raised, making Ricard's recipe legal and instantly popular.

After consolidating his local business on the Mediterranean coast, Ricard hit Paris with a wave of publicity and advertising impressive in its day. The push was aided by the arrival of the French Riviera as a popular vacation spot, no longer just for the aristocracy, but increasingly for the middle classes as well. Marseille took on an allure that Parisians found irresistible, thanks to influences like the films of Pagnol showing actors and writers relaxing in the south's sunny cafés sipping pastis.

Trading on this image, Ricard promoted his drink as he socialized his way through Jazz-Age Paris. Ricard explained:

'My father had the idea to produce a brand with a single taste … He launched his product before the last world war and he had a chance to start from Marseille when Marseille had a certain appeal for people from the north. A lot of people went there on holidays. Singers from the south were coming to Paris, actors and writers. My father was friends with those people and went to Paris with them. More than chic, I would say that the Ricard brand was exotic at that time.'

> **❝More than chic, I would say that the Ricard brand was exotic at that time. ❞**

The Second World War interrupted business, but both Ricard and Pernod Fils survived. They came back in the 1950s and entered a period of intense competition. Ricard supplanted Pernod as France's favourite anis. But Pernod held on to its pre-war notoriety overseas. In addition, Pernod Fils launched a new drink, Pastis 51, which proved eventually to be more popular than Pernod itself. Pastis 51 became a strong challenger to Ricard in France.

Both companies made some acquisitions into other spirits categories and fruit juices. Ricard went public in 1962. In 1975 Pernod Fils and Ricard formed a joint venture that led to a formal merger a year later. It was this transaction and the subsequent assignment of distribution responsibilities within the merged company that cast Ricard's role as a primarily national brand.

PERNOD FOR ANGLOS, RICARD FOR LATINS

The combined companies that became Pernod Ricard 25 years ago positioned Pernod as the anis brand it would use in one market, and Ricard as the brand it would use in another, based simply on their geographic origins – a decision that ended up doing neither one justice. 'At the beginning, we said that Pernod was for the Anglo-Saxon world and Ricard for the Latin world, only because Pernod was from the north and Ricard was from the south', Ricard recalled. Even now, he said, 'If you go to Switzerland, those who speak French drink Ricard, while those who speak German drink Pernod'.

For years, Pernod hung on inside and outside France, trading on the awareness and distribution strength it had achieved in the UK and the USA from returning tourists. At the same time, Ricard stayed close to home, making modest inroads into Spain and Italy while ousting Pernod at the top of the key French market and becoming the company's core product.

Pernod Ricard went on to diversify into other spirits, wine, soft drinks and fruit processing in the 1980s and 1990s, leaving its core anis business strangely divided between two brands unable to support each other overseas and vying for the same customer base at home. Growth in consumption of anis slowed and profit margins for Ricard declined. While this situation persisted, rivals to French anis went on to achieve truly global status. Spirits such as Scotch and rum, arguably no easier to drink than anis on the basis of taste, nevertheless became internationally accepted largely due to the marketing focus of the managers handling the leading brands, such as Johnnie Walker and Bacardi.

Had the more palatable and faster-growing Ricard been the one chosen by its owner for export to the expanding economies of Northern Europe and the New World, instead of declining Pernod, anis might be more widely consumed outside France today. Or it might not, Ricard said:

'There is a taste barrier. If you take Jamieson Irish whiskey [also owned by Pernod Ricard], it's a product that is easy to drink, smoother than Scotch whisky which is a bit more difficult to drink. If you take bourbon whiskey, it is even more difficult. If you take anis, it's very tasty but you have to get used to it … Bourbon and anis have much in common. Bourbon is very American, like anis is French.'

In any case, if a non-French bartender knows the name of any anis drink today, it is likely to be Pernod, although Pernod does not rank among the world's top 100 spirits brands, while global unknown Ricard ranks in the top ten. This paradox is now recognized by the company. 'Now, we let Ricard go when Pernod is in a market and vice versa', said Ricard. 'We let both go because when they are alone, it's more difficult to promote the brand than when they are together. And we notice that Ricard is easier to drink than Pernod.'

START AT THE TOP

When taking Ricard into a new market, the company follows the customary beverage-industry formula of targeting upper-income consumers with luxury buying power. Once established among the well-to-do, the brand is migrated downwards towards middle-income customers.

> 66 Once established among the well-to-do, the brand is migrated downwards towards middle-income customers. 99

This pattern contrasts sharply with the company's efforts within France, where Ricard in recent years gained a decidedly middle-income image, due in part to private label competition. Promotional efforts lately have been geared toward taking it up-market and re-establishing its hipness. As Ricard said:

'It is true that in France, as it is a popular drink, it was drunk by a lot of people. But it was more in the middle, so we have invested quite a lot of money in recent years to promote the brand among younger and more wealthy people. There still are some people who … have Ricard at home, but they will not really offer it to you because they say it's not chic enough. But this is improving. It's moving now.'

A market for super-premium anis is emerging, which could help the category in the same way that connoisseurs boosted the image of Scotch by paying top dollar for single malts. In addition, Pernod Ricard is promoting

Ricard on college campuses and in nightclubs, with some success. 'The image is changing ... We promote it now as a drink for the night', he said. He went on:

'It's everyday an aperitif in France because the cocktail before lunch or dinner is very important ... That is the biggest market for us and we don't want to hurt that. That is the core of the revenue. But we also are promoting it in the universities when they have their swinging evenings, and it works well. Or in the ski resorts, we have teams who promote the brand in the terrace for lunchtime and in the nightclubs. We always target new consumers. In New York, one of the happening places to go is called the Pastis Café ... It's for the young. It's a very swinging place and there are walls of Ricard. It's not operated by us, but just by the people who operate the café.'

Encouragingly for Ricard's ambitions to transcend its national base, upon enquiry it emerged the owner of the Pastis Café in Manhattan is Keith McNally. Doesn't sound very French.

3

NEXT DOOR NEIGHBOUR: LEINENKUGEL'S AND THE REGIONAL BRAND

'Our positioning, the flavour of the Northwoods, it's only going to work in a certain area'

Dick Leinenkugel, vice-president of sales and marketing, Jacob Leinenkugel Brewing Co.

FOLLOW THE DRIFTING BARBECUE SMOKE to the Rotary Club fry-out in just about any town in quiet, green Wisconsin on a summer Sunday afternoon and you will find the locals munching on bratwurst in the sunshine, swatting mosquitoes and knocking back more than a few cold bottles of Leinenkugel's. The same goes for Minnesota and northern reaches of Illinois, Iowa and Michigan. But outside the upper Midwest, the beer that made Chippewa Falls famous is mostly a stranger.

That did not deter Miller Brewing Co., the second largest brewer in the USA, from buying little Jacob Leinenkugel Brewing Co. in 1988. Since then, the mammoth Miller group has tried hard to take Leinenkugel's nation-wide. But the brand has remained stubbornly Midwestern. Trading on its whimsical image as a quality craft brew from the rugged Northwoods, after more than 130 years Leinenkugel's still does more than 80 per cent of its business in Wisconsin, Minnesota and Illinois.

In those states Leinenkugel's commands fierce loyalty. Not that folks in Wisconsin or Minnesota get fierce about much of anything. But they are loyal to their Leinie's. 'The Leinenkugel's consumer ... is a person who loves the outdoors – camping, hunting, fishing, canoeing, outdoor activities, loves to vacation in Wisconsin or Northern Minnesota or the UP [Upper Peninsula of Michigan]. That's what I call a rugged lifestyle', said Dick Leinenkugel, vice-president of sales and marketing, in an interview in Chicago. He went on:

'We're not a brand that's pushed. And we won't be successful that way. We are truly a brand that's discovered. Word of mouth is a big part of who we are. Even in the age of the internet, people want to connect locally ... People want to have a sense of place and I think as long as we can take people to that place, through our brands or through them using our brands, that's where we'll be successful. Chippewa Falls, the Northwoods. It's kind of mysterious.'

In a world where the search for identity can lead people to look back to simple and familiar things, brands with deep roots in a single region can and do succeed. This is an old-fashioned view of branding. It stands opposed to the trendier argument that commercial identities are becoming more global due to world-circling communication, transportation and entertainment. But it is a view that even corporate giants, such as soft-drinks leader Coca-Cola Co., are re-examining closely after some setbacks with global branding.

Coca-Cola's struggle to understand the reaction to an embarrassing 1999 product recall in Belgium, France and the Netherlands, as well as setbacks related to attempted acquisitions in Europe, are leading it to redefine its view of the global brand in a local light. The Atlanta giant's new CEO Douglas Daft told the German news weekly *Die Zeit*:

'What we are seeing is a reaction – people see globalization as a threat to their individual way of life ... Being seen as being truly everywhere is what the goal of the Coca-Cola Co. has always been. We have to now link that into being seen by our consumers as being a brand that is relevant to my local community.'[1]

Coca-Cola Co., owner of the most valuable brand in the world, could take a lesson in marketing from the quirky brewer from Indianhead Country. If the people at Leinenkugel's know anything, it is how its consumers live their lives in their communities. Why? Because the Leinenkugel family actually lives in those communities and so does its company, despite the fact that it is owned by Miller, a unit of New-York-based Philip Morris Cos. It's that simple. As Dick Leinenkugel, the great-great-grandson of the founder of the business, said:

'We are a 133-year-old brewing company that has family members running the brewery and a strong linkage to our Northwoods heritage. Primarily a regional brand, we focus on the Upper Midwest in our imagery and what we try to be – not only who we try to be when we meet people and live it, but also in our advertising and packaging, and everything we try to do. Regional brands like Leinenkugel's that have a strong local following and are able to maintain that local following by having a great dialogue with consumers ... are going to do well and survive. Not only survive, but thrive. That's our plan.'

THIRSTY LUMBERJACKS

Jacob Leinenkugel, the son of a Bavarian immigrant brewmaster from Sauk City, Wisconsin, moved north to Chippewa Falls in 1866, the year after the end of the Civil War, and founded a brewery. The sawmill workers and lumberjacks of the frontier town of 2,500 inhabitants were no doubt grateful. The business grew steadily. In 1888 Leinenkugel introduced a Bock beer, the first of many line extensions to come later. When he died in 1899 his son took over. The company survived Prohibition from 1918 to 1933 by bottling soda water, but promptly returned to brewing after repeal of the 21st Amendment.

The brewery expanded gradually across Wisconsin after the Second World War and, in the early 1970s, into Minnesota and Upper Michigan. In line with a national fad for low-calorie products, the company introduced Leinenkugel's Light in 1972. Another extension, Leinenkugel's Limited, followed in 1986. In the next year, Bill Leinenkugel, great-grandson of the founder, retired after 40 years with the company.

Miller – the huge Milwaukee brewer made famous by its powerhouse brands Miller High Life and Miller Lite – acquired Leinenkugel's in 1988. A corporate struggle for marketing control followed, with Jake Leinenkugel, great-great-grandson of the founder, winning out over ambitious middle managers at Miller. He was named president in 1989.

The brewery in 1993 launched Leinenkugel's Red Lager into a wave of national enthusiasm for 'red' beers. Rapid expansion followed, using Miller's vast sales and distribution network. Dick Leinenkugel, younger brother to Jake, recalled:

'We went into over 40 states at one time with Leinie's Red. But what we found was that as we got further afield from Chippewa Falls, our brewery, certainly the operating costs, the cost to get the beer there, were very high. Leinenkugel's was not familiar, so you had to spend more time educating your wholesalers, your sales people. We really found that Leinenkugel's didn't mean a whole lot to people that weren't familiar with it. We did well with accounts or people who had been to Minneapolis, or were from the Upper Midwest or went to school at [the University of Wisconsin in] Madison. But that wasn't enough to sustain the brand. What we realized was that for every ... five dollars we would spend in New York or California, that was just dollars we were more effectively able to use in our home market.'

As the red-beer fad faded, the brewery pulled back from its drive for a national brand presence. Leinenkugel's beers are no longer distributed so widely. Leinenkugel explained:

'Our positioning, the flavour of the Northwoods, it's only going to work in a certain area. We realize that. People are going to have different perceptions of the Northwoods in different areas. But we have a lot of room for growth up here in Wisconsin. No plans to expand coast to coast. We've done that. We've tried that.'

'We do over 80 per cent of our business in three states: Minnesota, Wisconsin and Illinois. What we've realized is that we're just scratching the surface here right now. There is still a lot of opportunity for us to grow in these three states. Chicago is a huge beer market. Minneapolis is a big beer market. Certainly, Milwaukee and the rest of Wisconsin. It's one of the top beer consumption states in the nation on a per capita basis. So there is a lot of opportunity for us to grow within these three states. But importantly, then, through contiguous expansion, looking at Iowa and Michigan, there are certainly opportunities.'

After the retreat back into the Midwest, demand for Leinenkugel's continued to grow. The company started rapidly extending its product line beyond its Original Lager, Bock, Light and Limited brands. Developing its image as a craft and specialty brewer, Leinenkugel's introduced Honey Weiss, Autumn Gold, Auburn Ale, Big Butt Doppelbock, Berry Weiss and Maple Brown Lager beers. It also relaunched its Limited beer under the new name of Northwoods Lager.

These line extensions allowed Leinenkugel's to ride a wave of consumer interest in specialty and craft beers, but they also may have led to some second thoughts about over-stretching of the brand. As Leinenkugel said:

'We recently have taken some steps to reduce our portfolio. At the beginning of this year we discontinued four of our brands. We'll be taking steps next year to further refine that portfolio. We really believe in spending behind and focusing our ... sales efforts on those brands that are delivering the most consumer satisfaction. Now in our portfolio, three brands account for 80 per cent of our sales. That's Leinie's original, Leinie's Red and Leinenkugel's Honey Weiss.'

> ❝We really believe in focusing our sales efforts on those brands that are delivering the most consumer satisfaction. ❞

Trimming the brand portfolio is not meant to signal a step back from speciality brewing:

'We're in a category where people want different styles and different flavours of beers. Thus, Berry Weiss. We are going to extend the seasonal availability of Berry Weiss ... We'll continue to do our Bock, which has been around since 1888. But we'll get out of things that don't make sense for us, or aren't being accepted by the consumer.'

ALMOST BEING THERE

In spite of being part of the massive Philip Morris group, which owns brands ranging from Miller beer and Marlboro cigarettes to Post cereals and Kraft foods, Leinenkugel's has managed to hold on to its regional identity. The latest advertising effort, managed by a firm from lovely Sheboygan, Wisconsin, is to exploit the Northwoods image by selling it to people who know it from holidays.

Northern Wisconsin is a popular playground for Chicagoans and the Windy City represents a big market. Leinenkugel said:

'We're embarking on a strategy called "vacation marketing". That is the concept that Leinie's is not only the beer that you drink when you're on vacation, but it's the beer to find and enjoy when you're back home. My dad always told us ... half of Chicago comes up and visits the resorts of northern Wisconsin. They love this beer up there. That's where people are first introduced to it. I think when you're on vacation, you're more willing to try something that's new, different and that's part of that area.'

Radio spots and billboard advertisements are aimed at catching Chicagoans as they drive in and out of the region with a message that will remind them of Leinenkugel's.

Playing off the regional identity in a different way, Leinenkugel's is also positioning the beer inside the Chicago tourist zone as a characteristic local brew:

'Even though we are 300 miles away from Chicago, our image is such that we're a strong regional brand. On Michigan Avenue, they get a lot of foreign visitors, people who are visiting the art museum or other museums down there. A lot of English people. They come in and say, I'd like a local beer ... Leinie's Red or Honey Weiss, our beers. So I think we're perceived as being this local regional.'

Leinenkugel's recognizes, since the Leinie's Red episode, certain limitations to its brand for now. As Leinenkugel said:

66 Until you stop growing in your local market, there is no reason to expand anywhere else. 99

'Until you stop growing in your local market, there is no reason to expand anywhere else. I'm sure that we could take Leinenkugel's and select a Northern California market or a New England market and achieve some level of success there, but would it be the right utilization of our marketing resources, our marketing dollars? No.'

At the same time, the brand has built almost a cult following that is in evidence on its website (www.leinie.com):

'I really enjoy writing the replies on our internet site saying, sorry, you can't have our beer in Seattle, but come and visit us in Chippewa Falls. I think I answered one last night ... It was Berry Weiss in Seattle. Her comment was my relatives are sick of carrying 12 packs when they come out to Seattle on the airplane. I responded something like, "You have really nice relatives. I would ask them to come and visit more often. But we're just not going to ship our beer to Seattle." I'd love to say Leinenkugel's could go to Hawaii because I was in the Marines in Hawaii ... But I'm sure there are limitations. The positioning is not going to work in Texas. We are in Arizona right now through a brew pub venture. But it really doesn't work in Arizona.'

Regional branding is especially common in the beer business and there are plenty of other breweries, not only in the USA but around the world, that take an approach similar to Leinenkugel's. Rolling Rock, a US beer owned by the Labatt unit of Belgian brewing giant Interbrew, stresses its origins in Latrobe, Pennsylvania, although its character is somewhat less distinctive. The German brewing industry is so highly fragmented that most German beer brands are still regional. Britain still has a number of regional brands, although most European countries are dominated by national brands.

Miller itself recently acquired the Henry Weinhard's brewery in the Pacific Northwest of the USA. 'It's got a great heritage there, a lot like Leinenkugel's and a real strong loyal consumer base', Leinenkugel said. 'I'm optimistic about regional brands. I think they'll continue to do well.'

NOTES

1 *Die Zeit*, 7 August 2000.

THREE DISTINGUISHING MARKS

Traditional Leinenkugel logo

Plain typographical UDV logo

Universal Shell Pecten symbol

CATERPILLAR The original product – which still forms the bulk of their business; an example of a new product; and the logo

one vision

The Coca-Cola swirl has been strongly defended by the company. It ranks as the world's most valuable brand.

I N THE MID-1970s A POPULAR T-shirt appeared on market stalls and roadside trestles around the world. It mimicked the famous soda swirl of Coca-Cola. But rather than promoting the world-famous fizzy drink it advertised an entirely different substance. 'Enjoy Cocaine – it's the real thing' read the stylised script. The 'joke' only worked because Coca-Cola was, even then, one of the world's most famous trademarks and the fact that the T-shirts were to be seen on the streets of London, the beaches of Majorca and in the clubs of New York reflected Coca-Cola's ranking as a truly international brand.

Not surprisingly Coca-Cola reacted swiftly. Executives may have privately sensed that imitation was flattery, but publicly their response was to sue retailers and manufacturers. Every now and then the same message reappears on garments and the response is always the same – quick and forceful litigation to defend the brand.

Brand value is hard won, but can be a company's most important asset. According to research by Interbrand, which earlier this year published its World's Most Valuable Brands survey, the value of the Coca-Cola brand represents 59 per cent of its US$84 billion market capitalisation. Coca-Cola heads the Interbrand rankings of brand values.

The Shell Pecten is another of the world's most recognisable symbols – and an important asset to the Group companies. It is arguably as well known as the Coca-Cola swirl or the McDonald's golden 'M', the Ralph Lauren pony or the Nike swoosh. But a three-year research project commissioned by the Shell Group Brand Committee found that Shell had not been as successful as it could in communicating the values that lie behind the

Brand Values: Actor Doughie Vipon (top) explains the Brand Vision in the video distributed to the businesses. Waves of change (middle) explores the natural power of the Pecten, one of the world's most recognisable brands.
A still (bottom) taken from the Shell Pura advertising, shown in Ireland and the Netherlands.

Goldmine: The golden arches of McDonald's (left) are readily identified the world over.

Below, Simon Saville, Global Brand Standards manager.

Reproduced from an original article by Mark Hannant appearing in Shell World, October 1999

ONE VISION Front page of the brand strategy publication

HEINEKEN The logo and the product, bottled or on draught

INTERBRAND Rita Clifton, CEO

LEO BURNETT USA Linda Wolf, CEO

CADBURY SCHWEPPES PLC Alan Palmer, International Marketing Director, Group Confectionery; the product, and the "C" swirl.

photo Simon Thong © Reuters 2000

YAHOO! IN SINGAPORE Promoters distribute leaflets to promote their new 35,000-item online shopping facility

photo Pierre Virot © Reuters 2000

THE BIRTH OF EASY RENTACAR Stelios Haji-Ioannou of easy Holdings and Joachim Schmidt of Mercedes-Benz pose in front of an A-Class Mercedes in Geneva

photo Mikhail Chernichkin © Reuters 1996

photo Rula Halawani © Reuters 1998

WAR IN THE UKRAINE A man looks at an advertisement in the Ukraine, where there's war between Coca-Cola with 25 per cent of the market and Pepsi-Cola with 22 per cent

NEW ARRIVAL An elderly Arab man tries the first Coke in Palestinian-ruled Ramallah, 1 August 1998

4

JUDO TACTICS: EASYJET AND THE UNDERDOG BRAND

'Never underestimate the importance of being seen as the little guy against the big guy'

Stelios Haji-Ioannou, CEO, easyJet

DECKED OUT IN AN ORANGE JUMPSUIT and with boarding pass in hand, the wily Greek airline entrepreneur Stelios Haji-Ioannou recently treated the world to a clinic on the slashing art of underdog branding, sponsored by none other than arch-enemy British Airways (BA).

It was the day of the inaugural flight of Go, then the discount division of long-suffering BA. The largest airline in Europe had been forced to 'Go' down-market largely due to short-haul business lost over several years to Haji-Ioannou's UK-based budget carrier easyJet.

The first Go flight was a staged media event. But BA had not counted on 10 tickets being bought by easyJet staffers. All 10, including the boss, turned up at the BA gate in unmistakable citrus-hued easyJet outfits, bearing coupons for free easyJet flights. BA agents had to usher the unwelcome but paying easyJetters aboard. Once aloft, the orange commandoes politely walked the aisles of the plane, in conspicuous view of the watchful media, distributing free flight vouchers to 148 fellow passengers. In no time, what had begun as a coming out party for Go turned into another brilliant publicity heist by the man who specializes in giving BA fits.

Haji-Ioannou, the millionaire son of a Greek shipping tycoon, regularly employs such judo-like marketing tactics, turning the power and weight of his lumbering opponents against them by clever manoeuvre that requires cunning, speed and the nerves of a cat burglar. Beyond air transport, he has diversified into online-only auto rental with easyRentacar.com, online banking with easyMoney.com and Internet cafes with easyEverything. All these businesses share the 'easy' name, the hard-to-ignore orange colour scheme and a generous supply of attitude.

'Never underestimate the importance of being seen as the little guy against the big guy', Haji-Ioannou told *The Guardian* newspaper after stealing Go's thunder. 'We have positioned ourselves as the Robin Hood of the airline business. People recognize me in the street and come up to me and thank me. They say, well done, keep up the good work and carry on fighting the bastards.'[1]

Underdog brands, or brands that promote themselves as scrappy alternatives to older and more established rivals, are becoming more common. Haji-Ioannou has been inspired by Dallas-based Southwest Airlines, and fellow UK business rebels Richard Branson and Sir Freddy Laker.

Underdog brands are often guided by charismatic business entrepreneurs – Steve Jobs at Apple Computer was an example before his company got big and bureaucratic – and by a spirit of innovation, risk and even, dare it be said, fun.

> 66 Underdog brands are often guided by charismatic business entrepreneurs. 99

Underdog brand managers like to roll the dice and take chances. That can be dangerous, of course. The ones who lose are the ones you never heard of. But for Haji-Ioannou and 'easy', the underdog style is a speciality. His story is an excellent model of how to run a brand that not only offers a real option to cost-conscious consumers, but gains much of its awareness on the wings of its rivals. For instance, at the time of writing, easyJet was running a contest on the web offering free flight vouchers to anyone who could guess how much money BA's Go would lose during the year.

'I didn't set out to build a brand. I set out to build a low-cost airline', Haji-Ioannou, 33, said in an interview during a recent conference in Geneva, where he was engaged in a guerrilla marketing action against national powerhouse SwissAir. 'The big thing that helped us build up the brand was that British Airways attacked easyJet and that gave us a lot of credibility. It made us recognized in the market as a threat', said the young CEO, whose stout physique and jovial style conceal a killer instinct.

AN EASY START

Born in Athens, Stelios – as he prefers to be known – is the second son of the Greek Cypriot shipping billionaire Loucas Haji-Ioaunnou, who owns and operates the huge Troodos shipping group. After high school in Greece, Stelios earned degrees from the London School of Economics and the City University Business School before joining his father's business. He started his own shipping company, Stelmar Tankers, in 1992, complete with a luxurious office and a retinue of well-dressed executives. He still manages the successful firm and its 12-tanker fleet, but the business is said to consume little of his time today.

Bored with shipping, Stelios travelled in the USA in the early 1990s and became familiar with the discount airline concept as practised by Herb Kelleher's audacious Southwest Airlines, whose colour scheme, perhaps not coincidentally, is also orange. Stelios over these years became an admirer of Branson, too, the ultimate rebel brand operator who has pushed his Virgin brand into music, air travel, condoms, cola, ballooning, vodka, financial services, radio, cinemas, cosmetics, clothing, a train line and holiday resorts.

Eyeing these two role models, and reckoning that Europe was ready for a Southwest-style airline revolution, Stelios borrowed £5 million from his father in 1995, rounded up £50 million elsewhere, and founded easyJet. The launch party was at Planet Hollywood.

He set up shop at under-used Luton Airport in London's northern suburbs. Luton is a tough town of car factories and council estates – just right for the no-frills image that he wanted for easyJet. The company was housed in a warren of offices off the runway that Stelios named easyLand and painted bright orange. He hired mostly young people to work in a vast room without walls. In the middle of it, he installed his own, plain desk, usually littered with Diet Coke cans.

Profitability came after about two years, Stelios claimed. Some industry analysts were sceptical, however, given the razor-thin profit margins of the discount airline business, which is getting crowded these days in Europe with companies such as BA's Go, Ireland's Ryanair, Buzz from the Netherlands' KLM, and Branson's Virgin Express.

THE WEB'S FAVOURITE AIRLINE

Inside easyLand, the only people who put on ties are the pilots. Hundreds of headset-wearing sales agents work the telephones, making reservations and explaining easyJet's procedures to callers. Another part of the staff manages the flow of business over the internet. EasyJet claims to sell more than two-thirds of its seats over the web – a higher internet sales ratio than any other airline.

Advertising and promotion is handled in-house and often on the run. A recent ad attacking Go was conceived by two executives in the back of a taxi one morning, designed and mocked up that afternoon and appeared the next day in London newspapers.

EasyJet doesn't issue tickets and it doesn't use travel agents. Individual passengers reserve their seats on the phone or via the web. Fare structures are simple – no black-out periods, holiday surcharges, advance-booking requirements and other dodgy details that make other airlines so aggravating.

On the day of the flight, easyJet passengers show up at the check-in counter with proof of identity and get a plastic-laminated, reusable boarding pass. At Luton, it takes less than five minutes to get to the gate from the main terminal, compared to a half-hour at major airports such as Heathrow.

EasyJet's planes usually leave on schedule. When they don't, there is a reasonable explanation and an apology. At boarding time, passes are collected and passengers file out on to the runway apron guided by battered, hand-painted signs reading Liverpool or Amsterdam or Malaga. On board, there are no assigned seats. Passengers sit down where they wish. There is no first class or business class. All the seats are the same. The planes are clean, new Boeing 737s.

The upshot of this bare-bones style – which starts at the top with Stelios and flows down to the flight attendants who clean up the planes themselves after landing – is that fares are dirt cheap. A round-trip Amsterdam–Luton weekender recently went for £85, versus £102 on BA. Overnight hops could be made to Barcelona for £145 on easyJet; £198 on Go.

The big drawback of easyJet at the time of writing was that it did not fly to Paris, Milan, Frankfurt, Rome or anywhere outside Europe, limiting its usefulness for business travellers. Stelios knows this. Although he has hunted for more business passengers, he told *The Guardian* recently:

'I realized there are two types of customer in the airline business: those who pay out of their own pocket, and those who don't. The industry was set up with the fat cats who don't pay out of their own pockets in mind. There was never price competition. Airlines set up all sorts of freebies and bribes so that people would choose them. What we have done is give price competition. The other thing I realized is that quality is all about meeting customer expectations. The priorities are, it has to be safe, cheap and on-time. So if you don't promise anything else, no one can be disappointed.'[2]

> **❝Quality is all about meeting customer expectations.❞**

NO EASY VICTORIES

As easyJet has expanded, it has clashed repeatedly – and eagerly – with the deeply entrenched national powers of European commercial air travel, most of which are former government monopolies only recently privatized. British Airways, for instance, went private in 1987. Many of these clashes, while seemingly stacked against a small brand like easyJet, have been turned to its favour by artful underdog public relations and advertising, as well as aggressive legal tactics. The losers in easyJet's counter-punching display have been industry heavyweights.

When Stelios started out in 1995 BA initially watched and waited, and it appeared to be safe in doing so. For a year it appeared that not much was happening around easyLand. Then in May 1996 a ValuJet DC9 crashed into the Florida Everglades, killing all 110 people aboard. The accident instantly resurrected public fears about discount airline safety. For a while, 'cheap' once again meant 'dangerous'. It was not a good time to be in the budget carrier business.

EasyJet soldiered on through the slump that followed, and managed to do so safely. 'The way we combat possible perceptions that we will be unsafe or unreliable is by showing that we are not', Stelios said.

'The proof of the pudding is in the eating. If you have a good safety record then you are okay. If you started to lose planes, you would have a big problem.'

But BA sensed that the ValuJet disaster might present an opportunity to pick off its young, orange challenger on the cheap. According to easyJet, BA chief executive Bob Ayling bumped into Stelios at a Salomon Brothers airline conference in New York and asked to arrange a formal meeting. The two met, according to Stelios, and Ayling said that he thought easyJet had 'cracked' the secret to running a low-fare airline profitably. But he added that easyJet would benefit from being brought under BA's so-called 'safety halo', possibly through a partial acquisition.

Stelios, who has said he has a sell-out price like anyone else, was inter-ested in Ayling's approach. He said he even allowed a group of BA executives into easyLand to have a peek at his business plan. But then, he said, he got a letter from BA in March 1997 saying that any possible deal was off due to BA's belief that government regulators would block its entry into the discount market.

Try to picture easyJet's surprise, therefore, when BA announced in November 1997 that it planned to launch its own no-frills carrier to be run out of Stansted Airport. Modelled closely on the Southwest Airlines/easyJet prototype, the BA low-fares unit was later officially named Go. Stelios was furious and charged BA with plotting to drive him and others out of business.

Branson, a veteran of battles with BA, responded angrily to the Go ven-ture. In remarks to the Associated Press, he said: 'Today's announcement by British Airways is typical of their approach to business. They hate competition and Europe's new low-cost carriers are genuine competi-tion.' The *enfant terrible* of British business charged that BA would continue to 'rip off' customers at crowded Heathrow and Gatwick with high fares, but somehow 'miraculously find they can offer rock-bottom prices against their new competitors at Stansted'.[3]

In February 1998 easyJet filed a lawsuit against BA in an attempt to block Go, charging that BA had abused its dominant market position to stifle competition, breaching Article 86 of the European Community Treaty. A UK judge ruled three months later that the launch of Go would be allowed to proceed, but that easyJet could continue to pursue its case.

EasyJet discovered in the meantime, however, that it continued to grow even with Go in the market, thanks undoubtedly in part to the huge publicity boost received from the BA episode. Stacks of newspaper articles and television news reports appeared about it. Stelios looked like a hero and passenger volumes at his airline soared. This lesson was not lost on him.

EasyJet afterwards made a habit of courting controversy, which has, so far, been kind to it. The airline became the subject of a regular ITV television documentary show called *Airline* that still appears throughout the UK. The programme uses a day-in-the-life-of format, zeroing in on individual easyJet staffers and passengers as they try to get off the ground. Stelios himself has appeared in a cameo role as the cheerful host who soothes tired customers with free drinks.

More combative parts have come his way in other recent easyJet productions, including the airline's lawsuit in 1999 against Olympic Airways of Greece. The action alleged unfair competition and misleading advertising involving promotion of discount flights between Athens and London. EasyJet claimed that British Airways executives had been put in charge at Olympic and were bringing Go-style tactics to Athens to combat easyJet's gains there.

EasyJet also recently took a swing at SwissAir. The spat involved the larger airline's attempts to limit easyJet's access to Geneva Airport. EasyLand staff took to calling the SwissAir chief 'Darth Vader' and campaigned in Switzerland for passage by public ballot of a European Union law opening Swiss skies to more airline competition. The measure passed overwhelmingly in May 2000.

Barclays Bank, one of the largest financial institutions in Europe, became the target of an easyJet propaganda war. In advertisements and web postings, easyJet lambasted the bank for trying to raise landing fees at Luton Airport to between £6 and £7 per customer from £1.68 per customer – a hike that easyJet claimed would wreck its cost structure. Calling Barclays 'greedy investment bankers', easyJet asked passengers to e-mail their concerns to the government.

Barclays, through its venture capital funds, controls 62 per cent of the fast-growing airport, which recently added a new terminal and a new commuter train station to link it to central London – all thanks largely to the boost in passenger traffic brought by easyJet.

THE BIG EASY

In five years easyJet grew to 1,000 flights per week with 18 destinations. It has more than 1,000 employees and a fleet of 18 Boeing 737-300s, with orders for dozens more new 737-700s to be delivered over the next four years. Besides Luton, hubs have been added at Liverpool and Geneva.

Even as it has expanded, easyJet's rivals have struggled. In May 2000 British Airways reported an annual loss of $360 million before exceptional gains, its worst financial result since it privatized 13 years ago. Ayling has resigned as CEO, having inadvertently done more to boost the fortunes of his upstart rival than anyone could have imagined possible.

Stelios, flush from easyJet's success, began pushing his 'easy' brand into new areas in 1999. 'Once you've built a brand ... then you start to try and stretch it', Stelios said.

He opened the first in a chain of easyEverything internet cafés opposite Victoria Station in central London in mid-1999. The huge store had 400 internet screens offering access for as little as £1 per hour to the public. More stores later opened in London, New York, Madrid, Edinburgh, Amsterdam, Rotterdam, Barcelona and other cities, moving towards a goal of 60 stores by the end of 2001. The young internet café industry still had no clear leader by mid-2000. So Stelios had no obvious giant to pick a fight with, putting him on uncertain ground with easyEverything. But this was absolutely not the case with his two other new 'easy' brands.

> **❝Once you've built a brand then you start to try and stretch it. ❞**

EasyRentacar.com got started in early 2000. The company rolled out with a stunningly simple business model positioned predictably as an alternative to Hertz, Avis and the usual rental agencies. The 'easy' upstart offered one car, the Mercedes A class, at 10 sites – including London Bridge, Amsterdam, Nice, Paris, Birmingham, Manchester, Malaga, London – Chelsea, Barcelona and Glasgow – at a fee structure much simpler than those of the giants of the business. Plus, the 'easy' cars can be reserved over the internet, a feat that remains so difficult to accomplish with the established agencies that it is clear they don't really want business on the web.

Finally, an online financial services concept called easyMoney.com was unveiled by Stelios, but its website was still under construction in late 2000. Branding against the UK's big, impersonal banks would be a natural fit for Stelios, but details of his venture remain unclear.

In our interview, he said:

'You have to build up a brand country by country. With us, it's helped to be attacked by the flag carriers in other countries, like KLM in Holland and SwissAir in Switzerland. We were unknown in Switzerland before SwissAir objected to our application for a route licence between Geneva and Barcelona. So for us, building a brand is being recognized by the incumbents. Brand recognition takes time to establish. It take effort and a lot of battling, which sometimes looks like warfare.'

NOTES

1 *The Guardian*, 16 November 1999.
2 *The Guardian*, 16 November 1999.
3 The Associated Press, 17 November 1997.

5

BULLDOZERS TO BOOTS: CATERPILLAR AND BRAND EXTENSION

'We've literally been asked to do everything, even condoms'

Mark Jostes, marketing manager, Caterpillar Co.

WHEN I WAS GROWING UP IN GEORGIA, wearing a black baseball cap with a bright-yellow Caterpillar logo on it meant you were a redneck.

Not that there's anything wrong with that, as Jerry Seinfeld would say. But in the Deep South in the 1970s the Cat hat was definitely associated with the hound-dogs-and-pickups crowd, and I'm pretty sure it had the same image from Maine to California. So, imagine this redneck's surprise when he arrived 25 years later in London – crowned the coolest place on Earth by gushy magazines that know – and saw the Cat logo all over the place on boots and shoes, T-shirts, book bags and, yes, even hats.

Moreover, it was not being sported by tobacco-spittin' good-old-boys, but by those spiky-haired, nose-pierced urban youth you only see in big cities after about 3 o'clock in the afternoon. Think of Soho or Tribeca or Capitol Hill in Seattle. I was, to use a Britishism, gob-smacked.

Caterpillar Inc., the world's largest maker of construction equipment and engines, has pulled off one of marketing's most extreme brand extensions. In the UK and much of Europe, this conservative, Illinois-based builder of bulldozers and backhoes is now known as a rad brand of hip-hop streetwear. 'No industrial equipment company has ever transcended into a soft goods market with the success that we have', said Mark Jostes, mass retail marketing manager at Cat. 'In America, if you ask people who Caterpillar is, they'll tell you it's a construction equipment company first, and they sell workboots. Here, they'll say it's a workboot company, and maybe they've heard of the equipment', Jostes said in an interview.

In a back alley in London's trendy Clerkenwell section are the offices of shoe and apparel design and distribution firm Overland Group Ltd, whose speciality is stretching the Cat brand to the outer limits. On the ground floor, a bullpen of sharp-eyed young designers and marketers collaborate to gin up next season's lines of shoes, sandals, shirts, trousers, jackets and accessories that Jostes assures me not only say Cat on multiple hard-to-miss logo tags, but also exude a rugged, engineered Cat style. Jostes told me:

'Kids view us on the street ... as this chunky, solid, authentic American thing that they don't totally understand, but they know it's a real American work thing. What we have to do as a brand for young people is keep it fresh, keep it fun and energetic ... Our people are out on the street taking that pulse every day. And we have young people developing the product. That's part of the secret.'

> **❝What we have to do as a brand for young people is keep it fresh, keep it fun and energetic. ❞**

Back at headquarters in rock-ribbed Republican Peoria, where sober engineers pore over designs for elevated sprockets and planetary gears, heads are shaken occasionally in puzzlement at Jostes and his odd venture. But, he insists, the suits-and-ties back home are getting their heads around the brand extension programme.

'We've sold 32.6 million pairs of shoes since 1994. Any way you slice that pie, that's 66 million billboards walking around on this planet carrying our brand, and those people have paid for the opportunity to extend us into places where people may never have seen us before. So, smart managers at the company have recognized that Cat is getting a lot of value out of this.'

As an exercise in popularizing a brand whose conservative owner was once best known for labour problems and being slow to respond 20 years ago to the Japanese competitive challenge, the Cat brand extension is worth a look. As an example of pure, unmitigated marketing chutzpah, it's a must-see.

CREEPY CRAWLERS

Agricultural equipment manufacturer Benjamin Holt substituted crawler tracks for wheels, and then gasoline engines for steam on his farm tractors back in the early 1900s in Stockton, California. He called his powerful, go-anywhere vehicle the Caterpillar tractor. Sales grew slowly as farmers and heavy equipment users tried the machines. Early exports went to Mexico, Canada and Argentina. Holt added a plant in East Peoria, in the heart of the Midwestern farm belt.

As the First World War approached, both the British and German military drew on Holt's ideas to develop track-driven tanks. With the outbreak of fighting, Holt declined to fill German orders, but his factories worked overtime to meet the demands of British and US forces. After the war Holt merged his business with rival Best Tractor Co. They renamed their joint operations Caterpillar Tractor Co. and established headquarters in Peoria. Sales boomed through the 1920s, then fell sharply during the Depression. Cat pioneered diesel engines and rubber tyres during this troubled period, and began painting its products in the 'Hi-Way Yellow' that would become its signature colour.

The painting lines shifted to olive drab during the Second World War, when Cat cranked out shiploads of military equipment. With peace, Cat's business boomed on post-war reconstruction demand worldwide. Explosive growth came in the 1950s and 1960s as plants opened around the world.

By the 1970s Japanese challengers such as Komatsu were chipping away at Caterpillar's global dominance, but the company largely looked the other way. Cat was fat, dumb and happy by the time of the 1982 Reagan recession, first in a series of severe blows. A seven-month US strike followed. Sales plunged to $6.5 billion in 1982 from $9.2 billion in 1981. Cat lost money for the first time in 50 years. It slashed its workforce to 58,400 in 1983 from 83,400 in 1981. Nine plants closed. Dealers cut prices on inventories. But losses continued throughout 1983 and 1984. Economic recovery in 1985 put the company back into the black, leading to a broadening of the product range and a reorientation towards smaller equipment. The company name changed to Caterpillar Inc. in 1986. Three years later, it adopted its present logos – Cat and Caterpillar in blocky, black capitals with a bright yellow triangle below the first A (*see* Fig. 5.1).

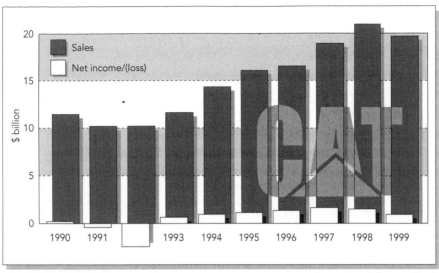

FIGURE 5.1 Caterpillar annual figures

Source: Hoover's Company Reports

In 1988 a trademark merchandising and licensing division was set up with the idea that the Cat brand might bring in a licensing revenue stream. Early licensing ventures included scale models of Cat vehicles for collectors and children. Videos, books, trading cards, and a few shirts and hats followed. But the big move was to hire a licensed contractor to make Cat workboots, not for the fashion conscious, but for real workers on construction sites and other places where Cat equipment was used. Cat distributed through mass merchandisers, such as Wal-Mart, to the blue-collar backbone of America.

Launching the boots into mass-merchandise discount stores put the Cat brand in front of people who knew it, but limited the potential of the venture due to the inability of discounters to move the brand much beyond its core audience. As Jostes said:

'Initially we targeted the mass-merchant footwear environment in the US ... because most American workers were going there to buy hunting equipment, toys for their children, tobacco and hair and make-up products ... So we felt that was the place for us to start.'

BROWN HELPS YELLOW

Then one day London shoe designer and merchant Steven Palmer happened to notice a sturdy Cat workboot in the display window of a workwear shop. He liked it, but more importantly, he knew that there was a major change getting under way in the world's footwear markets. The so-called 'brown shoe revolution' hit in 1989–90, when young consumers suddenly turned their backs on the flashy basketball and running shoes that had been making Nike and Reebok rich. In their place, the youth market started snapping up boots, sandals and shoes with a more rugged, outdoorsy look.

Palmer had a hunch that the Cat boot could ride this wave. So he sought out Cat's licensee and won the contract to be European distributor. In 1990 he began distributing Cat boots across Europe through his firm Overland Ltd. He felt the Cat brand had potential beyond the construction site. So he began trying to expand the shoe programme. But his initial efforts stumbled after Cat and its US-based licensee became embroiled in a legal dispute. The two ended up in court and parted ways.

In 1994 Cat assigned a new global footwear manufacturing licence to Wolverine Worldwide, a larger and better-known shoe and boot group, which already owned the Hush Puppy brand. At the same time, a new team came aboard to run Cat's trademark merchandising and licensing division. Jostes was part of this group and it quickly came to a meeting of the minds with Palmer, who had retained the European distributorship through the transition to Wolverine. Working with the new Cat licensing team, Palmer started again to push the Cat boot beyond its initial conception and towards the streetwear category. Design work centred on Overland's studios in Clerkenwell, with practical input from the industrial boot people at Wolverine in Michigan.

In the USA, Cat stayed with a worksite approach, but was moving way past that in Europe and was soon scoring big with a very urban, 16- to 26-year-old, mostly male target market. The Cat streetwear line took off, with the familiar bright yellow logo becoming an urban fashion icon in places about as far removed from Peoria, in more ways than one, as could be imagined. Although the licensing venture was bringing in a trickle of revenues, reaction to it in Peoria was not uniformly favourable. 'There were people offended, I would say, up until two years ago', Jostes said.

But the numbers and sustained growth began winning over even the most sceptical. Cat shoes on average sell for about $90 a pair. The trademark licensing and merchandising division's retail-level annual revenues grew to $900 million in 1999 from $250 million five years earlier. Only a portion of that returned to Cat in royalties and licensing fees. But the brand was getting out there.

Cat boots and shoes are tagged with the hard-to-miss yellow-and-black Cat logos, usually in multiple locations. The book bags have flaps covered with a large Cat insignia. 'When you pick up a Cat bag or a pair of shoes, you get a little injection of Caterpillar', Jostes said. 'We're trying to touch consumers in a different way.' As a heavy equipment maker, Caterpillar annually sells about 200,000 pieces of equipment. The prices are impressive – $1 million for a bulldozer, for instance – but the volumes are not huge. 'Plus, that's spread across 200 countries. So we have a limited market base. That's not that much stuff ... We need to reach out to a larger, global audience. We have to grow our market base', Jostes said.

> 66We're trying to touch consumers in a different way. 99

The key question, of course, is the one asked of any brand extension: it may be a success in its own right, but how does it help the core business? How does selling Cat shoes and shirts to kids in London help Cat sell more bulldozers or pipe layers or wheeled excavators?

STRETCHING EXERCISES

Brand extension – or taking an established brand and tying it to a new product or service that may or may not be related to its origins – is a practice that occupies much of the time of brand marketers these days. Extension is so routine, in fact, that most new brands are actually extensions of old ones.

Marketing experts differentiate between two broad types of extension. One is the common and familiar 'line extension', which involves moving within a brand's accustomed category. For example, the Marlboro cigarette brand extends to Marlboro Lights. But the more rare and riskier version is known as 'category extension', or moving a brand out of its present market segment into an entirely new area. This is also known sometimes as 'image transfer', 'cross-branding', 'brand bouncing' or 'brand stretching'.

Besides the extreme case of Caterpillar, some other successful examples would be the Mars bar brand extending into ice cream, the BiC brand extending from disposable pens into disposable razors and lighters, or the Virgin mega-brand stretching from recorded music into soft drinks, trains, vodka, radio, financial services, cosmetics ... seemingly anything Richard Branson takes a fancy to. 'Most new products are line extensions. In 1990, 63 per cent of products introduced were line extensions, and another 18 per cent were category extensions', reported Kevin Keller of Dartmouth College.[1]

Both line and category extensions present major potential advantages to a company, such as cost-savings. Writing in a 1994 *Harvard Business Review* article, London Business School Dean John Quelch and marketing expert David Kenny estimated the cost for launching a genuinely new brand at about $30 million, versus a comparatively cheap $5 million for launching a line extension.[2]

Extensions can target established customer segments more narrowly, win all-important in-store shelf space, satisfy consumers' desire for 'something new' while keeping them loyal, exploit excess production capacity, boost sales in the short term and block competitors, Quelch and Kenny pointed out. But they also stressed that extensions have their pitfalls. Among them are the risks of confusing consumers, disrupting their buying habits and encouraging them to experiment, complicating trade relations and production and distribution logistics, increasing exposure to competition, and, perhaps worst of all, missing out on the promise of an all-new brand that could have been big.

The dangers of extension are shown by failed efforts such as Budweiser Dry, Crystal Pepsi, Cadbury milk powder, Levi's Tailored Classics, BiC Perfume, Harley-Davidson wine coolers or the Cadillac Alante, commented David Andrew, managing director of consulting firm Interbrand Pacific.[3]

'It goes without saying that before making any brand extension it is imperative to know the brand well. What are its attributes? What is its personality? What identity does it convey to its buyers and users?' advised HEC's Jean-Noël Kapferer.[4]

As long as these questions are all answered, extension may very well be preferable to creating a new brand because it is much cheaper and it creates new opportunities for brand synergies, according to Aaker of the

University of California-Berkeley. He wrote: 'The development of a new or separate brand is expensive and difficult. ... A separate brand should be developed or supported only when a compelling need can be demonstrated.'[5]

In the case of Caterpillar, of course, development of a new brand of boots or clothing would have been nonsensical. It was the strength of the brand itself, not a new product, that drove the extension's logic.

YELLOW BLOOD

Caterpillar, known for its deliberate approach to technological innovation, studied its brand closely before deciding in 1988 to pursue the workboots extension. The time and effort expended on understanding the brand is evident in materials distributed to employees and dealers about it.

One booklet, *People Know Us When They See Us: An Introduction to Caterpillar Identity Standards*, outlines Cat's 'corporate identity system' and lists words the brand is meant to bring to mind. Some – such as 'reliable', 'honest', 'professional', 'leader' – are found in any boiler-plate mission statement. Others indicate the brand's true character, such as 'strong', 'down-to-earth', 'rugged', 'enduring', 'powerful', 'gritty'.

The booklet stresses brand consistency. If it goes over the top, it shows how seriously Cat takes the topic. One passage reads:

'Think about what the Cat and Caterpillar names mean to you. We've all felt it. You pass a construction site and see a big yellow machine. You slow down and look for a familiar name. You see a stranger wearing a Cat hat. You feel like you've found a friend. That's yellow blood. Personal pride and a sense of ownership in one of the world's most successful and respected companies.'

> **You see a stranger wearing a Cat hat. You feel like you've found a friend.**

Guidelines tell employees how to deal with trademarks, design issues, logo use, colour schemes, signs and packaging. Another booklet, *Communicating Caterpillar: One Voice*, discusses Cat's values, competencies, personality, attributes, positioning, voice, audiences, images and identity. Unsurprisingly, Jostes said he has a checklist of 16 brand attributes memorized. He claimed he reviews it mentally each day to make sure his decisions hold true to it. Half of Overland's 245 employees have been through an eight-hour Cat workshop to teach them the company's values and brand attributes. 'We make them attend that. We make every licensee do that', Jostes said.

Clearly, Cat is nothing if not thorough about its brand. But the bottom-line question remains. How does $1 billion in sales of boots and clothes help add to Cat's $20 billion in annual equipment sales? The key, said Jostes, is to influence 'future decision makers', even if some of them are highly unlikely ever to be in the market for a tractor-scraper or an articulated truck. He went on:

'When we talk about future decision makers, that young chap who might have an earring and green hair, or who might be as normal-looking as somebody else's child, may never and probably will never buy a bulldozer. But if he decides someday to invest in the stock market, and he's looking at a portfolio of Dow Jones top 30 companies, maybe the experience he's had with a piece of Cat something ... will influence his decision.'

Likewise, said Jostes, future apparel buyers, contractors or retail equipment renters may be swayed subtly towards a favourable association with the Cat brand by their experiences with Cat soft goods.

There is downside risk to the footwear and clothing venture, Jostes acknowledged. For instance, a flawed pair of $90 workboots could give a bad impression to a 'decision-maker' who really is in a position some day to spend $1 million on a bulldozer. If that happens, Cat could lose business. To prevent this, Jostes and associates maintain tight control over Wolverine and Overland to ensure that Cat products are durable and strong and no shoddy goods go out. Efforts to extend the brand further than it is already stretched are also policed and considered carefully.

Cat has said no to a lot of brand licensing proposals from outside manufacturers. Jostes explained:

'We've literally been asked to do everything, even condoms. You have to be careful in picking categories. You have to constantly remind yourself and the licensees every day what it's about. I mean, I could get greedy. I could call a licensee tomorrow and say, we now want to sell to every distribution channel in Europe. But that's a short-term view ... We have to be responsible. You don't want to take a brand and try to extend it too quickly without foundation, like if we went out and put our logo on computers or skateboards or underwear or perfume. What would we make it smell like, diesel fuel? So, there are brand extensions we can't get into, especially in the early stages.'

However, Cat does plan to expand into other soft-goods markets beyond shoes, shirts, bags, belts and hats. It has started branding jackets, shorts, watches and will soon move into sunglasses. The brand is expanding into new toys, scale models, computer games and retailing. 'We are reviewing the possibility of benchmark stores. London is under discussion, and a few other cities. But those are still a way off for us', Jostes said. He added 'We will probably also be stepping into the kids' market with apparel very soon'.

Cat's retail licensees spend over $1 million a month advertising Caterpillar in an effective programme that hits young consumers where they live, on the streets and in the tube. 'We target those categories for advertising and we relate to them visually', Jostes said. 'Kids are more visual today than they've ever been ... That's part of the reason this yellow Cat logo works on Cat footwear. It's bright, it's iconic.'

TACKLING TOMMY

Cat views just about everyone in the leisurewear market as its rivals. According to Jostes, 'We're competing with The Gap, with Tommy Hilfiger, with Abercrombie & Fitch, with Diesel. So we're in those same categories and we do have to steal some market share from everybody to be viable.'

Youth brands come and go, of course, as shoemakers Sperry Top-Sider or Fila can testify. So Caterpillar recognizes it is riding a wave that could close out at any time. 'The internet-paced world that we're in changes every minute. So we do think we'll be a viable brand. I'm not sure we're going to grow our footwear the way we did the first couple of years', Jostes said.

In its first few years, annual sales growth ranged from 35 to 50 per cent. 'We've levelled off somewhat now, but we're still very viable. And as the globe shrinks, there are new economies for us to step into, plus the strong ones that we're already in.'

For Caterpillar, perhaps the best thing about the extension into soft goods is this – if it all ended tomorrow, barring some sort of negative public relations disaster, Cat would keep humming along as a heavy equipment maker without missing a beat. As Jostes put it:

'If a new CEO started tomorrow and said, we don't want to do boots anymore, and we just walked out of it, our dealers would be disappointed for a while, but it probably wouldn't affect our global construction equipment brand negatively. I don't think it would, and that's good in a way. So we haven't hurt the cause, but we have probably helped it.'

NOTES

1 Kevin Lane Keller, *Strategic Brand Management: Building, Measuring and Managing Brand Equity*, Upper Saddle River, New Jersey: Prentice Hall, 1998, p. 453.

2 John Quelch and David Kenny, 'Extend Profits, Not Product Lines', in *Harvard Business Review on Brand Management*, Boston: Harvard Business School Press, 1999, p. 109.

3 David Andrew, 'Brand Revitalisation and Extension', in Susannah Hart and John Murphy (eds), *Brands: The New Wealth Creators*, London: Macmillian, 1998, p. 192.

4 Jean-Noël Kapferer, *Strategic Brand Management: Creating and Sustaining Brand Equity Long Term*, London: Kogan Page, 1997, p. 260.

5 David Aaker and Erich Joachimsthaler, *Brand Leadership*, New York: Free Press, 2000, p. 123.

6

ONE TRICK PONY: HEINEKEN AND BRAND CONSISTENCY

'I consider a bad bottle of Heineken to be a personal insult to me'

Freddy Heineken, former chairman, Heineken

PEER INTO THE BEER COOLER at your neighbourhood off-licence and dis-cover a dizzying showcase of brand extension. Famous names that once fronted for just one brew have been stretched to cover sub-brands ranging from light to ice, dry, draft, red, berry, honey, weiss, bock and so forth.

Miller, a top-selling mass-market beer brand in America owned by Miller Brewing of Milwaukee, is sold in seven different versions. Arch-rival Budweiser comes in four; Canadian market leader Molson in seven. And it's not just beer. Soft drinks, snack foods, cleaning products, electronics, media. Even banks and utilities play the brand stretching game with amazing elasticity.

Then there's Heineken. With precious few exceptions, a Heineken is a Heineken no matter where you go or what the latest fad is in brewing. It's the familiar beer in the green bottle with the red star and Dutch roots. For nearly 140 years the brand has largely defied the trend towards extension, yet it is still among the world's two or three most powerful beer brands, along with Budweiser and Guinness.

Unmatched international reach, premium market positioning, a supportive portfolio of smaller brands that can be stretched, and committed, brand-savvy upper management have saved Heineken from diluting its brand image and personality over the years in search of short-term gains. While compromises have been made and new challenges to growth are emerging, Heineken has remained remarkably true to itself since third-generation chief executive Freddy Heineken steered the company into the modern marketing era following the Second World War.

As a result, Heineken offers a strong example of brand consistency – a hallmark of branding success that is paid lip service by most companies, but actually practised by few. Not many firms can back up a record as steady, yet flexible and growing, as Heineken can with regard to its flagship brand, the second-biggest selling beer in the world after Budweiser.

René Hooft Graafland, marketing director at Heineken NV, said the brewer has tried extending the Heineken brand in the past, but with only mixed success. Unlike many other brand owners these days, he said, Heineken is increasingly sceptical of the wisdom of such moves. 'The brand has opportunities to be leveraged in other areas, but for the time being we are very hesitant to do that', he said in an interview in his office on a rainy spring day in Amsterdam. He went on:

'We have the luxury not to go into line extensions. We at Heineken have, up to now, had the opportunity to grow geographically. Secondly, we have been able to grow from a niche brand into a slightly bigger brand. We enter markets at the top, but over time we can attract more consumers … We are not forced to extend the brand into other areas.'

Heineken, as one of the world's biggest brewers along with Anheuser-Busch of St Louis, Missouri, and Interbrew of Belgium produces dozens of beers besides its namesake, such as Amstel, Murphy's Irish Stout, the Asian favourites Tiger and Anchor, and others including Primus, Kaiser, Aguila and Piton. It owns more than 100 breweries in over 50 countries. No brewer is nearly as international. Yet the crown jewel has remained fairly constant. There has never been a Heineken Light or Heineken Ice or Heineken Dry. Not that Heineken has not considered it – it has, especially when looking at the stunning success of extensions such as Miller Lite or Asahi Dry. Hooft Graafland said:

'We have these debates and we will continue to have these debates. And that is good that we have these debates. But we have other ways to tap into these markets. Heineken cements all the other parts of our company together, but the brand represents only just over 20 per cent of our total group volume. We have other very strong brands that we use to tap into these market opportunities.'

For example, Heineken has had success with Amstel Light, a low-calorie beer, particularly in the USA where light beers now outsell all other categories. Heineken has also launched Amstel Malt and is heavily promoting a non-alcoholic form of the Buckler brand in many markets. But the group's lead brand has stood apart from such efforts. HEC's Kapferer took note of this: 'Aware of the boom in the sector of "light" foods, many companies jumped at the opportunity to profit from it. But, it was a wrong move for quite a few, which is why there is no "Heineken Light".'[1]

Said Hooft Graafland:

'I have not seen many successful line extensions of great brands, unless they were very close to the original. ... In beer, the alcohol percentage and the taste perception and the craftsmanship are very much a part of all that a brand stands for. So if you start saying light beer – why not a Heineken Light? ... Well, that has different connotations that we say don't fit the Heineken brand.

'There are not many real successful extensions of brands. We still see no need for it. We still see huge growth opportunities for our single-minded position.'

DUTCH TRADING, GERMAN BREWING, AMERICAN MARKETING

Heineken was founded in 1863 when Gerard Adriaan Heineken bought a brewery called De Hooiberg ('the haystack') in Amsterdam. The brewery, in existence since the 16th century, was the largest in the city and the new owner made it the foundation of Heineken & Co. After hiring a German brewmaster and expanding with another brewery in Rotterdam, Heineken commissioned the development of the yeast that is still used today in brewing Heineken.

By 1893, the year of Gerard's death, his company ranked among the Netherlands' largest brewers along with Amstel. On the brink of the First World War, his son Henry Pierre took over. The company suffered in the 1920s and 1930s due to economic depression and reduced Dutch beer consumption. In response, the board of directors boosted exports of Heineken, principally to Belgium, Britain, West Africa, the USA, the Dutch East Indies and West Indies.

Prohibition soon killed the US business. But one of the highlights of the company's history came in 1933, when Heineken managed to be the first imported beer to reach the US market just three days after the end of the national ban on alcoholic beverages. For 65 years after the arrival of that first shipment by freighter into Hoboken, New Jersey, Heineken was the USA's number-one imported beer.

At about the same time, Heineken took tentative steps into Asia, opening its first foreign brewery in Indonesia and establishing a brewing company along with soft-drinks producer Fraser & Neave that was the forerunner to today's Asia Pacific Breweries.

Business ground to a halt during the Second World War and the German occupation of the Netherlands. During this period Heineken's managers came to question the company's heavy reliance on the on-premise trade, or sale of beer through bars and taverns under exclusive supply relationships. One of the chief proponents of reorienting the company towards off-premise sales through retail shops and towards exporting was Alfred 'Freddy' Heineken, grandson of the founder.

Immediately after the liberation of the Netherlands and war's end, Freddy went to the USA to work and study. There he saw the rise of supermarkets and took note of the power of advertising. When he returned home in 1948, he personally nailed a sign to his office door that read 'advertising department' It was a first at Heineken.

In the 1950s Heineken broke away from the rest of the staid Dutch brewing industry and vigorously embraced marketing. The idea of branding was understood by Freddy Heineken. He came up with the green colour scheme, the Heineken script with its 'smiling e's' and he standardized the packaging look. But it took time for him to gain complete control of the company. Meanwhile, Heineken made one of few notable compromises that it has brooked with its lead brand.

DILUTING THE MESSAGE IN BRITAIN

As the Dutch brewer had expanded, it had hungrily eyed the UK market just across the English Channel. But its hopes had been frustrated by consumers who still favoured traditional British ales and bitters, as well as by a tax code that penalized stronger beers, hobbling a brand like Heineken.

To break into Britain, Heineken introduced in the 1950s a new formulation of its premium beer that had a lower alcohol content. The brand succeeded at first, leading a transition among UK beer drinkers to lagers from ales. But when the lager market opened up to full-strength beers, Heineken was left with a proposition that diluted, both literally and figuratively, the Heineken brand. Later, full-strength Heineken was brought into Britain, but the legacy of the earlier move left the company with a confused profile in the UK, where it has suffered recently at the hands of rivals such as Belgium's Stella Artois and Australia's Foster's. Hooft Graafland explained:

'We have this strange situation in the UK. With hindsight, you would say, how could we have done this? But at that time [in 1951], we were very eager to get the beer into another market. To be in another market, you had to make a number of concessions, otherwise you were not a player in that market. That was the feeling.'

In another notable exception to its more recently strict approach to brand consistency, Heineken introduced a Heineken Dark sub-brand into parts of the USA:

'In the past, we have been less consistent and less rigorous than we would be now. So there is a Heineken Dark in a few states, only in America. In the Netherlands, we do have a number of seasonal beers which are very much linked to the tradition of being a Dutch brewer.'

But Hooft Graafland said that the UK and Heineken Dark experiences were lessons for the company, which embraced a more focused approach to branding as Freddy Heineken took control:

'It shows how brand-building now has a completely different notion than it did 30, 40, 50 years ago. Mr Heineken had a vision for the brand. He really understood what brands were. As a young guy, he went to the States. He learned about marketing when people in Europe hardly knew how to write the word. So he brought that back and combined it with huge creativity … and the power to continue doing things as he thought they should be done. This gave us, as a company, an enormous consistency, when you have a guy with a vision, the creativity to shape it and also the power to bring it into practice ... Alfred Heineken's father and grandfather built the company, but Alfred Heineken really built the brand.'

Heineken became the Netherlands' leading brewer throughout the 1950s and 1960s and exports soared, especially in the USA and France, requiring the construction of a third brewery in the Netherlands. It acquired former rival Amstel in 1968 to consolidate its Dutch market leadership. Two years later it bought the James J. Murphy brewery in Ireland. At the same time, it expanded exports into southern Africa, the Caribbean, the Persian Gulf and the duty-free markets, while cutting important licensing deals in France, Ireland, Spain and Italy.

Expansion over the next 20 years followed a familiar pattern, based on Freddy's often-quoted conviction that 'beer can travel'. He was appointed chairman of the company in 1971. Typically, the 'Heinekenization' process would begin with direct exporting into a new market with the objective of building brand awareness and an image of quality and prestige. The export operation would be accompanied by an in-depth market-research effort. As volumes increased, a licence for production would be granted to a local brewery. Its activities would be carefully guided. Then as business improved further, Heineken would take the final step of either buying all or part of the local brewer, or building its own local brewery. The final outcome would depend on local regulations, market circumstances, costs, the attractiveness of potential partners and, of course, the competition.

> 66 The 'Heinekenization' process would begin with direct exporting into a new market with the objective of building brand awareness and an image of quality. 99

In country after country, Heineken followed this familiar model and the company grew to a size by the 1980s that its founders could scarcely have imagined. Sales of beer brewed under the control of Heineken in 1960 totalled 3.8 million hectolitres. That number rose to 11.3 million by 1970, 25.9 million by 1980, 53.5 million by 1990 and 73.8 million by 1997.

Success brought great wealth and public attention to Freddy Heineken, who became one of the best-known business figures in Western Europe. Trouble followed in 1983 when he was kidnapped and held for a ransom of $10 million. Blackmail and extortion attempts also dogged the company, like many in Western Europe, throughout the 1980s. In 1989 Freddy Heineken stepped down as chairman of the board and was named chairman of a supervisory council. Although he largely removed himself from day-to-day affairs, it was known in the industry that he remained keenly involved in management.

In the 1990s Heineken became Europe's largest and the world's second-largest brewer as it set out on a rapid series of acquisitions, making it the trend-setter in global brewing consolidation. It bought its US distributor Van Munching & Co. in 1991. Then it scooped up a host of mid-sized European brewers, including Italy's Interbrew Italia in 1994, France's Fischer Group in 1995, Italy's Birra Moretti in 1996, Poland's Zywiec in 1998 and Spain's Cruzcampo in 1999, as well as part or whole stakes in breweries in Hungary, Switzerland, Italy, Slovakia and throughout Southeast Asia.

Acquisitions like these and many others reshaped Heineken so that in 1999 its lead brand generated only about 20 per cent of total beer sales by the group and affiliated companies, down from 25 per cent in 1997. Amstel and Murphy's had assumed greater importance, along with regional brands. Hooft Graafland said:

'We believe that the Heineken brand prospers much better within a portfolio of brands because it allows you to increase your systems strength substantially. We often have had discussions about what Heineken would be if we only went after the Heineken brand. But you would lose so much on your systems and commercial strength, and you would lose synergies in distribution, that in the end it would not be better off.'

Difficulties arose in the 1990s, as well, with Heineken handling some better than others. In 1994 it was confronted with its first-ever labour dispute, but the episode was brought to an end with minimal disruption. Heineken opted in 1995 to pull out of an 18-month-old brewing venture in Myanmar (formerly Burma) amid political controversy over the repressive regime there. Many other companies took the same action.

In the following year an internal memorandum leaked out in which a Heineken executive made some embarrassing complaints about a UK television show for young people that the company was sponsoring. He griped there was 'too high a proportion of negroes in the audience'. A Heineken spokesman said these comments stemmed from the executive's assessment of the show's suitability for use in Italy, which has a low black population, and were made worse by his poor command of English. Nevertheless, a public furore erupted and Heineken was forced to issue a formal apology.

The company's long-time hold on American imported beer drinkers slipped a bit in the last decade of the century. Mexico's Corona, a cheaper brew with a lighter taste, made serious inroads as consumers demonstrated a declining degree of loyalty to beer brands. By the end of the decade, despite these troubles, Heineken was still immensely profitable and selling in more than 170 countries worldwide (see Fig. 6.1). Although considerably smaller than world beer-market leader Anheuser-Busch, Heineken was widely regarded by brewing industry analysts as having greater growth potential and a superior market position in premium categories with heftier profit margins.

> **66** To differentiate ourselves only on quality became a difficult thing. So we got more emotional aspects. **99**

Heineken ranked as the 64th most valuable brand in the world, with an estimated worth of $2.2 billion, in the 2000 edition of the annual global top brands survey by consulting firm Interbrand.[2]

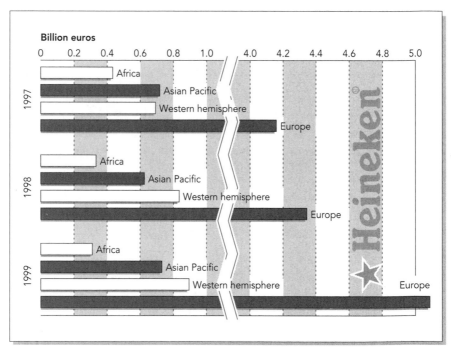

Source: Company reports

FIGURE 6.1 Heineken annual sales proceeds by region

MORE THAN QUALITY

At its birth and for over a century, the Heineken brand used quality as its chief differentiator. It was a characteristic that mattered a lot in a period when brewing standards still varied widely, especially during and after the world wars, and in the less developed markets that furnished much of the company's post-war growth. But by the 1980s, while quality remained crucial, more was needed.

'The Heineken brand all over the world has been built on quality', Hooft Graafland said. 'Over time, we have seen that quality levels are coming closer to each other. To differentiate ourselves only on quality became a difficult thing. So we got more emotional aspects.'

Unlike the more aggressively promoted American power brands of the 1980s, such as Marlboro, Coca-Cola or McDonald's, the Dutch brewery with the green bottles cultivated a less costly, more low-key style that emphasized an understanding of local cultures and a dash of worldly wit. As Hooft Graafland said:

'The word power brand is not right for Heineken. Power brands, with all respect due to the great achievements of a couple of the American brands, are like a slap in the face. That's not what we are. Although I'm often jealous of what these guys can do on branding, I think that sometimes they hit the wrong buttons with consumers. We are much closer to the local communities. We are not saying we are out to build the brand with one type of advertising all over the world. No, we want to get closer to local cultures.'

Within this context, Heineken has added to its image for quality by playing subtly on its European, if not specifically its Dutch origins, especially in the USA. According to Hooft Graafland:

'In the US we say on the label "Brewed in Holland", although people there think Holland is part of Germany. But still it is from Europe, from someplace far-away. Our brand DNA is influenced by the fact that we are from Europe, although we don't play that very strongly. It's implicit in the brand. The name sounds German. Mr Heineken always says, I'm happy that I have the name Heineken because it's a great name for beer. And I think he is right.'

'Green-ness' is another brand trait that Heineken has sought to develop. In Britain the brewer has also had success portraying its brand as a source of cool refreshment and fun, scoring against the stuffy personalities and lukewarm drinking temperatures of most local brands. Most recently, the company has begun experimenting with stretching its good-times persona a bit further. In Amsterdam Heineken has built a movies-and-music hall, and is involved in other music projects. Both are radical departures for the brand and are still in early days.

DUTCH PRAGMATISM

Heineken has not been in the habit of trying such experiments. As a result, it has not overly suffered from brand manager careerism in the way that some companies have. 'Sometimes a new brand manager has an ambition to grow his own career and he wants to add something to the brand because it should be visible that he has been there', Hooft Graafland said.

That has been largely prevented at headquarters in Amsterdam and in the field, although marketing managers across the organization over the years have been allowed more freedom of action within certain limits, while taking on wider responsibilities. Hooft Graafland added:

'Where the marketing function in the past was very much the nice pictures and the nice stories and very isolated, we see now that marketeers should grow much more into business managers. You can't market a brand in isolation. Marketing departments should have a broader view than just being great advertising or promotional guys.'

As is the case at most branded goods companies, market and consumer research has played an important part in guiding strategy. Here again, however, an over-arching vision from the head office has kept the work of the survey-makers in useful perspective:

'One of the big advantages we have is that we are a single product company. We're not a single brand company, but we are only in beer, which makes it possible to go really deep into understanding beer markets and beer cultures and beer drinkers. So we do a lot of research. But we try to avoid letting the research make the decisions for us.'

Similarly, Heineken has restricted its use of some of the more technical brand-valuation techniques that are increasingly prevalent, such as applying economic-value precepts to individual brands and businesses, or using valuation methods like Interbrand's. 'We manage our company based on concepts like EVA [economic value added, a trademarked financial method by New York consulting firm Stern Stewart]. We make decisions in-country also on that basis, although we have an overriding strategy that can't all be put into figures', Hooft Graafland said.

Finally, Heineken has squared up strongly to the internet. Unlike many consumer goods companies, it was an early mover on the web, although Hooft Graafland said much remains to be done. 'Nobody knows how it will work out. But you have to force yourself to get a vision on this. And you have to be prepared to renew that on a regular basis.

Heineken started on the net with a corporate website and treated it as a new communication channel for advertising. 'We were quite happy because we were one of the first', Hooft Graafland said. 'But it was just a way of advertising … Then after a while, we saw that, hey, people were not coming back to our site. With hindsight, it's logical because why would you go back?'

To make the site more 'sticky' with consumers, Heineken added service components, such as concert-ticket booking services and chat rooms:

'That worked quite well and we felt good about it. We were at a level where we were getting about 300,000 people every month. So we are one of the bigger consumer brand sites. But if you compare that with the people America On-Line or Amazon.com gets, it is peanuts, it is nothing. So then we said, we've done it the wrong way.'

Heineken most recently has begun moving towards forming web partnerships to create portals and communities targeting much larger population segments than Heineken drinkers. In the process of enhancing its sites and linking them to others, Heineken has sensed a need to overhaul its entire view of the net. Rather than bringing people to Heineken through the new technology, Hooft Graafland said, the notion is spreading that Heineken could bring people to the net:

'We've discovered we have something in our hands that not many companies have, which is the consumer contacts. If you talk to big players in the new economy, what they miss is the relationships with consumers, the almost physical contact. We have with the Heineken brand 10,000 contacts every minute around the world. If you start using these contacts to direct people to your site, you can be a very powerful player.'

BRANDING FROM THE TOP

Broadly, the lesson to be learned from Heineken is that it has stayed consistent with its lead brand while broadening its message. It has constructed a supportive portfolio around it and risen to the elite of its industry, chiefly thanks to its steady, family leadership and a commitment at the top, at least since the 1950s, to branding. This was largely due to the influence of Freddy Heineken, who even in his late seventies remained involved in company affairs in 2000, although more as a sounding board than a daily manager. According to Hooft Graafland:

'What is important is that the notion of brand-building is anchored really at the top of the company. To manage brands you need stewardship, absolutely from the top. We have been very fortunate. Even when Mr Heineken stepped down, his successors were very keen on this. They realized that the company is the Heineken brand, that that is our most valuable asset. That the brand is not something you delegate. It doesn't mean the board and the CEO of a company have to do it all themselves. But the organization should feel that it's really coming from the top.'

NOTES

1 Jean-Noël Kapferer, *Strategic Brand Management: Creating and Sustaining Brand Equilty Long Term*, London: Kogan Page, 1997, p. 266.
2 Interbrand, *The World's Most Valuable Brands Survey*, 18 July 2000.

7

TRADITIONAL VALUES: CADBURY AND THE BRAND FAMILY

'We try to make this Cadbury thing work for us'

Alan Palmer, international marketing director, Cadbury Schweppes

WHEN I STARTED TELLING BRITISH FRIENDS and co-workers that I was going to visit the 122-year-old headquarters of Cadbury to do research for this book, there was a telling pattern of replies. To a person, every one of them smiled faintly and said, 'Ah yes, Bournville'.

As an American, I was a bit puzzled by this, having little experience with the Cadbury name beyond seeing its chocolate bar vending machines in London Underground stations. But Cadbury is one of those brands that strikes a deep chord with consumers in countries where it dominates confectionery markets, such as the UK, Australia, New Zealand and South Africa.

For a long time the company that built a model workers' community in little Bournville outside Birmingham, England, seemed to forget about its priceless heritage. But in recent years it has begun to reclaim the Bournville legacy by pushing for more 'Cadbury-ness' in its branding efforts. The Cadbury project, still under way and gaining momentum, shows how individual product brands can gain from being promoted under the umbrella of a strong and characterful family brand name.

Brand family strategies are used by many companies, including Cadbury competitors such as Nestlé and Hershey, as well as other food groups, virtually all car manufacturers, most cosmetic and perfume houses and many leading computer and software makers. The concept is to create and maintain a single, powerful parent name – such as Heinz, Wrigley's, Pillsbury, Kraft, Honda, Chanel or Microsoft – then roll out individual product brands or sub-brands under its aegis and with its support.

Branding experts chop this idea rather finely by differentiating among range brands, line brands, endorsement brands, umbrella brands and other brand hierarchies, but the central idea of the brand family covers the concept.

Different from the brand family strategy are stand-alone brands like the hundreds marketed by the faceless consumer goods giants Procter & Gamble, Unilever, Diageo or Philip Morris. Stand-alone brands – such as P&G's Ariel and Tide detergents or Philip Morris's Marlboro cigarettes – may be extended, but they function largely independently of any overarching symbol, word or idea.

Stand-alone brands are becoming more rare these days because the costs and difficulties of creating successful all-new brands, at least in a traditional way, are so staggering. The price-tag for a typical US new brand campaign is about $80 million, twice what it was just five years ago. As a result, most brands launched today are derived from existing brands or are members of brand families. Seventeen out of 20 all-new brands fail, it has been estimated. No surprise then that out of 16,000 new products launched annually in the USA, 95 per cent are extensions of existing brands, pointed out John Murphy, founder of the consulting firm Interbrand.[1]

66 Most brands launched today are derived from existing brands or are members of brand families. **99**

The money-saving trend towards brand families and extensions certainly reduces brand clutter and aids consumers, but its downside risk is the danger of diluting the meaning and impact of the parent brand. Brand managers wrestle with these issues daily, and will continue to do so as long as advertising inflation continues, making derivative branding a cost-effective tactic.

For Cadbury, making more of its brand family in the chocolate business was a case of returning to family values in more ways than one, said Alan Palmer, international marketing director for confectionery. 'I suppose the world could have gone on quite happily with 25 separate brands being advertised on television by Cadbury, with each one making its own approach to the consumer. But then the economics of advertising started to change', said the precisely spoken career marketing executive in an interview in his office overlooking the leafy grounds of Cadbury's historic Bournville industrial campus. He went on:

'Advertising inflation has caused food manufacturers, and indeed ourselves, to have to rethink the dynamics of communication. We could no longer afford to advertise 25 brands on television ... So in the very early 1980s there was this rethink undertaken by the marketing department as to what one should and could do with the high-ground position that we knew we had with consumers. The Cadbury brand was very powerful, much more powerful than our market share at the time warranted. In a sense, we've been redeveloping the role of Cadbury ever since, over the last 18 to 20 years, as we push greater emphasis on the iconography and the integrity of the Cadbury message.'

AH YES, BOURNVILLE

Quaker businessman John Cadbury started selling tea and coffee out of a Birmingham shop in 1824, expanding later into cocoa and drinking chocolate, which soon became his sole business. Joined by his brothers, Cadbury moved into chocolate manufacturing. His sons took over around mid-century and began advertising a new, additive-free Cadbury's Cocoa Essence that they developed. The bean press used to make this drinking chocolate generated volumes of cocoa butter by-product, which had the happy result of allowing production of more and better solid eating chocolates. By the end of the 1870s the family enterprise was a UK market leader and had outgrown its Birmingham quarters.

The socially conscious Cadburys fled cramped and smoky Birmingham for new quarters on 14.5 acres outside the city in 1878. They built a state-of-the-art factory, shops for artisans, offices, dressing and reading rooms for the workers, a kitchen and mess hall, gardens, playing fields and a dairy. All of it formed the nucleus of one of Britain's most ambitious and earliest planned industrial communities – Bournville.

As chocolate consumption rose, the Cadburys benefited. They expanded to Canada, Australia, New Zealand, South Africa, France, India and the USA. Efficiency improvements led to shorter working hours for employees and above-average wages. Progressive workplace policies, coupled with the factory's park-like setting, attracted thousands of workers from Birmingham. Bournville came to be known as a model workers' community.

In 1905 the company launched a product that would become its defining brand – Dairy Milk. Using a higher and fresher milk content than competitors, it was an instant hit, helped greatly by an advertising and promotion budget in its first year of £40,000, impressive in its day. 'The concept of marketing at Cadbury predates marketing as such. This business was doing marketing before it knew what marketing was', Palmer said.

Dairy Milk sales grew ten-fold in its first decade. By 1918 Cadbury was the leading UK producer of chocolate and cocoa. Ads appeared in 1928 using the 'glass-and-a-half of milk' design that would become a Cadbury icon, along with the flowing script of the company name and the colour purple. Further international expansion followed, as did a policy of allowing the general public to tour the Bournville plant in operation. It became a popular day-trip for schoolchildren and reinforced the brand.

The Second World War brought the business to a halt. When milk, sugar and chocolate rationing was lifted in 1953, Cadbury had to work hard to re-establish itself. It became a pioneer in television advertising. As Britain rediscovered sweets, growth surged at Cadbury. Soon, it was swept up in the 1960s craze for diversification. It launched an instant milk called Marvel and an instant potato mix called Smash. According to Palmer:

'This was slightly odd. The name Cadbury began appearing on products that weren't chocolate or even derived from chocolate. So the logic that had sat behind Cadbury prior to that time became a bit deconstructed. The value of the Cadbury name was respected ... but you had this contradiction. What was the connection with chocolate? There wasn't any, apart from corporate branding.'

In 1969, in another flurry of diversification, Cadbury bought out UK drinks group Schweppes, putting it in the soft-drinks business and back into the tea and coffee business that it had left behind a century before. By this time the company's advertising was highly specialized, with the Cadbury name sometimes attached as if an afterthought, and the glass-and-a-half logo and purple colour scheme neglected.

Taxes and cocoa bean prices rose in the 1970s. At the same time, consumers shifted their chocolate buying to the supermarket from the sweet shop, changing the ways that chocolate treats were packaged, distributed, displayed and sold. In the ensuing turmoil, Cadbury's financial results suffered and it began rapidly losing market share to more nimble rivals such as Nestlé and M&M/Mars. Cadbury tried making popcorn. It tried reducing the thickness of its chocolate bars, but backed off after consumer complaints. It acquired the Peter Paul confectionery group in the USA in 1978. Then in 1980 Dominic Cadbury was named managing director of the confectionery division.

CLEARING THE PURPLE HAZE

Bringing a new sense of urgency to the business, the descendant of the founders began speaking publicly about a 'marketing precipice' beyond which Cadbury could not slip without its market share going into a free-fall. He set in motion a reassessment at Cadbury and a period of radical change. 'His remarks became the inspiration for rethinking what Cadbury should be and should deliver', Palmer said, adding that renewed emphasis was focused on the traditional branding icons.

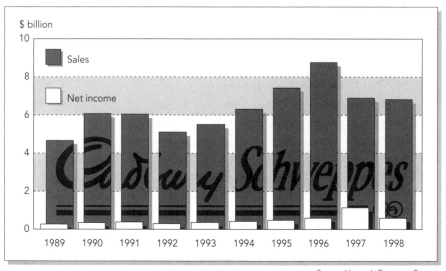

Source: Hoover's Company Reports

FIGURE 7.1 Cadbury Schweppes annual figures

A movement started within the company to make the Cadbury name a more powerful part of the business. 'There was considerable debate as to how to execute this', Palmer said. 'Some people said, well, we don't sell Cadbury, we sell chocolate ... So we needed to understand the motivators that lay behind the corporate brand and the actual purchase intents among the product brands.'

> 66 A movement started within the company to make the Cadbury name a more powerful part of the business. 99

At the same time, painful changes were made in Bournville. Several departments were closed. Jobs were eliminated and much work hired out to contractors in a back-to-basics drive. 'Lots of product lines were axed, rationalized, reconfigured, so that they would operate on efficient, new modern equipment, enabling mechanization to take over from what had been a very labour-intensive industry', Palmer said.

The first big new product of restructuring was a winner – the Wispa chocolate bar launched in 1983 with a blast of promotion. 'It was a revolutionary approach to mass marketing – blitz marketing almost – which kick-started that brand, but also provided an impetus in the marketplace with our customers that gave us a new authority and credibility', Palmer said. 'Off that success, we've built over the years.'

Dominic Cadbury became chief executive. He sold off Smash and other food businesses acquired over the years. He also removed the Cadbury name from products not related to chocolate. 'We reverted to a purity where the Cadbury name was only associated with cocoa products', Palmer said.

In 1985 the company started to experiment with something it called 'Cadbury-ness' in an effort to capture the favourable image of the corporate name and apply it as a parent brand to the product line. Palmer explained:

'We were trying to bottle what we meant by this brand Cadbury ... We wanted to be more "Cadbury". So we put more emphasis on the purple, more emphasis on the script, more emphasis on putting the Cadbury purple under the brand name on our products. That process went on through the back end of the 1980s. We started to associate advertising with Cadbury in each television commercial.'

In 1995, to underscore the new approach, the Cadbury name started to be called the 'master brand' within the company. As Palmer said:

'We reinvented it under a new title, which is the Cadbury master brand, and that is the central part of our thinking today. We then started to remarket from that basis. We made a thing called a master brand commercial ... in which we addressed the emotional values of Cadbury and the sensual values of eating chocolate. But it was non-specific. It had an ambiguous product shot in it. We used that to raise the value of Cadbury.'

The company cut a sponsorship deal for the popular UK television show *Coronation Street*:

'That was a terrific investment for us. It put Cadbury back in front of the consumer. It recaptured the high ground. So what we try to do is to make this Cadbury thing work for us, as a competitive advantage and as a spearhead for the development of the category. This is a great example of how one can make a brand living and relevant in the 21st century, even when its antecedents come from the 19th century. It should be as relevant today as it's ever been.'

On the international front, Cadbury moved to standardize its branding style around the world, following a trend in brand marketing towards more globalization. 'We've taken the marketing programme across countries where we have an established presence', Palmer said, showing off chocolate bars from Russia, Pakistan and elsewhere, most wrapped in uniformly purple packages with closely similar graphic designs, the Cadbury script and the glass-and-a-half logo.

'Most recently we've been engaged in internationalizing the graphics for what we call the Cadbury Dairy Milk mega-brand ... The iconography for this brand is now consistent worldwide', Palmer said. The drive to standardize globally around the master brand has confronted internal challengers who cite a recent step back from globalization by Coca-Cola. Palmer added: 'People ask, if you globalize too much, do you lose the local flavour? My own view is that you have to get that balance right.'

CHOCOLATE TREATS

Cadbury's conception of a master brand sweeping across a family of sub-branded chocolate products is aided by the versatility of chocolate. It can be used not only in confectionery, but in baked goods such as cakes and biscuits, beverages, dairy products and other items. Palmer explained:

'For that reason, the Cadbury brand is the biggest single-product food brand in the British Isles ... We only got to that fact by adding up the value of all chocolate confectionery sales, all the biscuit sales ... a vast variety of product formats. The purple and the iconography provides a linking piece that holds this all together.'

Cadbury's consistent personality and appeal has been reinforced by the fact that chocolate, as a product, has changed little in a century. So Palmer concluded:

'The top 30 brands in chocolate are dominated by brands that have been around for more than 50 years. A lot of what the consumer perceives in Cadbury, the brand, today is derived from the values associated with the family, the environment and the brand over time. You couldn't create it overnight today. It's why Cadbury the company is a consumer brand rather than just a corporation. Nestlé is something that will always be a corporation to consumers in this country where Cadbury is something that is more profound ... People identify with the values in the brand and, in a funny sort of way, I think with the company itself.'

> **“Cadbury the company is a brand rather than just a corporation.”**

NOTES

1   John Murphy, 'What is Branding?' in Susannah Hart and John Murphy (eds), *Brands: The New Wealth Creators*, London: Macmillan Business, 1998, p. 5.

8

A BRAND TOO FAR: COLUMBIA/HCA AND THE LIMITS OF BRANDS

'We're looking now to be invisible, not visible'

Victor Campbell, senior vice-president, HCA-The Healthcare Co.

CAN ANYTHING BE BRANDED? Every book about brand management and marketing asks this question hypothetically, then implies that the answer is yes. But the answer is actually no. Proof that there are limits to branding lies in the story of the former Columbia/HCA Healthcare Corp., the largest for-profit hospital company in the USA, where health care is a unique and ever-changing jumble of private and public sector systems.

Columbia/HCA, based in Nashville, Tennessee, was at the forefront of the industry in 1996 when it launched a massive, $90-million-a-year campaign to brand its coast-to-coast chain of 350 hospitals. Within months, every unit of the sprawling organization adopted the corporate 'Columbia' brand – so that Hoffman Estates Medical Center became Columbia Hoffman Estates Medical Center, for instance. An intensive advertising programme was launched, including television and radio commercials, print ads, airport kiosks, sports sponsorships, internet ventures, signs and billboards.

Just months after the campaign got going, however, several Columbia/HCA offices were raided by federal agents as part of a sweeping government probe of the company's business practices that dragged on for years, forcing Columbia/HCA to agree in mid-2000 to a $745-million legal settlement. More importantly, the probe set off a storm of controversy around Columbia/HCA and its hospitals that illustrated perfectly one of the main theses of this book – that major brands in the information age bring social and political risks to their owners along with economic power. If any company has paid the ultimate price of having a well-known brand name, it has been Columbia/HCA.

Today, the company is recovering from its three-year nightmare. It has dropped the Columbia brand entirely and changed its name to HCA-The Healthcare Co. The television commercials and magazine ads are gone. Scores of hospitals have been sold off. Of the roughly 200 remaining, only one still uses the Columbia brand in its name. 'This is a debranding project, not a branding project. We're looking now to be invisible, not visible', said Victor Campbell, senior vice-president, in an interview.

Two lessons can be gleaned from the Columbia/HCA saga. First, the patient–physician relationship in America is so unusual that it makes health care a business to be approached by brand marketers only with great caution. Health care may very well be best left unbranded.

Second, no company today with a well-known brand can get away with letting its executives run foul of the law to the extent that Columbia/HCA did. The misdeeds of a handful of Columbia managers might have resulted in an isolated and manageable problem at a company with no national brand profile. But the power of the Columbia brand, and all it stood for, meant the probe was transformed by the business press, socially minded investors and web-savvy health care industry activists into a national scandal. In the end, it brought the company to its knees and destroyed the brand itself.

> **❝It is a much tougher world now for brands to compete. They're so tightly linked to their companies. ❞**

'It is a much tougher world now for brands to compete in some ways. They're so tightly linked to their companies. You can't get away with anything any more', commented Linda Wolf, chief executive of the advertising agency Leo Burnett USA in Chicago, in an interview.

TWO HOSPITALS AND AN IDEA

Rick Scott was an ambitious 35-year-old Texas lawyer when he and Fort-Worth financier Richard Rainwater in 1987 formed a partnership with 120 local physicians to buy out two El Paso hospitals. The facilities became the first properties owned and operated by the new Columbia Hospital Corp., a name devised by Scott. Over the next six years Columbia snapped up dozens of hospitals. Many of them were formerly not-for-profit operations run by community trusts or charitable boards. Columbia clamped down hard on costs and turned its hospitals into powerful profit centres. The company went public in 1990 on the New York Stock Exchange and rapidly became a superstar stock.

American health care at the time was notoriously inefficient. Costs were skyrocketing. Medicare and Medicaid, the two main federal health care subsidy programmes, seemed to be heading towards insolvency. Millions of Americans were uninsured or under-insured, while physicians lived in mansions and drove luxury cars to the golf course. Bill Clinton, governor of Arkansas, won the presidency in 1992 in part by promising to end what was then known as 'the health care crisis'.

In this environment Columbia thrived as the standard-bearer of a new way of managing health care – the free-enterprise way. While some health-care reformers (among them First Lady Hillary Clinton and her husband) called for sweeping governmental solutions, free-market advocates pushed to reform health care by exposing it to the forces of competition. Columbia was a key player in this scenario and it made a number of people rich in the process, but not without making enemies.

From the beginning in El Paso, Scott had a notion that branding his hospitals would give them a competitive advantage. He wasn't the first to try it. In the early 1980s Humana Corp. of Louisville, Kentucky, had set about branding its comparatively small chain of for-profit hospitals with mixed commitment and success. By the 1990s Humana had evolved chiefly into a health-insurance organization and the hospitals had been spun off into a separate company called Galen Health Care.

The purchase of Galen in 1993 by Columbia gave Scott the opportunity to expand his branding programme. But it was the merger in the following year of Columbia and the giant Hospital Corporation of America, or HCA, that took Scott and his idea for a national hospital brand into the big time. 'When the branding came, everything was branded Columbia, not Columbia/HCA. That was the name of the company, but all of the branding was Columbia. That was the name on the hospitals and in the ads', recalled Campbell, put in charge of investor relations after the 1994 merger. He had come from the HCA half of the business, which had never tried branding its hospitals.

With Scott at the head of the merged Columbia/HCA organization, a separate brand marketing staff was set up. Substantial branding programmes were put into development at great cost with the intention of revolutionizing health care services, then largely free of commercial brands.

DOCTOR'S ORDERS

Like other professional services in the USA, health care is a free market, unlike the socialist medical systems of Europe and Asia. US consumers face a multitude of roughly equal options from which to choose in meeting one of life's most basic needs. On the surface, these fundamentals would seem to suggest that a strong brand could be advantageous to its owner, while helping health care consumers by giving them valuable cues about quality, accessibility, trustworthiness and value.

But US consumers are not in the habit of shopping critically for health care. The primary reason is the physician. In the USA, physicians (as well as dentists, surgeons, psychiatrists, etc.) are highly skilled at branding themselves as individuals, mostly through word of mouth. Even poor doctors enjoy remarkable loyalty among their patients. Traditionally, whether you are ill or healthy, you do what the doctor says in all matters ranging from drugs to hospitals. The intimacy of the patient–physician relationship reinforces this obedience. Moreover, the morass of red tape pervading US health care discourages patients from switching doctors because of the hassle involved.

Physicians had ruled over the health care system in this way for decades when Columbia started its branding programme, which some physicians immediately condemned as a threat to their autonomy. And, of course, they were right. Scott had correctly judged that better-educated patients by the 1990s were fed up with ever-rising doctors' bills and were trying to play a greater role in choosing their own health care. The Columbia campaign approached patients directly with the suggestion that one brand of hospital was better than another. The goal was to attract patients to Columbia hospitals over others, thereby helping physicians affiliated with Columbia and leaving others out in the cold.

The branding message had added appeal when viewed in the context of a mobile society in which consumers were increasingly forced to shop for health care after relocating to a new city. As Campbell said:

'Part of Rick's belief was that consumers increasingly were going to be involved in the decision making in health care services. The thought was that by branding, over time, the name Columbia would get recognized as the leader in health care services, as the place to go for quality health care ... and the company was going to get much larger as we entered new states and countries, and other health services. All those factors were behind using the brand Columbia.'

Consumer focus groups and surveys by Columbia prior to the branding campaign found most Americans did not know and did not care who owned hospitals. Alarmed by this lack of awareness and understanding among consumers, Scott set out to make the Columbia name known and valued.

In August 1996 the campaign was launched. Over several months company hospitals added the Columbia prefix to their names and changed their building signs. Advertisements appeared in magazines and newspapers touting Columbia hospitals as the best, as did flights of television and radio commercials. Columbia distributed branded merchandise and sponsored a tennis tournament in the resort town of Hilton Head, South Carolina. Internet ventures and airport kiosks were set up. Efforts got under way to make Columbia the official health care provider of National Football League teams.

Anecdotal evidence suggested that consumer reaction to the Columbia campaign was largely neutral. Some physicians resented it. But *Time* magazine named Scott one of the 25 most influential Americans of 1996, while industry analysts, investors and senior executives voted Columbia the nation's 'most admired' health care company in *Fortune* magazine. Detailed studies of consumer reaction were started but never finished, due to a twist in the Columbia story that stunned the industry.

SHOWDOWN IN EL PASO

Early on Wednesday morning, 19 March 1997, federal agents burst into two Columbia/HCA hospitals and several offices in El Paso and ordered employees to back away from their computers, hand over their passwords and leave. Within minutes, the agents were trundling out boxes filled with thousands of pages of billing, medical and financial records and loading them into trucks. The El Paso raid marked the beginning of a massive government investigation of Columbia/HCA.

In Nashville, Scott reacted initially by dismissing the raid as routine. Nine days later *The New York Times* began running a multi-part series of investigative articles about the company that suggested it was not so much the hero of US health care as the villain. While government officials kept quiet about their inquiry, *The Times* raised questions about allegations of illegal conduct, questionable financial ties between the company and physicians, diversions of charitable assets, and the company's so-called 'brass-knuckle' business tactics.[1]

Columbia/HCA quickly became a major news item as reporters picked up on the ubiquity of the Columbia brand name. What might otherwise have been an innocuous affair in far-away El Paso became a local-angle story in newspapers nationwide. Columbia had almost 350 hospitals at the time scattered across much of the country. Each one was named Columbia and each one was instantly seen as potentially involved in the investigation. From Florida and Texas to Illinois and California, the Columbia branding campaign was working, although not exactly as intended.

> **Reporters picked up on the ubiquity of the Columbia brand name.**

In July 1997 hundreds of agents swooped on 35 Columbia hospitals and offices in seven states, seizing more documents and records. It emerged that the probe was focused on the company's practices in filing Medicare cost reports and laboratory bills; its financial relationships with physicians; allegations of fraudulent diagnostic coding practices; and other matters. Numerous government agencies were at work, including the FBI, the Securities and Exchange Commission, the Department of Health and Human Services, the US Postal Inspectors Service and state legal authorities.

The nationwide sweep in July put Columbia/HCA on full alert as the stock price plunged. While Scott tried to hang on, the board of directors began looking for options. Dr Thomas Frist Jr, former head of HCA, had sold out to Scott intending to retire, but as events spiralled out of control he was drawn back into the business. In late July, Scott and his second in command, David Vandewater, were ousted in a boardroom coup. Frist was named chairman and chief executive.

One of the first steps he took was to dismiss the chief of brand marketing and most of her staff, along with many other Scott lieutenants. Campbell was put in charge of the communications department with orders to shut down the branding campaign, then on a $90-million annual budget. 'We nixed that', recalled Campbell, who has worked for Frist for almost 30 years.

Hospitals owned by the company were given the option to drop the Columbia corporate brand. Many promptly did so. Amid a torrent of shareholder lawsuits, Frist imposed a radical restructuring in which Columbia/HCA sold off more than 100 hospitals and its home health care services business.

Four Columbia/HCA mid-level managers in Florida were indicted on fraud charges; two were later found guilty by a jury. Their cases were on appeal at the time of this writing. After two more years of investigation and negotiation, Columbia/HCA announced in May 2000 that it had agreed to settle civil claims actions against the company relating to Medicare diagnostic coding, outpatient laboratory billing and home health care services issues, at a cost of $745 million, subject to expected approvals. One week later, the company announced it was changing its name to HCA-The Healthcare Co.

The name change was conceived with the help of a brand consulting agency. Campbell explained:

'Our directive to them was to make us invisible to the patients in our markets … I told the guy that runs the firm early on, this is a debranding project, not a branding project. We're looking now to be invisible, not visible. It's sort of interesting. That was his challenge.'

By August 2000 only one company-owned hospital was still using the Columbia name and the total portfolio of properties was down to 200 hospitals. 'We have restructured this company based on the principles on which the company was originally founded and our name reflects that change', said Frist in a press release. 'Health care is delivered locally and should be focused locally.' In complete opposition to the Scott strategy, Columbia today has no national brand marketing programme and no corporate marketing department. Its corporate communications unit supports local hospitals involved in local initiatives.

Rather than trying to convince consumers of the desirability of company facilities through a traditional brand-building effort involving advertising and other overt communications programmes, Campbell said the company is happy to let its reputation build slowly by experience.

Looking back, others at the company observed privately that if Scott's branding campaign accomplished anything it was to smear with the brush of scandal some hospitals in the organization that had nothing to do with the ones under investigation. This was not the outcome Scott had hoped for, but it is an example of what can go wrong in today's branding world. Columbia/HCA misbehaved badly and attracted government investigators, whose activities were reported and interpreted nationwide with the lightning speed and power of the business press and the internet, throwing the company into crisis and finally destroying the Columbia brand in a short three years.

NOTES

1 *The New York Times*, 28 March, 6 April, 27 April, 11 May 1997.

PART 2

BRANDS IN
THE COMPANY

'Managing brands is going to be more and more about trying to manage everything that your company does'

Lee Clow, chairman, TBWA Worldwide

TRY TO IMAGINE THE SORT OF BRAND MANAGEMENT that leads to a company choosing a name for a product like Pschitt citrus soda or Creap coffee creamer or Pocari Sweat sports drink. These are actual brand names of goods from France and Japan. Perhaps their manufacturers never meant to export to English-speaking markets; perhaps they did; perhaps they just didn't think about it.

In any case, linguistic short-sightedness is certainly not unique to non-English speakers. US and UK companies, with brand names using the word 'mist', for instance, including a nasal inhalant and a hair-styling wand, have had to rebrand in Germany upon discovering 'mist' in German means manure.

Brand management mix-ups like these pale in comparison, however, to decisions like that of Quaker Oats Co. in 1994 to pay $1.7 billion for Snapple, a soft drink brand that promptly peaked in popularity and became a money-loser. The Chicago food and beverages group sold it in 1997 for just $300 million.

Or Volkswagen's $645-million purchase of Britain's Rolls-Royce in a 1998 deal that neglected to nail down permanent rights to Rolls' valuable brand name for VW. Arch-rival BMW later cunningly scooped up the rights to the brand beginning in 2003 for just $60 million in a separate deal.

Whether the task is naming a brand, determining its value, tracing its ownership or understanding its power in the marketplace, the business of managing commercial identities can be perilous, and it is getting more so as brands struggle with new challenges inside the companies that own them.

From finance and accounting, to investor relations and marketing, corporate executives from the CEO on down are having a hard look at brands. The bean-counters want more accountability for advertising budgets, while the deal makers want a firmer grasp on valuations. Investor relations wants more disclosure for analysts, while legal wants less, and a broader role in choosing brand names to ensure their trademark defensibility. Human resources wants to rotate executives through numerous jobs for training, but that conflicts with marketing's need to maintain brand consistency. Research and development says it can only move so fast, but sales is crying out for technical innovation to make its brands more competitive.

Most importantly, the CEO is interested. At many firms, chief executives are casting a more curious and better-informed eye on brands these days. When asked who the top brand managers were at their companies, several of the CEOs interviewed for this book effectively responded, 'I am'.

As brands assume more prominent roles in the marketplace and society, the businesses that own them are wrestling with ways to better look after them. This has led to a wide reassessment within companies and the academic community of brand management processes and structures. Much of this discussion is conducted in business school-speak, but it gets down to some simple concepts:

- Somebody must be in charge of a brand, whether it is a designated brand manager, a so-called internal 'brand champion' in marketing or corporate communications, a committee (generally frowned upon), a communication co-ordinator, the CEO or an advertising or branding agency. Whoever is in charge should respect the need for continuity in the brand, rather than being determined to make changes for change's sake as a way of leaving a personal stamp on a brand. This sort of careerism is a constant danger among brand marketers.

- The importance of brand strategy must be understood throughout the company, from marketing to sales to operations to accounting to investor relations, requiring the CEO to make this message clear from the very top of the organization.

- The brand strategy, and the brand identity and image, must be clearly enunciated, accessible to all, adequately funded and managed in a co-ordinated fashion both horizontally across geographic markets and vertically up and down the business. Even when times are tough, the temptation to chop branding expenditures should be resisted. Brands need constant and consistent support.

■ The brand should be made to stand for more than sales and profits. It should become an icon of everything that a company aspires to be and to do. Managers should be in the habit of evaluating all major decisions in relation to their potential impact and influence on the brand.

Aaker, of the University of California-Berkeley, observed that maxims such as these are sometimes preached, but seldom followed, especially when times are tough. 'At some organizations, there is a tendency to give lip service to building brands. If one listens carefully, though, one finds the assumption that brand building will occur only after the business "makes the numbers".'[1]

> 66 The brand should become an icon of everything that a company aspires to be and to do. 99

Companies that adhere faithfully and conscientiously to brand building, even when the hatchet men are swinging wildly, are usually the ones that prevail in the end.

TALES FROM THE TRENCHES

Part 2 of *Brands in the Balance* presents eight in-depth case studies of brand managers in the trenches, dealing with internal management issues. The case studies are based on interviews with some of branding's most dynamic leaders:

■ Alan Harris, president of the European unit of US food group Kellogg Co., talks about dealing with the tough and unrelenting issue of private-label brands, showing the courage to experiment but the wisdom to retreat when faced with an unfavourable outcome.

■ Bernard Arnault, CEO of French luxury goods giant LVMH, describes how he handles a wide-ranging portfolio of brands from behind the curtain of a largely anonymous holding company, displaying a flair for managing creative talent within a structured framework.

■ Clive Butler, corporate development director of Anglo-Dutch consumer goods group Unilever, discusses how to handle under-performing brands, showing a willingness to question fundamental assumptions within a large corporate bureaucracy.

■ Jack Keenan, deputy CEO of British beverages and food group Diageo, tells how he merged two massive spirits brand portfolios using the principle of economic profit, applying a new brand calculus to the old problem of portfolio management in a merger scenario.

■ David Powell, vice-president of marketing at diversified US industrial group Minnesota Mining & Manufacturing (3M) reviews efforts to defend trademark rights to two brands owned by 3M that have won household-word status, a coveted but problematic achievement.

■ Rita Clifton, CEO of world-leading brand consultancy Interbrand, and her colleague Jan Lindemann discuss the latest concepts in brand valuation and their origins in the 1980s corporate takeover battle for British bread baker Ranks Hovis McDougall.

■ Domenico De Sole, CEO of Italian luxury goods maker Gucci Group, relates the amazing story of the Gucci brand's return from near ruin, thanks to skilful application of brand control, discipline and respect for key branding principles: exclusivity and perceived quality.

■ Dimitri Katsachnias, head of the Parfums Cacharel unit of France's world-leading cosmetics group L'Oréal, talks about creating a new fragrance brand, demonstrating scepticism towards market research as a creative force while using it adroitly to measure marketing effectiveness.

GETTING WHAT YOU ASK FOR

Brand managers used to complain about the lack of recognition given to the role played by brands. For a long time, companies with strong branding traditions, such as Procter & Gamble, Coca-Cola, General Motors and Heineken, were unusual and confined to the consumer goods and auto sectors.

Today that is changing. Inside many companies brand managers are getting the respect they have so long craved. Technology-driven firms such as IBM and General Electric now intensively nurture and study their brands, as do financial institutions such as Merrill Lynch and Citibank. But along with recognition are coming new challenges. Finding ways to value and analyze brands is one. Others include constructing systems to protect a brand's heritage while leaving room for change, as well as co-ordinating complex brand-management teams across geographical borders and departmental lines.

The struggle inside companies over brand control and brand power has been researched and documented for many years by top consultants and academics. Aaker and consultant Erich Joachimsthaler wrote:

'When brand equity became the hot topic of the late 1980s, it may have seemed like another management fad that would last only a few years. Instead, however, one industry after another has discovered that brand awareness, perceived quality, customer loyalty, and strong brand associations and personality are necessary to compete in the marketplace.'[2]

Some of the executives interviewed in Part 2 embarked on their brand-management careers with an instinctive feel for it, while others learned about it on the job. All have valuable lessons to share.

NOTES

1 David Aaker, *Building Strong Brands*, New York: Free Press, 1996, p. 343.

2 David Aaker and Erich Joachimsthaler, *Brand Leadership*, New York: Free Press, 2000, p. ix.

STORE WARS:
KELLOGG AND PRIVATE-LABEL
BRANDS

'We're certainly not prepared to become a global private-label supplier at this time'

Alan Harris, president, Kellogg Europe

AFTER STARING BRAVELY ACROSS THE BREAKFAST TABLE at one of the branding world's scariest ogres for years, Kellogg Co. flinched at last in 2000. The maker of well-known brand-name cereals said in February of that year that it had agreed to manufacture private-label breakfast cereals for Aldi, the German supermarket chain. The arrangement was on a one-year trial basis and involved only five products to be sold strictly in German Aldi stores, but the deal nevertheless stunned the world consumer goods industry.

Proud and principled Kellogg, world leader in the $15-billion world cereal market, had always before scorned the 'if you can't beat 'em, join 'em' private-label game. Finally, it seemed, the pressure had grown too grrrrr-eat, even for the master of Tony the Tiger, after years of seeing rivals spoon up its market share. But six months later, to the surprise of many and the disappointment of Aldi, the deal was off.

Kellogg said the Aldi contract caused more problems than it solved and cancelled it, having discovered the hard way what many fast-moving consumer goods manufacturers are realizing about the private-label challenge – you can run, but you can't hide.

Private-label – also sometimes known as own-label or store-brand – marketing is one of the most vexing and enduring problems facing name-brand consumer goods companies. No matter how hard they try to ignore it, it won't go away. Moreover, strategies to combat it keep returning to the same basic marketing precepts: innovation, quality and a strong brand. No amount of selective co-operation or product-line diversification or other flanking manoeuvres will work.

The way to beat private label, say the experts and the veterans in the trenches, is to make a better product that is functionally unique and supported by a compelling brand at a price premium that people will pay. Yet this elementary proposition continues to elude some of branding's biggest players, perhaps because while it is the simplest solution to enunciate, it is also the most difficult to achieve.

'Packaged goods manufacturers have been remarkably slow in responding to this situation', wrote Susannah Hart, director at consultancy Interbrand UK. As things stand, Hart wrote, 'We would not be surprised to see many of the famous brand names of today, across a wide range of industries, turn into nothing more than own-label suppliers to retailers'.[1]

A private-label is a brand owned by a retailer, such as Wal-Mart's Sam's Choice, Tesco Own or Safeway Select. They have been used for a long time to sell products like canned peas and dog food, but gained market prominence about 30 years ago when they began spreading into high-profit margin areas once seen as the sole turf of name-brands, such as soft drinks, beauty aids, medicines and breakfast cereals.

Private-label goods are bought by retailers at low wholesale prices from manufacturers under contract, and then sold in the retailers' stores for 10–40 per cent less than similar, higher-priced name-brand products. Private-label and name-brand goods usually appear next to each other on the same shelves. They may sometimes even be made by the same manufacturer, although consumers seldom know it. Giants such as Unilever, Nestlé and Procter & Gamble make private-label goods, for instance.

Retailers like private-label goods because they fatten their profit margins, and give shoppers cheaper options to expensive name-brands. But name-brand manufacturers hate them because they steal their market share, cut their pricing power, compete for shelf space and erode name-brand loyalty.

'Undeniably, the presence of private label, and not just in cereal but in groceries overall, has grown over the last 30 years ... In certain countries, it has certainly become a bigger issue than it used to be', said Alan Harris, president of Kellogg Europe in an interview in his office in the largest industrial park in Manchester, the hard-working heart of England's Merseyside factory belt. He went on:

'It's a much smaller issue in the United States than it is in Europe ... But it's at a fairly pivotal point in America right now because of significant trade consolidation, which is taking place and I think will continue to take place. That will be followed by a much greater emphasis on private label. So I would say it's right there, right now in the States.'

The rising popularity of private-labels puts name-brand manufacturers in a tough spot. If they refuse retailers' demands for a line of private-label supply, they risk losing market share and profit margin to less-principled rivals. But if they play along, they risk looking deceptive to consumers and hurting their name-brand image, as well as alienating those retailers to whom they do not offer a private-label supply line – all for the sake of taking on a distracting, defensive, low-margin line of business.

> 66 The rising popularity of private-labels puts name-brand manufacturers in a tough spot. 99

Kellogg, like many other name-brand leaders, was frozen in the head-lights of this dilemma for years until the trim, bespectacled Harris decided to act and broached the Aldi proposal. He recalled:

'I went to the main board about July [1999] and said, this is a test. I'm going to confine it by content. I'm going to confine it to one customer, to one geography. We're going to do it for a year, and I'm going to come back to you in a year and tell you how it's working ... If I find that it causes too much customer antagonism, then we're not going to continue it.'

Customer antagonism was exactly what Harris found, and not after a year. After only six months the Aldi deal had rankled so many of Kellogg's other retailer customers that Harris announced Kellogg, with no hard feelings on Aldi's part, would terminate the agreement after its end-of-year expiration. In a follow-up interview after he had the courage to shut down a programme that took some nerve to attempt in the first place, Harris said, 'The big game in town is still the development of our branded business. We're certainly not prepared to become a global private-label supplier at this time.'

Many forces led to the emergence of private-label brands. They include: rising retailer power; smarter consumers; excessive price increases and managerial arrogance by name-brand manufacturers; the maturity of many packaged goods markets; and the excess production capacity that resulted.

The spread of private-labels does not represent 'The Death of Brands!', as newspaper headlines periodically proclaim, but rather the rise of one sort of branding at the expense of another, and often to the benefit of consumers. Private-labels may never entirely replace name-brands. Some retailers that have gone too far down the private-label road have suffered. But the private-label tide is rising, and few of the world's name-brand manufacturers have a clear idea of what to do about it.

Just a month after cancelling the Aldi deal, Kellogg announced second-quarter net earnings of $150.9 million including a one-time charge related to European supply chain efficiency. Those earnings were down 2.1 per cent from a year earlier, on quarterly revenues of $1.8 billion, which was up less than 1 per cent from the prior year.

FLAKY FOREFATHERS

Kellogg, the giant of breakfast cereals, is based in little Battle Creek, Michigan, tucked away in the folds of the Kalamazoo River Valley, about halfway between Detroit and Chicago. The town, surrounded by gently rolling grain fields and abundant orchards, about a century ago became a popular settlement for the Seventh Day Adventists, a fundamentalist Protestant sect that observes the Sabbath on Saturday, disdains alcohol and meat and believes in the Second Coming.

Seeking to popularize its doctrine of healthy living, in 1866 the church set up the Western Health Reform Institute in Battle Creek. Serving up a mix of oatmeal, Adventist theology and exercise, it attracted lots of guests in an age when people went away to such places the way they go to retreats or to the beach today. To boost its image, the institute paid to send a local Adventist boy to medical school in New York City and then brought him back home in 1876, at age 24, to be physician-in-residence. He was Dr John Kellogg – visionary, hustling self-promoter, quack, genius, mesmerizer, he has been called all these things.

Like a true innovator, Kellogg held some views that turned out to be immensely valuable and others that look a bit hare-brained with hindsight. He thought the colon was the secret to good health and lectured about 'autointoxication', or poisoning of the body due to insufficient breakdown of food in the digestive tract. He supported a vegetarian diet, vigorous exercise, and frequent bowel movements.

Under his tutelage, guests at the institute – and they included some of the day's biggest celebrities such as industrialist Henry Ford, inventor Thomas Edison, explorer Richard Byrd, aviator Amelia Earhart and the hugely obese President William Howard Taft – exercised in athletic nappies, took multiple daily enemas, swam in electrified pools and did aerobic exercise to recorded music. Over the years, Kellogg marketed a series of health-oriented products, including granola, peanut butter and a mechanical horse for exercising. Each of these products had a separate brand name and some were quite successful. To handle this end of the institute's operation, Kellogg hired his younger brother, William K., as business manager.

Together, they discovered quite by accident a way to convert wheat into flakes by steaming and pressing it between heavy rollers, rather than pulverizing it into flour. They toasted the flakes and spooned them out to their guests at the institute, who gobbled them up by the bowlful.

Mail orders flooded in and Dr Kellogg founded the Sanitas Nut Food Co., with William in charge to handle the business. The younger brother also kept experimenting on his own, and in 1898 he developed a process for flaking corn. Dr Kellogg was uninterested in the breakthrough, however. So William left to start the Battle Creek Toasted Corn Flake Co. on his own in 1906. It was later renamed Kellogg Co. Corn Flakes were the company's main product and they flew out the door in boxes bearing the motto: 'The Genuine Bears This Signature – W.K. Kellogg'. Dozens of rivals sprang up almost immediately in Battle Creek to copy Kellogg, including the C.W. Post Co., forerunner of General Foods.

Kellogg led the industry in innovation, introducing the Waxtite inner lining for freshness in 1914, Bran Flakes in 1915, All-Bran in 1916 and Rice Krispies in 1928. Expansion had reached into Canada, Australia and England by 1938. Dr Kellogg died in 1943; William in 1951, both at the age of 91.

In marketing, Kellogg Co. pioneered the idea of the brand family, routinely attaching its strong corporate brand to descriptive, catchy individual product brands. For instance, it was almost always 'Kellogg's Corn Flakes', seldom just 'Corn Flakes'. The company also led in developing cartoon brand characters. Rice Krispies gnomes Snap, Crackle and Pop made their debut in the 1930s. Later they were the first animated figures to appear in TV advertising. Tony the Tiger followed in 1953; Toucan Sam in 1963.

Kellogg diversified beyond breakfast cereals with the invention of the Pop-Tart in 1964 and the acquisition of Eggo waffles in the 1970s. But, as it grew to become one of the world's largest food groups, Kellogg also began to encounter some of the forces that would shape its most difficult period to come.

BOWL OF CONFUSION

Private-label brands first appeared in the USA more than a century ago on the shelves of the Great Atlantic and Pacific Tea Co. (A&P). General merchandisers Sears Roebuck and Montgomery Ward also pioneered the field. But by the 1950s name-brands from specialized manufacturers – with their national reach, higher quality and better branding techniques – had far surpassed private-labels in consumer preference. The experience was different in the UK, where retailers such as Sainsbury and Marks & Spencer had a stronger position in the marketplace and kept a firm grip on consumer sensibilities with their private-label brands. But there, too, name-brands were in a leadership position by mid-century.

Then came the recurrent economic shocks and persistent inflation of the 1970s and early 1980s. Throughout this period, large name-brand consumer goods manufacturers sought and obtained regular wholesale price increases, which were passed on to consumers. Inevitably, these hikes were sufficient to compensate not only for the general increase in producer prices, but also to pad the profit margin a bit.

US retailers, especially in the supermarket sector, were still too fragmented to resist these hikes. When a multinational titan such as Kellogg or P&G ordered prices up, the typical response of US retailers was to ask, how high? As a result, cereal prices soared in these years and consumers felt the pinch.

In the UK, where retailing was more concentrated, manufacturers enjoyed less power. UK supermarket groups such as Sainsbury and Tesco, feeling squeezed by name-brand suppliers, responded by beefing up private-label brand programmes they had operated for years. They quickly found this provided them with useful leverage in the give-and-take of purchasing negotiations with Unilever or Nestlé.

Inspired by the UK example and confronted with consumer unrest at runaway price increases, US retailers in the 1970s began selling both 'generic' or 'white-box' goods, as well as new lines of private-label items. The generics fad shocked name-brand manufacturers, but faded quickly as consumers balked over quality issues. Private-labels staked out a space in the market, however, and have held it ever since.

In the depths of the 1981–2 recession, US private-label brand market share hit 17 per cent, according to a *Harvard Business Review* article by John Quelch, dean of the London Business School, and David Harding, a marketing consultant.[2] By 1994, Quelch and Harding wrote, that market share had declined to 14.8 per cent, as consumer purchasing power recovered and name-brands regained the offensive amid the longest peacetime economic expansion in US history. Still, Quelch and Harding said, US private-labels commanded higher unit shares than the strongest national brands in 77 out of 250 supermarket product categories by 1996. One of the categories hardest hit by private-labels was breakfast cereals.

The presence of private-labels was more pronounced in Britain, where retailers aggressively expanded their programmes. By the mid-1990s Sainsbury's was getting 54 per cent of its total sales from private-labels, and Tesco 41 per cent, Quelch and Harding reported.

As marketing executive Andrew Seth has commented:

'The manufacturer–distributor pendulum has swung violently in favour of the retailer in many western markets, notably the UK, Scandinavia and most of northern Europe. This diminished the resolve of yesterday's long-term brand custodians, who have compounded their brand problems by inserting their heads firmly in the retail noose and making "own-brands" for retail sale.'[3]

❝Private-labels came to be viewed as vital to developing the brand images of retailers themselves. ❞

As private-label branding took firm hold over the 1990s, retailers began to see it as more than a bargaining chip for use against name-brand suppliers at the purchasing manager's negotiating table. Private-labels came to be viewed as vital to developing the brand images of retailers themselves. Harris observed:

'A lot of those retailers have come to see the [private-label] brand as a way of differentiating themselves from their competition. So it isn't just about price. I think the Sainsbury brand, for what it's worth, stands for more than just low price ... That can help to differentiate them from Asda and from Tesco. So it offers different things.'

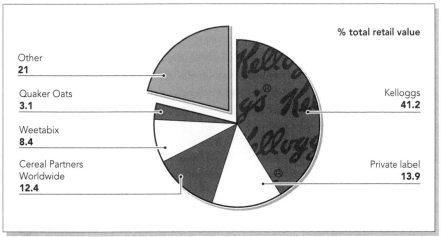

% total retail value

Other
21

Quaker Oats
3.1

Weetabix
8.4

Cereal Partners
Worldwide
12.4

Kelloggs
41.2

Private label
13.9

Source: Euromonitor International

FIGURE 9.1 Breakfast cereal market share in Western Europe by company, 1998

MORNING RUSH HOUR

Against this backdrop of private-label expansion, Kellogg was also hurt by changing eating habits, another legacy of the 1970s and 1980s.

As more women entered the workplace, commuting times lengthened and the pace of working life accelerated, the habit of sitting down at home with a bowl of Corn Flakes in the morning started to fade into history. Many people began believing, rightly or wrongly, that they didn't have time for it anymore.

New options appeared. Following the lead of McDonald's and its Egg McMuffin, fast-food restaurants started opening earlier and offering morning menus. People wolfed down a bagel and coffee while stuck in traffic. Instant breakfast shakes and breakfast bars came on the market. Harassed parents sent their children out to school with a bag of crisps and a drink.

After decades of rapid growth, sales volume expansion at Kellogg and other breakfast cereal makers slowed in the late 1980s and 1990s. Total US sales of ready-to-eat cereals from all manufacturers was about $7.3 billion in 1999, down by more than $1 billion since 1995, it has been estimated.[4]

Kellogg responded to these twin threats – loss of market share to private-labels and changing morning-eating habits – only slowly and with limited effectiveness. From 1983 to 1991 it introduced no major new brands, even as it began to lose its share of a breakfast cereals market in clear deceleration. The company formed a convenience foods division and teamed with food processor ConAgra in 1994 to create the Healthy Choice cereal line, which helped build a market niche for super-premium adult cereals.

But by 1996 Kellogg was forced to slash prices on 16 of its leading name-brands in response to market-share losses following price cuts by rivals and continued inroads by private-labels. More overseas expansion efforts followed, as well as restoration of higher prices on leading brands, the elimination of 25 per cent of the North American workforce and the departure of several top executives in 1998 and 1999.

By early 2000 the formerly unthinkable was occurring at Kellogg. Arch-rival General Mills, based in Minnesota and teamed in a joint venture with Nestlé in Europe, gained US breakfast cereal market-share parity at about the same time that Harris unveiled his private-label programme in Germany.

The Harris experiment, combined with some successes in the convenience foods business, showed a chastened Kellogg finally on the move. The company was also clearly looking for new ways to improve its branding efforts in the face of the private-label challenge.

A handful of consumer goods manufacturers, such as Gillette and L'Oréal, have shown in recent years how reasearch and innovation can block inroads by private-labels. Other recent boom brands, like Starbucks, Tropicana and Ben & Jerry's, have triumphed over private-labels by offering powerful brand messages that have transformed the pricing structures of their categories. These name-brand successes have been achieved by returning to branding basics, while also expanding the idea of the brand to cover a broader message beyond describing the contents of a package. 'To be a brand is not to be a name on a product', summarized marketing expert Jean-Noël Kapferer of HEC. 'Rather, it is, through constant investment in know-how, to become and remain the reference of quality at an acceptable price.'[5]

Kellogg, having taken a hard look at the dynamics of the private-label market, is confident today that it can meet targets something like Kapferer's by relying in part on a research advantage. 'If our product tastes and performs better than the private-label competition, then we see that in terms of sales performance in the stores', Harris said.

The critical edge that branded goods manufacturers claim to have against private-label is a focus on research and development and the product quality and performance that results. Kellogg, in theory, as a dedicated breakfast cereals producer with huge revenues, will be able to spend much more money and time finding ways to make better breakfast cereals than will a retailer like Sainsbury or a small manufacturer under contract to make private-label cereals for Sainsbury at razor-thin profit margins. The problem with a product such as Corn Flakes has been that its brand has become so well known that it is nearly a generic descriptor, critics say, while the product that it represents is so simple and easy to manufacture that legions of imitators are knocking it off.

Such private-label copycats behave in the marketplace as pure cannibals, eating the market share built up over years of hard work by Kellogg. 'I don't think they bring a lot of people to Corn Flakes that have never thought of Corn Flakes before … I don't think they increase consumption. It does tend to be more of a competitive steal', Harris said.

The consumers who defect to private-label cereals are not naturally a lower-income category. 'In all of the studies we've done, it doesn't come out that simply. What actually happens is they draw across a spectrum', Harris said. Private-label goods attract a psychographic category called the 'professional shopper' that takes pride in pinching pennies and is willing to experiment. These consumers often come from upper-income categories. Private-label goods buyers also do not tend to remain so forever.

❝The consumers who defect to private-label cereals are not naturally a lower-income category. ❞

As Harris said: 'People will move from the brand to the private-label depending on their experience, the offer, the environment, and some people who might have bought private-label before will move to the brand. So it's very fluid.'

KELLOGG BRAND POWER

When Carlos Gutierrez took over Kellogg as CEO in 1999 he made the following statement: 'I am convinced that the key to growth for our company and the category is investment in product innovation, in franchise-building marketing and in the accelerated expansion of our convenience foods business'.[6]

Where this summation of strategy left the company's top branded breakfast cereals was uncertain, although Harris said the company is confident the Kellogg brand itself retains considerable power. Consumer studies also show Kellogg elicits strong associations with nutrition and quality.

As an example of the brand's strength, Harris cited a new product that came to be called Pastry Swirls.

'It was a kind of premium Pop-tart, if you will, high in fat, high in taste. This thing was terrific. But we were concerned about what name to call it. So we said, we'll call it Mendelson's, this fancy name. We didn't want to call it a Pop-tart. So, we called it Mendelson's and we decided we wouldn't put the Kellogg name on it because we were a little bit concerned about the fat content. So we put it out there into test market and it did just okay. It did okay because the food was good, but it didn't do well. So then we brought it back in and said, now let's get real. Let's call it a ... Pastry Swirl, and let's put the Kellogg name on it. And, with very little else changed, boom. The business went straight up because the consumer goes in and there's that very, very strong Kellogg endorsement.'

Interbrand, the brand consulting firm, ranked Kellogg as the 33rd strongest brand in the world in the 2000 edition of its annual survey of the world's top brands, with an estimated value for the Kellogg brand of $7.4 billion, up 4 per cent from 1999.[7]

However, pushing the Kellogg brand into new areas that the founding Kellogg brothers might not necessarily have approved of is a delicate issue in Battle Creek. Harris commented:

'One of the things about being the guardian of a brand is that you try not to take it places where you think it could be damaged. But I think we've tended to find this brand will often travel further than you might think.'

NOTES

1 Susannah Hart, 'The Future for Brands', in Susannah Hart and John Murphy (eds), *Brands: The New Wealth Creators*, London: Macmillan, 1998, p. 208.

2 John Quelch and David Harding, 'Brands versus Private Labels: Fighting to Win', in *Harvard Business Review on Brand Management*, Boston: Harvard Business School Press, 1999, p. 25.

3 Andrew Seth, 'Managing the Brand', in *Brands: The New Wealth Creators*, p. 198.

4 *US News & World Report*, 30 August 1999.

5 Jean-Noël Kapferer, *Strategic Brand Management: Creating and Sustaining Brand Equity Long Term*, London: Kogan Page, 1997, p. 45.

6 Reuters, 22 April 1999.

7 Interbrand, *The World's Most Valuable Brands Survey*, 18 July 2000.

10

PUZZLE MASTER: LVMH AND THE BRAND PORTFOLIO

'The CEO of each of these brands is really behaving as if he were the owner'

Bernard Arnault, CEO, LVMH

WHEN THE SLEEK, 23-STOREY LVMH TOWER opened in December 1999 in midtown Manhattan, few passers-by would have recognized the name on the front door, even though they may well have known the high-profile brands sold around the corner on Fifth Avenue by the world's largest luxury goods group.

Louis Vuitton, Moët & Chandon, Christian Dior, Givenchy, Celine, Guerlain and Dom Pérignon are some of the chic names controlled by France's LVMH, whose chairman Bernard Arnault is becoming a master at managing top brands from behind the curtain of a largely unknown holding company.

Handling a large portfolio of brands is a precarious balancing act. On one hand, owning a number of brands, especially in related market areas, presents opportunities for cost savings by combining promotion, distribution and production efforts. On the other hand, too much con-solidation risks each brand in the group losing its distinct identity, and thus its competitive positioning in the marketplace.

Moreover, brands in a portfolio have to be regulated to prevent overlap and market share cannibalization. They have to be given a fair share of management attention, research and development support and financial backing, even when one is outperforming another and commanding the spotlight.

Nowhere are these imperatives more vital than in the high-strung luxury goods industry. Cost cutting can look so easy, but countervailing and intangible factors, such as brand personality, designer prestige and creative independence, mean all the difference between the penthouse and the poorhouse.

'We have a group culture that allows us to manage the contradiction between creativity, or the naturally unstructured part of designers and artists working with ideas, and the very organized part of this business, which is managing for growth throughout the world through a network of shops', said Arnault, a reserved and slender Frenchman, in an interview in his subdued Paris headquarters office. He went on:

'If you do not give freedom to your designers and creators, you don't get the right product and you have no real creativity. On the other hand, if the managers cannot really manage, then the business is not working as a great cash-flow machine ... So, the success of the group comes from our ability to manage well these two apparently contradictory forces of the business.'

For brand managers, LVMH offers a remarkable study in how to nurture and develop the creative forces of any brand, not just those behind $500 handbags and $200 champagnes, while also keeping a firm grasp on the business – a left brain/right brain conundrum that can often be vexing. Arnault succeeds at this, despite gaining a reputation through numerous merger and acquisition battles as one of Europe's most fearsome corporate raiders, as well as worrying some analysts on Wall Street about his ability to keep up with the fast increasing size and complexity of the LVMH empire.

66 Arnault's secret lies in understanding the style and personality of each brand under his control. 99

Arnault's secret lies in understanding the style and personality of each brand under his control, attracting and choosing the right people to cultivate those aspects and, at the same time, marshalling the cost and growth opportunities permitted by LVMH's unique scale and exploiting them to competitive advantage. As he says:

'It gives us really an edge on the market. We leave each company independent, but at the same time we bring them the power of being number one in the world. When a company needs investment, we can do it. We can put money in year after year until it works well. Some brands are more difficult than others. But we are there and we will not let them go; we will build them.'

GRABBING THE PIECES

Like a few other groups with portfolios of disparate brands, such as Swiss luxury goods rival Richemont or US bourbon-to-golf-balls conglomerate Fortune Brands, LVMH has been assembled over a relatively short period by a series of aggressive acquisitions and takeovers of much older companies to give it a huge sales lead (*see* Fig. 10.1).

Louis Vuitton was a Paris woodworker who carved his way into the luggage business in 1854. By the First World War, his son was running the world's largest travel goods store and the familiar LV monogram was being stamped on high-quality bags, cases and trunks sold across France, England and the USA.

In 1977 control of the Louis Vuitton (LV) business passed to Henry Racamier, a former steel executive who had married into the family. He transformed LV from an obscure status symbol for the in-crowd into a well-known status symbol for those much more numerous people hoping to look like part of the in-crowd. Annual sales rose to nearly $2.5 billion from $20 million in just a decade under his leadership.

Quite separately, Arnault was working in Florida in 1984 as a property developer at the head of a company started by his father. Informed that a weak French textile group was for sale, he returned home and snapped it up. He knew its sorrowful assets included a gem – the Christian Dior fashion brand.

At LV, meanwhile, Racamier was worrying that his company might fall victim to a takeover. It was the middle of the 1980s' junk-bond-fuelled takeover binge. In 1987 he made a defensive merger between LV and Moët Hennessy, the prestigious champagne and cognac group. Importantly, Moët Hennessy owned the rights to Christian Dior fragrances, which drew Arnault's attention.

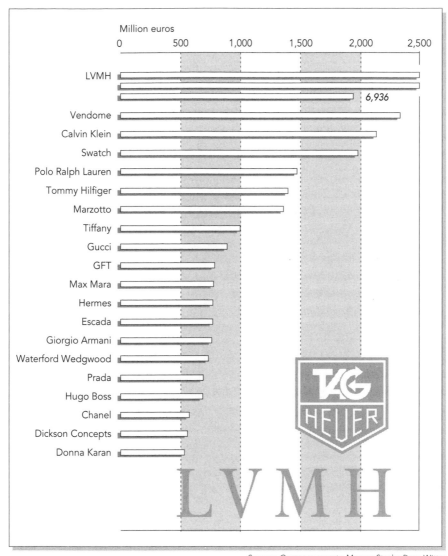

Sources: Company reports, Morgan Stanley Dean Witter

FIGURE 10.1 Luxury goods companies 1998 top 20 sales

Almost from the day of its creation, the new LVMH ran into trouble. Racamier and chairman Alain Chevalier fought over who was in charge and how to run the company. Seeking allies against Chevalier, Racamier invited Arnault and his investment partner Guinness, the UK drinks group, to boost their stake in LVMH. They did so and quickly gained control of 43 per cent of the company. Out-manoeuvred, Chevalier resigned and Christian Dior fragrances was within Arnault's grasp. Eighteen months later, Racamier was forced out and the LV half of the business fell to Arnault, as well.

Louis Vuitton ranked as the world's 34th most valuable brand, with an estimated worth of $6.9 billion, and Moët & Chandon as the 59th most valuable at $2.8 billion, in the 2000 edition of an annual survey of top brands by brand consultancy Interbrand.[1]

The bloody boardroom battle for LVMH laid the foundation of the Arnault empire, and he soon added to it by buying noted fashion and luxury brands Celine, Givenchy, Christian Lacroix, Kenzo, Berluti, Loewe and Fred, as well as luxury goods retailer DFS and control of publisher Desfossés International.

Arnault mounted a strong and sometimes acrimonious resistance to the merger of Guinness and GrandMet, UK food and drink groups in which he controlled stakes. In the end, the formation of Diageo, the world's largest spirits distiller proceeded in 1997, with Arnault realizing substantial profits. In the following months, LVMH gained control of France's number-one and number-two perfume retailers, Sephora and Marie-Jeanne Godard, as well as smart-set department store Le Bon Marché.

Arnault mounted a takeover bid for Gucci, the Italian leather goods powerhouse, in 1999. But French retailer and distributor Pinault-Printemps-Redoute (PPR) – headed by another French billionaire, François Pinault – rode to Gucci's rescue in a white-knight deal. At the time of writing, the PPR–Gucci transaction was being contested in court by Arnault, who still held a large Gucci stake.

After this setback, LVMH swooped into the prestige watch market by buying Ebel, Chaumet and a stake in TAG Heuer, making itself the world's third-largest watch group. LVMH also gained control of Britain's Thomas Pink shirts, several small cosmetics firms, an auction house, the fabled Château d'Yquem winery, and was rumoured to be among several potential acquirers of Italian design house Giorgio Armani.

LVMH revenues in 1999 hit $8.2 billion, up 23 per cent over 1998. Excluding acquisitions, sales growth was about 15 per cent. Net profits for the year more than doubled to $665 million. The company's stock, traded in Paris, rode out market concerns about Asian economic setbacks and ended 1999 up sharply (*see* Fig. 10.2).

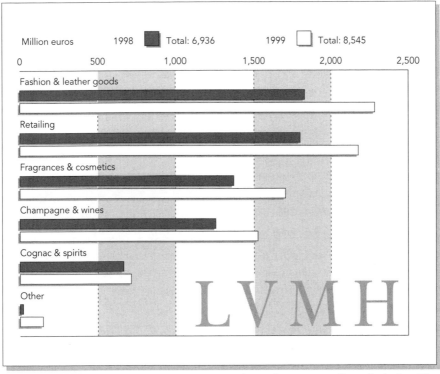

Sources: Company reports, Morgan Stanley, Dean Witter

FIGURE 10.2 LVMH annual net sales by business group

Amid the success of his luxury goods and fashion ventures, Arnault has indulged an enthusiasm for the internet with a string of investments, mostly through a family holding company. LibertySurf, the first internet stock floated on the Premier Marché of the Paris Bourse in March 2000, has netted him capital gains of more than $1 billion. He incurred losses on the collapse of fashion e-tailer boo.com, but other investments have been profitable. Arnault has also taken Sephora and the LVMH brands on to the web in a big way, with the launches of sephora.com and Eluxury.

In early 2000 LVMH widened its distribution net by acquiring Miami Cruiseline Services, an operator of onboard duty-free shops. It also bought a majority stake in Italian design house Emilio Pucci. But the latest deal to highlight Arnault's style as a brand master was the 1999 joint venture with Italian mogul Patrizio Bertelli, head of the legendary leather goods group Prada, to buy out the chic Roman fashion house of Fendi, one of the luxury-goods world's most glamorous and highly coveted names.

WOOING THE FENDI SISTERS

The courtship of the five Fendi sisters, who each owned a piece of the family business, was a long and dramatic contest ultimately won by Arnault and Bertelli partly because of their willingness to allow the Fendis and favoured designer Karl Lagerfeld to remain involved – a hallmark of the Arnault approach.

Founded in 1925 by Edoardo and Adele Fendi, the house of Fendi started out making fur coats. The parents turned the business over to their daughters in the 1980s and it took off, with the help of Lagerfeld. In 1999 Fendi handbags were on the must-have lists of celebrities like Madonna, Sharon Stone and Elizabeth Hurley. Fendi clothing, shoes, watches, ties and home products were moving briskly.

But the sisters, seeing the earlier $23-million buyout by France's Hermes of design house Jean-Paul Gaultier, sensed rightly that market values were peaking for companies like theirs. They hung out a for-sale sign. At the outset, Gucci chief Domenico De Sole was reported to have convinced four of the five sisters to sell to him, although the US private equity firm Texas Pacific Group (TPG) was seen as being favoured by one sister because it had pledged to allow her two children to remain company employees.

Arnault and Bertelli, normally business rivals, arrived late on the scene. But they won the day, ousting Gucci and TPG by acquiring a 51-per-cent stake in Fendi in a deal valuing the firm at $850 million. The Fendis retained 49 per cent of the business and 'important positions in the company including chairman, director general, style, planning and communications', said the deal announcement.

The final decision had been given by the sisters to Lagerfeld, who preferred the Arnault/Bertelli management team to those of Gucci and TPG, sources close to the transaction said. In our interview, Arnault talked about his relationship with Lagerfeld and the Fendis from the deal negotiations up until the present. 'Fendi today is one of the most desirable brands', Arnault said. 'We knew that when we were talking to them and trying to acquire them. It was a small company and they did not have many outlets.'

Arnault promised to increase the number of Fendi shops around the world, arguing, no doubt accurately, that no other company could do this as well. He also said that LVMH and Bertelli could most effectively bring about increased production in Fendi's Italian operations. Perhaps most critically, he told the Fendis and Lagerfeld that they would stay aboard, and they have. 'The family stays in the company. They are still there, for creativity, with the designer', he said.

He said he did not speak of setting limits on Lagerfeld and the Fendis to keep their brand's style and attitude from straying into market niches already occupied by other LVMH brands. Rather, he said, he left this issue up to them and trusted their vision, adding: 'The image of Fendi is very well-defined. It's different completely from Vuitton and from Dior. Karl and the Fendis have this type of genius and creativity and they know it perfectly. So they will follow it. They are not going to change the image of Fendi.'

MANAGING INITIATIVE

Here was the crux of Arnault's brand management philosophy. In most of the brands in LVMH's portfolio, managers are given considerable autonomy. They are motivated financially by equity interests in their respective businesses. They enjoy the support of a large organization and they must answer to it, but they are allowed to innovate by following their own creative inspirations. As Arnault said:

'Every brand has the possibility to really behave as if it were a family-owned brand. Most of these brands came from families and were developed by families. To be successful, they have to have the same feeling even if they belong to the number-one group of luxury products in the world. So it's very entrepreneurial. The CEO of each of these brands is really behaving as if he were the owner of the brand, and he has complete freedom to manage the brand. Everybody working in the company feels as if they were in a medium-sized company with all of the benefits attached to it. They do not feel they are working in a very big organization, à la P&G [Procter & Gamble], not at all ... Our ability is to create and inspire, but also because we are the largest and the best in the world, we can attract the best possible talent, young executives, young artists, young designers.'

> **❝ Every brand has the possibility to really behave as if it were a family-owned brand. ❞**

To prevent overlap in the portfolio, Arnault said the group starts from the ground up:

'When we add to the portfolio, we try to find companies in niches of the market that we are not in yet … When we bought Fendi with Prada, that was a niche of the market where we were not present. So we try to complete gradually and progressively the portfolio while trying to avoid direct competition, direct overlap, and trying to have positioning that is different. This being said, the fact that a customer can go to Vuitton and buy something and then buy something at Fendi does not mean that we compete directly.'

Some companies make the mistake of trying to 'uniformize' their businesses 'with one designer overseeing a lot of different things', Arnault said.

'This is not the right way. The right way is to leave each brand really independent in its creative image and innovation of production and image-building. That is what we are doing. We are completely decentralized, which means that every brand is independent.'

Reflecting this view, he said he sees the value of the LVMH name itself as limited chiefly to reassuring and inspiring employees and potential employees, as well as relating to investors.

'It's a corporate brand. It's not a brand under which we are going to sell products. The fact that Louis Vuitton or Givenchy or Fendi or Celine belong to the same group, the customers do not care and even do not know, and do not need to know. Each of these brands has to be completely separate. From a corporate standpoint, the fact that each of these companies know that they belong to the largest group of luxury products in the world, and that the people that we hire know this, is very important because of the corporate identity. I think it's key to the success that LVMH has as its identity being the corporate owner of all of these brands.'

So, the Manhattan tower with the LVMH sign at the front is meant to talk to Wall Street, Madison Avenue and the Garment District more than it is to consumers on Main Street.

QUALITY, IMAGE AND GLOBALIZATION

In addition to managing in a decentralized manner, Arnault said a key to LVMH's branding success is a focus on quality – a theme echoed by others in the luxury goods business, such as Gucci. 'Customers are used to quality now. When they buy luxury products, that doesn't mean they want to buy just trendy products that they recognize … It also means they want quality. So for us, quality is as important as innovation and creativity', he said.

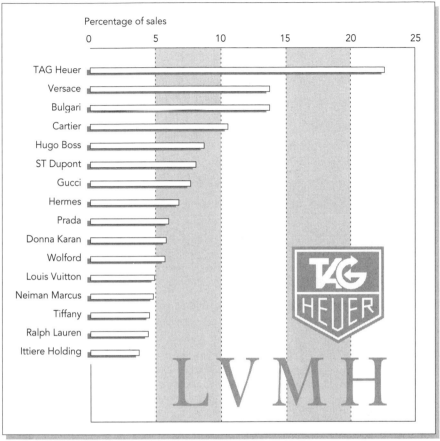

Sources: Company reports, Morgan Stanley Dean Witter

FIGURE 10.3 Luxury goods companies 1998 marketing expenditure

Assiduous attention to brand image is equally vital, which explains why LVMH spends about 10 per cent of revenues on advertising (*see* Fig. 10.3). Arnault explained:

'Part of our culture is the image of our brands. It is really key to follow and be extraordinarily protective of the image of our brands ... Image is something that we are working on at every level, not only in the ads, but also in the way that we present the product and the way we behave *vis-á-vis* customers. This is something that is built every day at almost every level of the company.'

Finally, he said, globalization is a reality for luxury goods companies, not just a debating topic as it is for many other brand goods companies:

'In our field, we will have more and more globalization. We are selling worldwide brands. As buying power goes up and up with economic growth, even in emerging countries, people are travelling more and more. So they want, with brands like ours, the same products in Paris, in Tokyo, in New York. Globally we sell the same products. For us and our field, it's important to have a global brand projecting the same image and having the same type of content all over the world. This was not the case 20 or 30 years ago because, at that time, buying power was very different.'

For instance, when Christian Dior entered Japan 40 years ago, the economy was very different and consumer buying power was low.

'The Japanese customer could not buy imported products because they were too expensive. So what Dior did at the time was to start licensing and contracting the products, and they were producing products that were affordable to the Japanese customer. Now, the world has changed completely. Today the buying power of the Japanese customer is one of the highest in the world ... So our strategy to approach them has to be completely different.

'Now that they can afford it, they want the real product coming from Europe. That is why seven years ago we decided to cancel the licensing agreements that we had in Japan. Globalization, for us, now is key. The Japanese customer travels to Paris, to New York, to Louis Vuitton shops in these cities, and wants to see good product. He does not want to see something different.'

The power of luxury goods groups like LVMH to go global and command unmatched profit margins stems in part from the *laissez-faire* approach taken by managers like Arnault to brand creativity, setting up a virtuous cycle that lifts both company and brand.

NOTES

1   Interbrand, *The World's Most Valuable Brands Survey*, 18 July 2000.

11

JUDGEMENT DAY:
UNILEVER AND BRAND DISPOSAL

'We have 1,600 brands, but we don't have 1,600 great ideas'

Clive Butler, corporate development director, Unilever

I WENT TO BUY SOME VITAMIN C the other day, to fight a case of the snif-
fles, and there were 30 or more brands, sizes and formulations on offer
at my local pharmacy. Tablets, chewables, time-release capsules, efferves-
cents, bioflavin enhanced, children's sizes, 200 mg, 500 mg, a store
brand, three national brands, a vaguely homeopathic-looking brand,
two 'natural' brands and hot drink mixes in cherry, orange and lemon.

It took 10 minutes to scan the labels and finally make a choice. Even
after that, I walked out unsure if I'd bought the right thing and asked
myself one question: does the world really need that many choices in
Vitamin C supplements? Plainly, the answer is no.

Yet a superabundance of brands exists, not just in Vitamin C but in a
great many consumer product categories, and it is one of the most critical problems confronting the branding business today.

The industrialized world is awash in brands. Walk down the aisle of a
supermarket or pharmacy and the evidence is stark. A mind-boggling
assortment of branded products presents itself, many of them registering
a whopping zero on the average consumer's brand recognition meter. At

a time when many consumers say they favour simplicity over choice, especially in routine purchases, the push is on inside many branded goods companies to cut back on the clutter.

Perhaps no company better exemplifies this trend than Unilever. The Anglo-Dutch consumer goods giant is in the midst of slashing its brand portfolio to 400 from 1,600 – one of industry's biggest-ever brand culls and a true test of the company's courage and commitment. At the last count Unilever owned and supported more brands in more countries than any other company in the world. Its big names include Lipton, Dove, Wall's, Ragu, Birds Eye, Sure, Snuggle, Obsession, Breyers, Suave, Vaseline, Close-Up, and that just scratches the surface.

Top brands like these will almost certainly survive the brutal disposal process under way at Unilever, but many, many others will not. In fact, the majority of brands in Unilever's stable are destined to be sold, subsumed into other brands, shut down or simply cut off from promotional support and left to wither away. The process, if Unilever sticks to it, will take years to unfold.

Other consumer goods makers are taking similar steps. French cosmetics giant L'Oréal was a pioneer of brand disposal. Swiss food group Nestlé SA and British spirits distiller Diageo are following suit. So are the diversified US titans Philip Morris Cos and Procter & Gamble Inc.

Unilever presents the most dramatic example of a branded goods company finally admitting that it has too many brands, and having to devise a way to deal with the problem. 'It's a very simple thing really. We have 1,600 brands, but we don't have 1,600 great ideas,' said Clive Butler, corporate development director of Unilever.

Butler, a bespectacled English gentleman with an academic manner and a long career in brand marketing, spoke with me on a momentous day in the 70-year history of Unilever. He explained how Unilever came to own all those brands, when it became clear it had far too many, and how it decided to take action. It was a long and arduous process and it had come to a head on the day we spoke.

THE AXE FALLS IN LONDON

22 February 2000 was a bright, cool day in central London. Outside Unilever House, the fortress-like corporate headquarters at the City end of Blackfriars Bridge, a stiff breeze was blowing off the River Thames and

buffeting the late-winter morning commuter crush. Inside, from the podium of the company's recently remodelled auditorium, Chairman Niall FitzGerald was announcing to the press that Unilever planned to axe 25,000 jobs (10 per cent of its global workforce), shut 100 or more factories and reduce its brand portfolio to 400 from 1,600 over a three- to four-year period.

Of the 1,200 brands left over, FitzGerald said, 'The remaining businesses that do not meet performance standards, or which are no longer part of our strategy, will be reorganized or divested'.

The announcement was a bombshell. It signalled a turning point for the branded goods business. Companies had previously sold off pieces of their so-called 'tails' of under-performing brands, allowing them to concentrate on brands offering higher profit margins. But Unilever had been slow to act. When it finally did, it proposed hacking off its tail right to its hindquarters. The reasons for such drastic action were clear to all, and had been sneaking up on the company for years.

On that same blustery day Unilever reported lower profits for 1999 compared to the previous year, and sales of £27 billion ($43.5 billion), a figure little changed from 1992 (*see* Fig. 11.1). Like many other consumer goods companies – such as Procter & Gamble and Philip Morris – Unilever had achieved immense size during the 1980s. But its core growth rate had slowed alarmingly in the 1990s as it wrestled with rationalizing a massive and diversified portfolio of businesses.

Growth, of course, is imperative in business. Without it, the stock price does not rise. Indeed, Unilever's had fallen throughout 1999, cutting into the personal fortunes of FitzGerald, Butler and thousands of other investors inside the sprawling company and outside it. Unilever is a blue-chip holding in many portfolios and its stockholders were demanding more. As Butler said:

'The moment when we began to think that less would be more … was when we began to be disappointed in our growth rate. All the things that brands are about – the kinds of brands that appeal to consumers, the way in which the trade responds, the way in which we are able to fund innovative resources – all of that in the end gets down to only one performance indicator, growth. Are you growing? And for many of the years of the last decade, we were not satisfied with our growth rate. That made us look very fundamentally at what kinds of brands were our instruments of growth.'

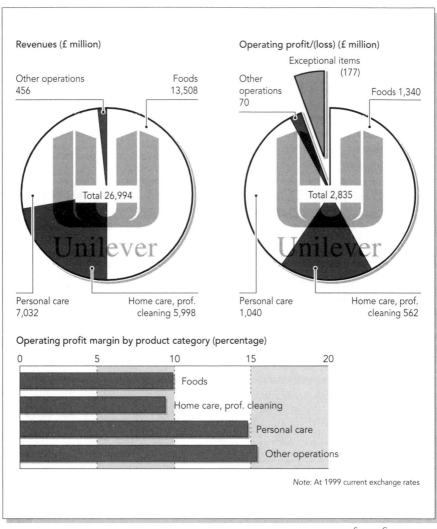

Revenues (£ million)

Other operations
456

Foods
13,508

Total 26,994

Personal care
7,032

Home care, prof.
cleaning 5,998

Operating profit/(loss) (£ million)

Exceptional items
(177)

Other
operations
70

Foods 1,340

Total 2,835

Personal care
1,040

Home care, prof.
cleaning 562

Operating profit margin by product category (percentage)

Foods

Home care, prof. cleaning

Personal care

Other operations

Note: At 1999 current exchange rates

Source: Company report

FIGURE 11.1 Unilever figures for 1999 by product category

Unilever plunged into a long overdue audit of its brand collection. It
revealed that most of its brands were simply not growing, or at least, not
at rates sufficient to fuel overall growth in a company as large as
Unilever. Butler said:

'We found that a proportion of the 1,600 brands are what I would call faintly
marketed – meaning they've inherited an annual marketing programme.
There's a routine allocation of some marketing funds. There are a few ideas
and a spot in the sales priorities. There's the annual television film. That

kind of approach, which sustained a lot of our companies and a lot of our brands for a good many years, isn't good enough now. You need to really understand consumers extraordinarily well to find unique things to say to them and unique ways to say them. And you have to invest significantly in resources for innovation, in technical and packaging areas.'

The realization that Unilever had the head of a greyhound but the body of a dinosaur hit home in Blackfriars just as some fundamental shifts were sweeping through the consumer goods industry. So-called 'global' brands were becoming more powerful in some major categories. Advertising and promotion costs were climbing. Retailers – such as America's Wal-Mart, France's Carrefour, Germany's Metro and Japan's Ito-Yokado – were getting much bigger and gaining purchasing leverage against suppliers. Consumer markets were maturing and price inflation was way down. In some markets there was even deflation, which cut deeply into manufacturers' pricing power. Unilever, a benign but sprawling empire not known for being fleet of foot, slowly came to understand these things.

Eventually Unilever came to see its vast brand diversity as outmoded. Strategic emphasis in the corporation shifted to a sharper brand focus based on global commonalities and efficiencies. As Butler said:

'It was a recognition that there are common themes in brands, particularly in an area like home and personal care. It says that some local differences are not worth the cost of those differences. Then in recent years you've had the emergence of [retailer] trade partners who not only have national, but international clout … They're going to be accounting for an increasing share of our business. And they're only interested in the brands that are number one or two or three in their markets. And of course they look for brands that are common across their markets.'

Finally, he said, Unilever had to face up to the fact that consumers were simply less interested in many products, such as soap and margarine, at the core of Unilever's business. Three generations ago, products like laundry detergent, toothpaste, deodorant, frozen fish and shampoo were still new. Today, although they may be dolled up with the overused words 'New and Improved', consumers know these products are not always new and not necessarily better. Many of these products have nearly been perfected. They all work more or less equally well, are safe and part of everyday life. Vitamin C, for instance, while not made by Unilever, is basically the same no matter what the brand.

People shopping for everyday consumer goods today are less willing to spend time making choices about such brands. They would rather think about other things. Butler explained:

'There is no doubt that the amount of time that consumers want to spend playing the brand game, or discriminating and making brand choices, is much less in our kind of fast-moving consumer goods market now than it was 20 years ago. If you just think, what do people want to make decisions about now? What do they really want to spend their time on comparing one brand to another? It used to be soaps and toothpastes and washing machines and that sort of thing. It's now likely to be laptops and mobile telephones and holidays and other kinds of entertainment.

> 66 People shopping for everyday consumer goods today are less willing to spend time making choices about such brands. 99

'So a lot of it is routine now for consumers, and we have to try harder to rise above the routine. That calls for some adjustments in what we expect brands to do and it may mean that we have to use fewer names to cover a broader area; that we can't have one particular product that just does hand-washing and something else for washing the dishes; that we can't have something just for cleaning floors, but not for cleaning bathrooms.

'You actually need names that have a broader authority because consumers are just not willing to make all the fiddly little bits of brand discrimination if you have brands in too narrow an area. I think that's a very big issue, and it's a dilemma because the broader an area your brand covers, the less specific its claim and its authority and you start to look more like a retailer brand name. But nevertheless, you can't always afford to have lots and lots of brands ... The consumer isn't always interested in sorting through ten brands that do the same thing.'

Unilever has taken some major steps to take on new brands and divest old ones since that blustery day in London. The company agreed in June 2000 to buy BestFoods in a major food industry deal valued at $24.3 billion. US-based BestFoods sells Hellman's and Best Foods mayonnaise and dressings, Mazola corn oil, Skippy peanut butter, Knorr soups, Thomas's English muffins and other brands. Unilever also snapped up the funky Vermont ice creamery Ben & Jerry's Homemade and diet-drink maker Slim-Fast Food, while agreeing to sell its European bakery supplies business.

While Unilever remains on the prowl for deals, it has joined the ranks of consumer goods manufacturers going on a brand diet. But how did the company get so fat in the first place?

THE FEDERATION OF UNILEVER

Understanding how Unilever built a vast collection of brands, with several hundred of only questionable value, requires going back in time to the days when packaged soap, ice cream, canned peas and, yes, even sliced bread were still exciting innovations.

The company was formed in 1930 by the merger of the young and aggressive Dutch margarine maker Margarine Unie with the long-established British soap maker Lever Brothers, founded in 1885. Both were competing for similar raw materials. Both were among the world's first companies to develop global marketing and distribution systems.

At a time when national governments were still armed to the teeth and pointing cannons at each other across defensive walls and trenches, globe-circling Margarine Unie and Lever were doing business in 40 countries. In those days, companies like the ones that came together to form Unilever represented the 'new economy', just as technology and other high-flying enterprises do today.

From the day of the merger that created it right up to the present, Unilever's corporate structure has been unusual. It is administered from twin headquarters in London and Rotterdam. It has separate stocks listed on the exchanges of both London and Amsterdam. It has one board of directors, but two equal chairmen – FitzGerald in London and Antony Burgmans in Amsterdam. Before any business school professor thought of a name for it, Unilever was a decentralized 'virtual' corporation.

It was also one of the first truly multinational companies. With operations in 40 countries at the time of the merger, Unilever expanded steadily throughout the British Commonwealth and into Latin America. Establishing semi-autonomous operating companies in each new market, Unilever gradually came to resemble a federation of independent states rather than a centralized empire. Today, it sells branded goods in 140 countries. Some of its biggest brands, such as Rama margarine and Omo detergent, are virtually unknown in the English-speaking world, but are household words in markets as far-flung as Brazil, Egypt, Japan, India and Russia.

Tellingly, in our interview Butler modified one statement by saying, half in jest, 'It's not the same in Malawi, of course'. This off-hand remark made me think – what other company in the world would have even the first inkling how things are in Malawi? Probably none.

As Unilever expanded around the planet, establishing itself as a provider of consumer goods in markets separated by thousands of miles, and sometimes centuries of economic development, headquarters staff had the good sense to give local managers considerable leeway. Brand expansion and acquisition were driven from the grass roots. Promotion and advertising took on a local flavour, within the confines of certain basic brand messages transmitted from the centre.

In the process, Unilever grew into one of the world's largest buyers of advertising. Today, it annually spends an estimated £3.5 billion ($5.6 billion) on marketing, including advertising. But most of its brands, no doubt including one or two in Malawi, are intensely local.

Picked up over the years through purchases or started fresh, many Unilever brands have stayed in the portfolio long after anyone can remember what purpose they originally served. This circumstance, while extreme in its vast size at Unilever, is certainly not unknown at many other companies, observed HEC's Kapferer: 'Brand portfolios are often overloaded, due more to successive acquisitions than to thorough planning'.[1]

66 Many Unilever brands have stayed in the portfolio long after anyone can remember what purpose they originally served. 99

At Unilever, by the late 1990s, some hard questions were being asked about the multiplicity of brands, and efforts in the household and personal-care products division were providing answers. Butler said:

'We had a lot of brands with different names and different designs, all managed by local brand managers. But at a higher level we found many of these brands were appealing to benefits shared by similar groups of consumers across many countries. The question then had to do with the value of the local twist that comes from having, say, a local Frenchman developing a local shampoo for France. Does that add so much that the loss of synergy between the same kind of shampoo, developed in Germany or Austria or Italy or the UK, is worthwhile? Do you really get a plus from all that "local-ness"?'

Queried thus, many field managers in the European home and personal-care unit, which had 187 brands five years ago, answered no. 'Those who managed it said, we can't flourish with 187 brands, so why don't we concentrate all our resources on 25 brands', Butler said.

With that goal in sight, the business group became the first to start chopping at its long and burdensome tail by consolidating, divesting or shutting down scores of under-performers. 'It has significantly improved the growth curve in Europe. Now, in fact, they've said even 25 is too much. We now have to go down to 15', Butler said.

A similar culling programme was tried in the personal-care business in Brazil, another critical market for Unilever. Butler said:

'We had 27 brands there and now we focus on five. This significantly altered the growth curve in 1998 and 1999 too. We're now growing much faster because the local company is allocating all the money, all the resource, all the energy to five brands. Not all the others have gone away yet, but they are slowly going away.'

The rationale was basic – wring more profits from a leaner operation by exploiting brand similarities across larger markets and killing off uneconomic brands. But would it be so simple for other areas of the sprawling enterprise, where product characteristics differed more widely? 'Our Brazil pilot was very encouraging, but it was only in home and personal care', Butler said.

FOOD FIGHT AHEAD

The question of whether brand culling will work in other divisions has not yet been answered. The big test will be food – the core of Unilever and the source of half its revenues and profits. Food is a very different business from home and personal care. Consumers have established expectations for food that vary remarkably from culture to culture. To reflect local tastes, companies like Unilever often vary the recipe for a product, even though it may be sold under the same brand.

Some foods require more variation than others. Products based on traditional recipes formerly prepared at home, such as pasta sauce, require the greatest customization. After all, Italians want pasta sauce to taste the way Mama used to make it, which can be quite different from the way an American Mom used to make it, for instance.

Ice cream requires less variation. Nobody's mother ever slaved over a Winner Taco Ice Cream sandwich, so expectations are much more flexible. They are even more so in personal-care markets. Shampoo and deodorant users want a product that works and are open to innovation. Little in the way of traditional benchmarks exists because businesses have always supplied such items of everyday life. For most of history, people managed without styling gel and fabric softener, for instance. As a result, consumers from Taiwan to Texas to Turkey are willing to accept basically the same product, thus presenting chances to consolidate regions under fewer, more powerful brands. In fact, if any part of the Unilever empire was best-suited to brand-culling experiments, it was home and personal care. 'In foods there often is ... a much bigger premium for maintaining local branding and a local livery than there is in personal care', Butler said.

But Unilever, faced with a slumping share price and revenue declines in food in 1999, moved ahead and tried the idea of focusing on fewer brands in its ice-cream business. So far, it has worked there, too. 'Ice cream also wanted to reduce the number of brands and they've had good experience', Butler said. 'What we're doing now is saying, let's do that Unilever-wide ... across all our businesses.'

The culling programme under way now within Unilever is huge and will go on for a long time. The scope of it was driven home at the 22 February press conference where FitzGerald was badgered by an aggressive London tabloid newspaper reporter into admitting that, no, he did not know all 1,600 of the company's brands. But then, probably no one at headquarters could recall all of them.

Wisely, the head office has turned to its field managers for guidance. As Butler said:

'We don't know all of the 1,600 brands around the world. Some of them are very local and you could not imagine undertaking an operation like this unless the local experts were fully and completely involved. What we have done is to say here are the principles and here's a deadline. Now, what we want to know is those brands that you feel are going to engage the consumer over the next 10 years and that you feel either do or can have the potential to warrant the amount of development, research, advertising and human resource needed to compete at the kind of level needed these days ... Every brand in Unilever has been assessed according to those principles.'

Political infighting over the process, with local managers squaring off to protect their turf, has been minimal, although no one is fooling themselves that the disposals will go off without a hitch. Butler said:

'It may be that when we actually get to implement the outcome there'll be some squeals. But oddly enough, maybe because it's come later rather than earlier, there is a very wide measure of agreement that we could not go on as we were. I think everybody knows that we will be a stronger business if we have fewer, stronger brands. Of course, there will be some tough discussions about brands which maybe do quite well in one country, but are rather weak in two or three surrounding countries. The right answer might be to stop sales in the weaker countries, but this in turn could lead to a reduction in scale that would impair the viability of operations in the stronger country. There will be questions like that.'

> **❝ Everybody knows that we will be a stronger business if we have fewer, stronger brands. ❞**

In such instances, he said, a combination of cold economics will be combined with local intuition. Many branded goods companies have turned to complex valuation systems, such as the one devised by consulting firm Interbrand, to place financial values on their brands. UK spirits giant Diageo, for example, applied a rigorous 'economic value' test to its brands recently when undertaking a disposal programme similar to, but much smaller than Unilever's.

Procter & Gamble, the US consumer goods giant, in 1992 killed its White Cloud line of toilet paper by merging it with its Charmin brand. It made a similar move with its Solo and Bold detergents. Beecham abandoned fading brands such as Serutan laxative and Rose Milk skin lotion. Unilever, some years ago, withdrew marketing support from its declining Pears soap brand, but the product has continued to cling to a small but loyal following, perhaps providing a glimpse of how Unilever intends to handle its host of similarly under-performing brands.

Like other brand owners, Unilever now carries financial values for acquisitions including brands as goodwill on its balance sheet. But it does not routinely determine values for homegrown brands. Still, in carrying out its disposals, judgements are being based on more than simplistic sales and market share measurements. Butler explained:

'The business is run on the basis of value creation, which we tend to do on a category and business-unit basis. It is quite possible that we will extend that to brands, or to the larger brands as a result of this exercise. We do have, of course, a developing system of measuring brand performance and brand health. In some ways, the shift from 1,600 brands down to 400 will mean increasingly that we actually run the business on measures that check the performance and the health of brands. So it's not just market share. Consumer measures that reflect the vitality of the brand will also be tracked.'

Aside from internally assessing brand health, Unilever is testing consumer responses to potential brand changes using psychographic mapping techniques:

'We have underpinned this whole exercise, in each of the categories in home and personal care, with a huge market-research exercise which has tried to produce some standard market maps in not all countries of the world, but key representative markets. We're trying to plot the main consumer interests in the market, what they want brands to do for them, trying to find the common elements. We have plotted our own brands and our competitors' brands.'

Global maps are being drawn in key categories. Each one puts Unilever's brands in their present and desired positions. Consumer responses to different scenarios covering changes in brand name, price, packaging and other variables are measured. 'We try to pull this all together in ways that the consumer will still find acceptable ... but which will enable us to get some synergies by having the same bottle or the same box, the same perfume or the same advertising', Butler said.

Through this process many strong Unilever brands, such as Lipton and Dove, will clearly be winners, while obvious under-performers will be cut loose. But most brands will probably fall in between. Selecting which of these will live or die will be the tough part. 'That's where brand scale comes in. It comes in when we say, in this market, how many brands can you afford to advertise? It varies. In hair, you find you probably can afford and need three or four brands to cover the waterfront. In other areas, toothpaste possibly ... one brand.'

Marketing professor David Aaker has outlined questions to ask of a declining brand before pulling the plug, such as:

- Is the rate of decline orderly and predictable? Are there pockets of enduring demand?
- What are the reasons for the decline – is it temporary? Might it be reversed?
- Are there dominant competitors with unique skills or assets?
- Are there many competitors unwilling to exit or contract gracefully?
- Are customers brand-loyal? Is there product differentiation? Are there price pressures?
- Is the brand strong? What is the market-share position and trend?
- Can the business manage a milking strategy?
- Is there synergy with other businesses? What are the exit barriers?[2]

Addressing questions of this type, Butler said:

'It's a mixture of how the brand fits the marketplace and the consumer, and second, how many brands can you afford to support at the level that big advertised brands require now. If you look at the cost of marketing a shampoo in the US now, I reckon that … ten, maybe even five years ago, you could launch a brand in the United States with a marketing budget of about $40 million. You don't get much change out of $80 million now and there are new launches under way right now which are spending in the region of $120 million.

'So how many of those can you afford? Now, it's not the same in Malawi, of course. But proportionately the cost of being good at marketing is going up and you cannot afford to have lots of little brands frittering away valuable advertising resource without the scale to make it really count. It's a question of picking absolutely the right positioning and then concentrating your firepower.'

> **❝You cannot afford to have lots of little brands frittering away valuable advertising resource.❞**

Unilever has not identified all the brands it will keep and all that will be disposed of. But it has said it expects to save $1.6 billion over three years. Industry analysts at the investment banks that follow the company are expecting big results. Said Butler in conclusion:

'The fact is that to compete in consumer goods markets now, with the strength of the competition and the cost of competition so high, you have to really reach higher to find the leading edge. The cost of competing to these standards means that you cannot do it for 1,600 brands. You can't find the energy or the resource to locate the competitive edge in 1,600 different ways … Unless there are real differences among products, consumers are not delighted by choices any more. They're actually confused by it. The old idea that consumers are pleased by all this choice, I just don't know. In mobile telephones, probably so. But toothpaste, for God's sake?'

NOTES

1 Jean-Noël Kapferer, *Strategic Brand Management: Creating and Sustaining Brand Equity Long Term*, London: Kogan Page, 1997, p. 68.

2 David Aaker, *Managing Brand Equity*, New York: Free Press, 1991.

12

SHALL THE TWAIN MEET? DIAGEO AND BRANDS IN MERGERS

'There hasn't been much classic marketing applied to spirits. It's been run on gut feel'

Jack Keenan, deputy CEO, Diageo

WHEN CONSUMER GOODS MARKETING VETERAN Jack Keenan set about merging two of the world's largest spirits distillers into global giant Diageo in 1997, he discovered a drinking problem. No, not that sort of drinking problem. Rather, the drinking public had made Johnnie Walker Red the best-selling Scotch whisky in the world, and arch-rival J&B the runner-up.

The two brands had competed fiercely over the years for the same customers. But now they were going to be allies, brought together by the $19-billion merger of their parent companies: United Distillers (UD), part of Guinness; and International Distillers & Vintners (IDV), part of Grand Metropolitan.

Keenan's job, as chief executive of the new Diageo spirits group combining UD and IDV, was to realign their brands to fight in the marketplace side-by-side, instead of head-to-head. It called for some tough decisions about brand positioning, value and strategy.

Mergers and acquisitions present these kinds of tests to brand managers with increasing frequency. Indeed, steering a brand portfolio through a corporate combination is becoming a speciality in itself, and few people have more experience at it than Keenan. A proven corporate fixer whose office is stacked with books of all description and interesting artefacts from around the world, the New-York-born and Harvard-educated Keenan managed the integration of General Foods with Oscar Mayer, General Foods with Kraft, and Kraft with Jacobs Suchard.

As he well knows, the tricky part of guiding brands through mergers is not the deal itself. Any back-slapping investment banker with a sharp suit and a briefcase full of someone else's money can do that. Witness the explosion in deal-making worldwide: 32,000 transactions in 1999, up from 11,000 in 1989. Rather, it's the part that comes after the bankers walk away, pockets jingling, that gets tricky.

'The classic example ... was J&B and Johnnie Walker Red. Johnnie Walker Red was the number-one selling Scotch in the world and J&B the number two', Keenan said. Diageo would gain little in the marketplace if it left the two alone. Vying for the same customers, they would only steal market share from one another, instead of from competitors, and their advertising and promotional efforts would walk all over each other. Clearly, changes were needed. But what changes?

To complicate matters, UD's parent Guinness and IDV's parent Grand Met both owned hundreds of other brands that needed to be reconciled in the same ways, including a truckload of Scotch whiskies. Some of the Scotches were big, such as Dewar's, Buchanan's and Bell's; some were bit players.

In other markets, Guinness and Grand Met owned an amazing assortment of brands, including Smirnoff vodka; Baileys Irish cream liqueur; Guinness, Harp and Red Stripe beers; Tanqueray, Bombay, Gilbey's and Gordon's gins; Beaulieu and Blossom Hill wines; Vecchia Romagna, Asbach and Metaxa brandies; Black Velvet Canadian whisky; parts of José Cuervo tequila and Hennessy cognac; and the largely American food brands Pillsbury, Green Giant, Häagen-Dazs, Old El Paso and Burger King.

Many of these threw up merger-related issues, and Diageo has recently moved to sell Pillsbury and spin off Burger King. But it was Keenan's handling of the heavily overlapping spirits lines in the deal creating Diageo that offers the most instructive case study in managing brands through a merger. As Keenan said:

'Earlier deals I had been involved in tended to be businesses where the brands complemented one another, rather than competing against one another. The interesting thing about putting together IDV with UD was … the brand portfolio question. Up-front, we knew we were going to have to prune the portfolio … There were a lot of casualties.'

A NEW YARDSTICK

Traditionally, brand portfolios in mergers are integrated using a good deal of intuition, along with some number crunching in the finance department that seldom follows predictable lines. Depending on who is managing the process and what markets are involved, brands may be assessed by market share, sales volumes, gross margins, cash flows, trading profits, return on assets or any combination of the above.

Those brands found to be superior in some way win the lion's share of marketing and research support in the newly combined organization, while weaklings are often left to struggle on with fewer resources, repositioned to fill new roles, sold off or simply shut down.

The trouble with this typical process is that real, core values of businesses and brands are often left undetected. Brands that generate huge sales volumes or command leading market shares may not, after all, be very profitable. Conversely, high profitability may mask inadequate long-term marketing and research support, or worse yet, inferior rates of return compared to competitors. Moreover, mixed bags of performance measures can send confusing and contradictory messages to employees, shareholders and other people involved in mergers, which are already unsettling enough.

> 66 Brands that generate huge sales volumes or command leading market shares may not be very profitable. 99

'Understanding the value of brands is never more important than in mergers and acquisitions, and the future will see many more of these', wrote Interbrand CEO Rita Clifton. She went on:

'Financial and organizational issues too often drown out what will really drive the company's future sustainable value: a new shared vision, clearly defined and executed values and vigorous brand marketing. Understanding the underlying hard value of each corporate brand within a merger will provide objective evidence for which corporate brand values should dominate, as well as which portfolio brands should be priorities for greatest value management.'[1]

Keenan, a scholarly 64-year-old known as both a sharp strategist and a boardroom diplomat, has been there, done that, when it comes to knowing the run-of-the-mill problems associated with merging brands. In the Diageo deal, he took a new tack – one being followed by a growing number of companies.

The former head of IDV, in merging with UD, applied the principles of 'economic value', or 'economic profit', to the scores of businesses and brands involved. Those that added economic value, a non-traditional measure of business worth, were retained and given new emphasis. Those that did not were put on notice as laggards needing to shape up, be sold or be killed off. It was a first in the spirits industry. In an interview at Diageo's London headquarters, Keenan said:

'I came out of the food business and we were just beginning to use operating economic profit analysis ... IDV had started doing it as part of Grand Met about three years before the merger. United Distillers did not use economic profit. They used trading profit ... So there was no real line of sight, by brand, by country, in terms of whether a brand was economically profitable or not. So when IDV merged with UD, we sent our finance guys over to their finance guys and said, here's what you have to do ... this rigorous analysis of where the economic profit is in our total beverage alcohol business, and it's really very clinical.'

Economic value analysis has been around for more than a century. It was first described in a rough sense by the economist Alfred Marshall in 1890. But it only caught fire as a business tool in the 1990s, when its converts included big US names such as Coca-Cola Co., Eli Lilly & Co. and Monsanto. A leading proponent of the method is New-York consulting firm Stern Stewart & Co., which owns the trademark rights to the term 'Economic Value Added'.

> **Many companies do not have a clear idea which of their business activities are truly worthwhile because they rely on traditional performance measures.**

The basis of economic value is the argument that many companies do not have a clear idea which of their business activities are truly worthwhile because they rely on traditional performance measures burdened by ill-conceived or outmoded accounting concepts. Stern Stewart, and its various imitators, calculate an adjusted net operating profit for a business and its operating units, then subtract from that figure a charge representing the cost of capital, or the rate of return a business needs to make to service its debt and to keep its investors from selling up and investing elsewhere.

Peter Drucker, the noted business scholar, put it this way in a *Harvard Business Review* article:

'Until a business returns a profit that is greater than its cost of capital, it operates at a loss. Never mind that it pays taxes as if it had a genuine profit. The enterprise still returns less to the economy than it devours in resources … Until then it does not create wealth, it destroys it.'[2]

Diageo chief executive John McGrath and Keenan adopted the economic value model at Grand Met and IDV, then imposed it on Guinness and UD when the organizations merged. This had sweeping ramifications for Diageo, but from a brand perspective it was a breakthrough because it gave Keenan a hard-edged rationale for making most of the tough decisions in the brand portfolio integration process.

In the case of Johnnie Walker, J&B and the merged company's many other brands, the numbers told the tale when examined by brand, by country and by target market using the new, unsentimental logic of economic value, although it was not always applied by Diageo as ruthlessly as it might have been.

IRISH STOUT TO AMERICAN WHOPPERS

Diageo is one of those corporate brand names born from a merger that says everything and nothing. Based on the Latin word for 'day' and the Greek word for 'world', it 'captures what this company is all about', according to the 1997 press release announcing the new name.

The company, which today has annual sales of around $20 billion and ranks as the world's largest spirits group, traces its history back nearly two-and-a-half centuries to Dublin, where in 1759 Arthur Guinness started a brewery. In 1821 the company that he founded launched a beer called Extra Superior Porter, later renamed stout. Guinness Stout formed the basis of a business that the third generation of Guinness family managers took public in London in 1886.

The company's trademark dark brew, known for its bitter taste and foamy head, was exported worldwide. Its distinctive advertisements pictured vigorous sporting scenes or loyal subjects in boots and pith helmets quaffing stout as a healthful pick-me-up in the outposts of Empire. Even today,

KELLOGG'S IS BREAKFAST Tony the Tiger, a familiar sight for millions every morning, with one of the most famous logos in the world

LVMH FOR LUXURY GOODS Bernard Arnault, Chairman and CEO, and two famous products: Hennessy cognac, Louis Vuitton bag

HARD TO AVOID A giant banner featuring Claudia Schiffer and Andie MacDowell on the tower of the ruins of the Kaiser Wilhelm memorial church in Berlin which was damaged during World War II and which will be repaired with the help of L'Oréal

MILLENNIAL MOUSE Lasers project an image of Mickey Mouse and Disney's Millennium 2000 logo across Sugar Loaf Mountain in Rio de Janeiro

DIAGEO

DIAGEO Jack Keenan, deputy CEO, with the range of Johnnie Walker products; and the Diageo logo

WHAT WOULD WE DO WITHOUT 3M? David Powell, vp, marketing, with some of 3M's most popular products, the indispensable Post-it range

RECORD BREAKER The "Ukraine" department store features a giant billboard which Unilever hopes will be a contender for the largest of its kind in the world

SHOPSMART SMART SHOP Daniel Gestetner, CEO of ShopSmart, in front of an ASDA store. ShopSmart has a co-promotion deal with ASDA and its US parent, Wal-Mart

A CLASS ACT: GUCCI Domenico De Sole, CEO,
with chief designer Tom Ford and the highly distinctive Gucci bag

Guinness is the only Irish name on Interbrand's list of the world's top 75 brands in the 73rd spot.[3]

In the 1950s, managing director Hugh Beaver started the *Guinness Book of Records*. Then in the 1970s, like many consumer goods businesses, Guinness lost its way. The company bought more than 200 companies and had disappointing results with most of them. It divested 140 companies in the 1980s, then went on another acquisition binge. It snapped up news-stands, health spas, convenience stores and other beverage groups. It won a takeover battle to buy Distillers Co. for $3.7 billion in 1986, bringing it the Johnnie Walker, Gordon's and Tanqueray brands.

Disaster hit when Guinness CEO Ernest Saunders was linked to a stock manipulation scam as part of the US government's probe of financier Ivan Boesky. Saunders was fired in 1987 and later convicted on criminal charges. The company refocused on beverages in the late 1980s, selling non-core assets and acquiring firms such as Schenley with its Dewar's Scotch whisky brand, and a minority stake in LVMH Moët Hennessy. The deal-making streak was capped off by the 1997 mega-merger with Grand Met, a very different animal.

Real-estate agent Maxwell Joseph started Grand Metropolitan in 1931 by buying London properties for resale. He scooped up a war-damaged hotel in 1946 and more hotels in following years. In 1961 he went public. Diversification came in the 1970s with purchases of catering firms, restaurants, betting shops and – in what was then the biggest ever UK takeover – the brewer Truman Hanburg. Soon after came the purchase of Watney Mann, owner of IDV and the Baileys, Bombay and J&B brands. Grand Met later bought US cigarette maker Liggett Group and Intercontinental Hotels.

Sir Maxwell, knighted in 1981, died and the company restructured around food and drinks, selling off its hotels and other businesses. In 1987 it bought Heublein, picking up Smirnoff, Lancers and Cuervo. Two years later it bought Pillsbury in a hostile deal that netted it the number-two US hamburger chain in Burger King, the ice-cream maker Häagen-Dazs and the frozen foods group Green Giant.

By quite different paths then, Grand Met and Guinness were competitors by the late 1990s, and both were feeling similar market pressures. Spirits consumption was flat to falling in many countries as wine and beer gained popularity. Competitors were merging, raising the ante for everyone. Burger King worked hard, but could not catch up with McDonald's, and remained number two in US fast food. Guinness Stout, Johnnie Walker, Dewar's, Häagen-Dazs and J&B were spinning big profits. But neither Guinness nor Grand Met owned a brand with the compelling power of something like Coca-Cola or Marlboro – staples that retailers must stock. Finally, the consumer-goods business generally was losing pricing power due to low inflation and retailer consolidation, even as the costs of advertising continued to soar. The rate of meaningful product innovation was flattening and developing markets, once promising, were unstable.

'We had both become tired', former Guinness head Sir Anthony Greener was once quoted as saying about the reasons and attitudes leading to the deal.[4]

Towards the end of 1996 the UK giants edged towards a merger. An official announcement came on 12 May 1997. In the ensuing weeks, a very public dispute broke out between the merging parties and dissident French minority shareholder Bernard Arnault of LVMH. But all the while in the background Keenan and his staff were busying themselves with the deal's real challenge – bringing together the massive spirits businesses of UD and IDV. The way they did it turned out to be a textbook example of smooth merger integration, even if the initially rosy forecasts of growth for Diageo were over-optimistic.

DEWAR'S ON THE ROCKS

The integration process was initially driven by regulatory authorities. In Europe and the USA competition watchdogs restricted the companies from sharing competitive information for seven months. To get part of the way around this roadblock, the companies hired consulting firm McKinsey & Co. Market-sensitive data was turned over to its experts with orders to compare the two businesses down to fine details. 'We gave them trade deal rates, by market by customer. We gave them all our procurement data, how much we paid for glass and that sort of thing', Keenan said. 'McKinsey put that all together.'

While McKinsey pored over the books, Brussels and Washington did too, emerging with the verdict that a combined UD–IDV would unfairly dominate the Scotch and gin markets. 'The European regulators basically said, you've got too much Scotch whisky and you're going to have to sell something here, something fairly major', Keenan said.

The demand from the European Commission helped Keenan resolve the thorny issue of what to do about Johnnie Walker, J&B and Dewar's. All three were profitable, both in the traditional and economic value sense. Number crunching was not a great deal of help in differentiating among them. But Johnnie Walker was the biggest-selling Scotch in the world, so it was off-limits. 'It really came down to whether it was going to be Dewar's or J&B' to be sacrificed to the bureaucrats, Keenan said. He went on:

'They had similar kinds of volumes. J&B on a global scale was number two and Dewar's was three or four ... In a sense, Dewar's looks a lot more like Johnnie Walker Red. It's more of a mainstream kind of brand. It was trying to say to people, you're grown up now, so switch to Scotch because you're mature enough now to drink it – that kind of positioning.

'So we really said, that's not going to be very useful to work with as a brand because it sits too closely to our conventional Scotch whiskies. J&B, with its unconventional, colourful label and stuff, can be a counterpoint much more nicely to the traditional United Distillers portfolio ... So we said, okay, Dewar's is the one we'll offer up. The European Commission said, that's great.'

But the American regulators were not satisfied. They, too, had objected to the potential dominance of Scotch markets posed by the merger. But they also were concerned about gin and demanded a divestment. 'Quite clearly, they wanted another scalp to hang on their belt', Keenan said.

By late 1997 18,000 employees of the two companies worldwide were waiting anxiously for answers about how the merger would play out. Top management was eager for regulatory closure. 'We said okay fine ... It was pretty hard to defend what they were asking us to do, but we did it', Keenan said of the agreement to divest not only Dewar's, but Bombay gin, as well. Both were put on the sale block. Shortly after they were both bought by arch-rival Bacardi for the steep price of $1.9 billion. Keenan explained:

'We had an auction and we got a lot of money. We were very happy with the result. Bacardi stepped in. Here was a great chance to broaden their portfolio a bit ... They were buying the number-one Scotch whisky in the United States, and the fastest-growing premium gin in the US, the UK and duty-free. It was a big deal for them and they were very aggressive bidders. When you're selling something you like very aggressive bidders. And off they walked, saving us the whole trouble of figuring out what to do with Dewar's in our portfolio, in a funny way.'

Regulatory approval was granted in December 1997. Immediately afterwards Keenan said, 'Everybody took big, fat books home for the Christmas holiday full of the other company's data. I know I did, and I spent three weeks in Florida at my desk looking at where UD made their money.' After the holiday break, general managers, finance directors and human resources directors were appointed for each country market within the combined corporation. Each manager received a packet that Keenan called the 'integration kit'. It included the McKinsey analysis and an explanation of economic value methods and how to apply them to specific brands, categories and markets. A 200-person integration team was named to assist the country managers and the internal process of merging UD and IDV was under way. Keenan said:

'Each anointed general manager was given the tools to understand in his market where the economic profit lay, by brand, by competitor, by route to market, by piece of the value chain. So they could then begin constructing a brand portfolio and a first-year profit plan and a little three-year strategy. They then had to design an organization to execute that strategy.'

The economic-value approach made decisions comparatively straightforward in many instances. But immediately, Keenan said, the integration team found problems of a predictably political nature.

ROLLS-ROYCE STRUCTURE FOR SKODA MARKET

'We found people were right away trying to build organizations. They were saying, okay, I've got me, and I've chosen my sales manager and my HR guy … The new general managers tended to have their old glasses on and were designing something very familiar. The portfolios had everything because less is not more, more is more, more is better, right? So we caught that really early, and we said wait, wait, think.'

To halt the trend towards empire-building, Keenan instituted 'stop-and-think sessions', forcing managers to slow down and reassess their plans regularly with advisers from London. Keenan said:

'These turned out to be hugely important. I remember the first stop-and-think with the Czech Republic. They showed me their structure and I said, what you've succeeded in doing here is designing a Rolls-Royce structure for a Skoda market, and we're going to have to think differently about this.'

For example, he said, some managers had built wholesalers into their plans because they had always used wholesalers to cut per-case sales costs. These managers had to be told: 'You're now twice as big and you now have the scale that you can deliver direct at a lower cost per case than you can with a wholesaler. So think about having a direct sales force now in certain markets.'

Similarly, reliance on third-party brands had to be discouraged as the integration process went along through 1998:

'Both companies had a lot of third-party brands. We used them for scale. It gave us more cases for the sales force and helped to cover the sales force overhead. If you got the sales force scales right and then you put some additional third-party volumes through, it helped with the overhead coverage. But that was beginning to make less sense when you looked at the new scale of things.

'By and large, we gave up most of our third-party brands, except for ones where we had some equity interests, like José Cuervo or Moët Hennessy … Or another big exception is Jack Daniel's in the United Kingdom where IDV had sold the brand for many years and it was truly economically profitable.'

As the logic of the economic-value yardstick took hold, it was revealed quickly that hard decisions were in order for some large brands that had long been considered beyond reproach. Top-selling brandies, especially, were shown to be laggards under the new calculus. Metaxa, number-one brandy in Greece; Asbach, number one in Germany; and Vecchia Romagna, number one in Italy, went on the hit list.

So did big-selling Christian Brothers brandy in the USA. Cinzano vermouth and sparkling wines, number two in their markets, several small US bourbons and some Canadian whiskies, including Black Velvet, were found wanting. 'We decided to sell those', Keenan said. 'They weren't in core categories. They tended to be in categories that were in secular decline. They had maturing stock. So from an economic profit standpoint, they were destroying value, even though they had a trading profit.'

While certain brands came under fire, the focus on economic value also exposed some country organizations as over-stuffed under-performers. Italy, for instance, had a large staff and sales overhead. Keenan said:

'It was big because there are 60 million people in Italy. Cinzano and Vecchia Romagna had huge volume. But we reasoned it's better to get out of brands in secular decline that are destroying value and resize the company. We said, instead of worrying about your volume budget, start worrying about your value budget – J&B, Johnnie Walker Red, Smirnoff, Bailey's, Gordon's and Tanqueray.'

The new style was young, spare, aggressive and focused on what the company started calling its nine 'global priority brands'. Inevitably, the changes ruffled some feathers. Keenan recalled:

'Our Italian general manager left. He didn't want to be part of a small, lean and mean structure. He liked big volume. So there were people that said, don't like the new way. The funny thing is that I think even some of the old management felt that what we were doing was "not quite right". As economic-value decisions were made, there were a few people around the patch that were kind of saying, hmmm. I would say this though – I was brought into IDV because they wanted someone who hadn't had years of experience in spirits, they wanted an outsider who could approach the business with objectivity.'

DISCO FEVER

The new method for assessing brands may have forced the young Diageo to face up to some uncomfortable truths about itself, but it had limits, as Keenan discovered when the discussion came back around, as it inevitably always did with the company, to Scotch.

Part of the big Scotch problem had been solved by the regulators forcing the sale of Dewar's, but still there was no resolution of what to do with Johnnie Walker and J&B. As Keenan said:

'First of all, we looked to see if they were economically profitable and which one was more so. But the maths were not much help. It was self-evident that when you're number one in Spain, you're certainly more economically profitable than the guy who's number six or whatever … So the next thing was, we said, we're going to have to position these in a different way.'

While the two brands had competed bitterly for the same customers for many years, they did have differing appeals in many markets, if not all. In most places Johnnie Walker was the gentleman's standard, much like Dewar's had been, while J&B was more of a status tipple favoured by hip night-clubbers.

This contrast did not hold true everywhere, as Keenan explained:

'Johnnie Walker Red, in some cases, was trying to be J&B. France was a good example. J&B was a brand for trendy young people, a brand of the night – the trendy discos was J&B. But for the last several years when we were competing with UD, there would be the Johnnie Walker Red trendy disco night kind of thing. You know, we're trendy too! So we had to say, no, you're not trendy. You're part of the fine Johnnie Walker family created in 1820 by John Walker Sons. So you're going to be over here, you're going to be traditional ... and J&B is going to own the night and the disco and so forth because it's a much more relevant brand. It's lighter in colour and flavour. It's got a vibrant look, with a yellow and red and green bottle. It's a pretty flashy kind of a brand ... So we said, in the portfolio, here's the role of Johnnie Walker Red and here's the role of J&B.'

Further down the Scotch line-up, other problems arose as the economic-value method turned over stones that many in the company might sooner have left undisturbed. In some of these cases management stuck to its rigorous value programme; in others, it wavered and followed different priorities.

At stake were former category leaders that had lost their punch, such as Vat 69. Some still led in selected Scotch markets, such as Black & White in Ireland, Bell's in England and Buchanan's in Latin America. But their numbers didn't add up. The same held true for UD's many classic malt Scotches, such as Craggamore, Dalwhinnie, Glenkinchie, Lagavulin, Oban and Talisker. As Keenan said:

'Some of them are quite small and, in the past, some of them did not create economic value. So one of the folks in corporate strategy at the Diageo level said, we'll have a sale. It will be terrific – former leading Scotch whiskies for sale! Buy Vat 69, get two Scotty dogs for the price of one!

'We basically said, look, we are not going to sell any of those Scotches. We are going to find a way, because they've got great value ...Intuitively, I think people felt that the classic malts can't be destroying value. They're so wonderful and they're growing in double digits. We've grown them from nothing to 400,000 cases. They've got to be good. They can't be bad and, of course, they're not bad, they were just priced too low. So there were some instances where we had to get prices up to create value for the smaller Scotch brands.'

In place of cutting and running on the classic malts and similarly borderline businesses, Keenan said the company opted for a category management tactic:

'This turned out to be extremely insightful of me, if I do say so, but it occurred to me that you probably never want to sell a brand in one of your major categories. For us, that's Scotch, gin, vodka and cream liqueurs. So I said, let's not sell these for some small or medium price. But let's see how we can use them to manage a category ... *vis-à-vis* competitive brands.'

As an example of 'category management', Keenan cited the handling of Scotch whisky in Greece:

'In Greece, we market six main whisky brands. All of them have clearly defined roles within the market and all of them are profitable, growing brands. The way we manage them is to identify our consumers, identify what they want to drink on different occasions and then target them effectively. Johnnie Walker Red Label, for example, heads up the Scotch category in Greece by setting the standard for Scotch whisky – Greece has the highest per capita consumption of Johnnie Walker in the world. Johnnie Walker Black Label plays a role in encouraging middle to upper income 25- to 40-year-olds to trade up from standard Scotch.

> **❝ We identify our consumers, identify what they want to drink on different occasions and then target them effectively. ❞**

J&B on the other hand is the young "maverick" recruitment brand which is drunk as a mixed long drink – particularly with cola. It is seen as a spirit rather than a Scotch and is aimed at male drinkers aged 21 to 24. The other Scotch brands in our portfolio also play key roles.

'Dimple is positioned to be the ideal gift and allows us to directly target Chivas, while the marketing of Haig builds on its Scotch heritage and targets Famous Grouse and Grants. Finally Cardhu plays the role of introducing consumers to the UDV Malts range.'

Some industry analysts have questioned the category management concept, arguing that it has allowed Diageo to avoid parting with brands that are still dragging on its profitability. But Keenan responded that these critics, who tend to complain that Diageo is still dragging a heavy 'tail' of under-performing brands, are missing the point.

The company has picked nine brands as its 'global priority' names: Johnnie Walker Black and Deluxe, Johnnie Walker Red, Smirnoff, J&B, Baileys, Cuervo, Gordon's, Tanqueray and Malibu rum. In addition, it has selected 'local priority brands' such as Buchanan's in Colombia and Venezuela, Bell's in South Africa and the UK, and Pimm's in the UK. Keenan said:

'As we designed the new portfolios, we built them around the nine global priority brands. We then had about 30 brands left over that we decided were important local priority brand. Beyond these, there's not much left. The security analysts keep writing about our huge "tail" of brands, but it's not worth writing about.'

'We're looking at brands that we love that were not creating economic value, like classic malts … We're fine-tuning those by saying to some countries, you're going to have to get the price up on classic malts because you're destroying value on every bottle you sell. There are markets that create value on every bottle they sell. So if you can't sell those brands at this high price, you're going to have to give up selling them.'

NOT SO BLACK AND WHITE

If the economic-value programme pushed some brands out of the fold and raised the hurdles for others, it also had the unintended impact, at least initially, of discouraging new branding projects. Keenan said:

'I'll tell you one thing we did have to watch for. By definition, any new product destroys value for some period of time because it's not economically profitable in year one or year two or year three. What we found was that when the UD guys were presented with how we looked at economic profit, they'd say, oh my goodness, this new product is destroying economic value, we'd better get rid of that. So we'd say, no it's okay. All you have to do is show how you can get it to be economically profitable.'

As an example of the problem with new brands and economic value, Keenan cited the Sheridan project at IDV's Baileys unit. The cream liqueur business had developed and launched a product with an unusual double bottle containing black coffee liqueur on one side and white cream liqueur on the other. At the top was an expensive and complex pouring spout that preserved the different viscosities of the bottle's contents, allowing them to be poured with an unusual layering effect. As Keenan explained:

'When I joined IDV, Sheridan was hugely unprofitable at the trading profit line, as well as the economic profit line. We were always trying to figure out if we could get that into a positive economic profit mode. We gave it one year, then two years. Finally they started finding ways to get the glass cost down. Then they took this very special pourer made in China with 40 different parts and found out they could make it cheaper in Switzerland, which is probably a first. But they finally got that thing going with enough volume to just edge into positive economic profit. So there are cases where you have to decide, do I keep going with this? Is it going to be worthwhile someday? Or should I cut and run?'

Beyond the economic-value equation having its impact, intended and other-wise, the Diageo merger has also resulted in new internal structures and ways of handling brand promotion and advertising. Before the deal, Keenan said, Grand Met's IDV had global brands teams based in London. There were teams for Smirnoff, J&B, Bombay and Malibu. Bailey's had a team in Dublin:

'The big teams like Smirnoff and J&B were about 45 people each. They would create the new blockbuster commercial ... Somebody would spend a million pounds producing it and then they would put guys on planes to Asia, Latin America, North America, Europe and off they'd go to present the new Smirnoff commercial.'

Often the result of this top-down approach was resentment and rejection in the field by country and region managers. Keenan said he jokingly labelled IDV's unwieldy system the 'matrix muddle'. He went on:

'The guy in Tokyo would say, I'm sorry but the Japanese will never understand this commercial, we couldn't possibly run it ... Then, of course, it would escalate. The other guy would come back from his trip to Japan and report to the Smirnoff brand director that the Japanese didn't want the new commercial. Then the Smirnoff brand director would tell the head of marketing, who would then come see me. Meanwhile, the region manager would say to me, did you know that young kid came out here and tried to make me run this commercial and it wasn't even in Japanese and I'm beside myself. And I've got the marketing manager saying, you must make the Japanese run the new global Smirnoff campaign!'

Keenan said he sized up the mess for a while and, after a failed attempt at centralizing brand promotion decisions in his office, took more radical action. 'I finally said, this is really crazy', he recalled. When the merger came, out of the window went the London-based brand teams and in their place Keenan set up smaller, transnational management groups comprised of essential brand directors with a global team of key managers. All work together on new campaigns. So far, in-fighting has been minimal.

BRANDS BY THE MEASURE

At present, while Diageo has not boosted its growth profile and profitability as much as hoped in the euphoric early days immediately following the merger, it has won praise in the markets for the management of the merger integration and its systematic approach to brand valuation. As Keenan said:

'We are at the point now where we're fine-tuning portfolios. We're closing down some minor brands, but we basically have the portfolios that we want by country. We're doing a lot of test marketing of brand positionings and advertising levels.

'In some markets, we're saying, what if we doubled the advertising? A lot of it is just what I would call classic marketing. But there hasn't been that much classic marketing applied to the spirits business over time. It's been run on gut feel, and a lot of that gut feel was great. You need intuition as part of it. But we weren't doing enough clinical marketing segmentation and marketing testing.'

The new twist brought to this picture has been the economic-value method and the fresh view it has brought to analyzing the underlying value of Diageo's businesses. 'Before we merged, each company was really not putting people and monetary resources appropriately against brands', Keenan said. 'They weren't applying the ruthless focus against brands looking at their economic value creation.'

NOTES

1 Rita Clifton and Esther Maughan (eds), *The Future of Brands: Twenty-five Visions*, London: Macmillan, 2000, p. 106.

2 As cited by Stern Stewart in *What is EVA?* section of firm's website, www.sternstewart.com 2000.

3 Interbrand, *The World's Most Valuable Brands Survey*, 18 July 2000.

4 *Independent on Sunday*, 14 March 1999.

13

HOUSEHOLD WORD:
3M AND BRAND TRADEMARKS

*'There is only one thing in the world worse than being talked about,
and that is not being talked about'*

Oscar Wilde

HUNT AROUND ON THE AVERAGE AMERICAN desktop and you will probably find two familiar items. One is a roll of clear, adhesive-backed
cellophane ribbon in a plastic dispenser; the other is a neat stack of little
note papers, usually yellow, with a weak adhesive on the inside of one
edge. The names of these products are … Scotch tape and Post-it notes.

Except, these are not generic terms. They are brand names owned by
Minnesota Mining and Manufacturing Co., or 3M, the research-based US
manufacturing group that is one of the world's only companies to possess more than one brand that is a household word.

This, of course, is the dream goal of many brand managers. Companies
spend billions of dollars trying to elevate their brands to household-
word status. Some marketers would kill for the power 3M has with
brands such as Scotch and Post-it, and so they should, up to a point.

Owning a brand that is a household word gives a company a powerful
marketing tool, but as 3M can testify, it is not without its complications
and headaches, and it requires constant vigilance. The great danger is

that such a brand could slip into the public domain, becoming fair game for use as a generic descriptor of the product it represents, whether the product is made by the brand owner or not.

'Anytime we identify somebody who is misusing or who has misappropriated our brand name, we take action with them. We start out by writing them a nice letter. Then if they don't stop, it could eventually develop into some form of litigation, but we try to avoid that', said David Powell, vice-president of marketing at 3M, in an interview in which he talked about the importance to the research-driven company of its brands and the lengths to which it will go to protect them.

The opportunity cost of not policing and protecting the trademark rights of a brand so popular that it enters the everyday lexicon can be high. Just ask Bayer Co., the German drug maker. Until 1921 Bayer held the US trademark rights to the word 'aspirin'. But it failed to act when the term began to be used as a catch-all description of acetylsalicylic acid pain relievers. Now, aspirin is no longer a trademark-protected brand and it can be used by anyone to describe such an analgesic product.

A similar fate was in store for an eye-opening array of former brand names now in the public domain, such as cellophane, elevator, escalator, granola, kerosene, linoleum, mimeograph, mineral oil, nylon, phonograph, trampoline, yo-yo and zipper, just to name a few.

Many brands in recent years have suffered from 'over-adoption', as trademark lawyers call unintended general usage, but have kept their trademark rights thanks to aggressive public education and legal efforts by their owners. Post-it brand notes and Scotch brand tapes are examples. Others are brands such as Xerox, Jeep, Kleenex, Coke, Frisbee, Walkman, Band-Aid, Chapstick or White Out.

Protecting brands from becoming over-adopted and losing their rights is costly and time-consuming. 'We have several people whose full-time job is monitoring these brands', Powell said. But, he added, a recent study of brand values put a price tag on the Scotch and Post-it brands of about $1.3 billion each. 'If you have assets worth that kind of money, then you're going to defend them, even if it means going to court and spending a significant amount of money to fight the battles.'

❝Protecting brands from becoming over-adopted and losing their rights is costly and time-consuming. ❞

SANDPAPER AND TWO-TONE CARS

Minnesota Mining & Manufacturing was founded in 1902 on the shores of Lake Superior in a part of the USA better known for iron mines than inventors' workshops. The company stumbled in early attempts to make sandpaper, but became established with a waterproof version useful to the burgeoning auto makers of the Great Lakes region for smoothing the finishes of car bodies.

Young 3M researcher Richard Drew, while visiting an auto body paint shop, noticed the painters struggled with two-tone jobs because of the flimsy, messy strips of glued paper they used to isolate one paint zone from another. He went back to the lab and, on his own initiative, invented masking tape.

The auto painters liked it, but complained because Drew applied adhesive only to one thin edge of the tape. As a result, it kept falling off. The painters told 3M to 'stop being so Scotch' and put adhesive over the entire surface area of the application side. Thus modified, the tape and the name stuck.

After much experimentation, Drew later applied his idea to clear strips of cellophane, a material invented by DuPont. In 1930 Scotch brand transparent tape appeared on the market. Like many other 3M inventions to follow, it was a first and its brand name became synonymous in the USA with the product.

In Britain and the Commonwealth countries, 3M was barred from registering Scotch as a brand name because the word was considered descriptive of anything Scottish. In addition, UK-based Sellotape Co. developed a similar cellophane tape in 1937 that had become the British standard. The Scotch branding restriction was eased over the years, but even today, most Britons still know clear tape as Sellotape.

Scotch tape made 3M's fortune, becoming a ubiquitous household and industrial product through the middle of the century. The company followed up with a remarkable series of innovations, including automotive undercoating, electrical tape, reflective sheeting, magnetic audio and video recording tape, Scotchgard brand fabric and upholstery protector, disposable face masks and surgical drapes.

In the late 1960s 3M chemist Spence Silver discovered an adhesive that didn't stick to anything very well, but retained its stickiness even after being moved from one surface to another. He didn't quite know what to do with it, but 3M patented the formula anyway. The adhesive hung around until Art Fry, another 3M chemist, applied it to slips of paper to use as bookmarks in his church hymnal. One day he wrote a note on one and attached it to a report to a colleague.

Fry had a hunch that his note represented a new way to communicate on paper, but hardly anyone at 3M shared his belief. After much persuading, he won a test-marketing programme of 'Press and Peel' notes. The test was a failure, but some sales success was noted in situations where consumers were able to sample the product. 3M tried a massive free-sampling programme and repurchase rates for the product shot up to 90 per cent. A national launch of the rechristened Post-it notes followed in 1980. Today, 3M makes 400 different Post-it brand products.

STAKE YOUR CLAIM

When 3M started at the beginning of the 20th century, only a few hundred trademarks were registered in the USA. By the time Post-it notes appeared almost 80 years later, that number was nearly 1.5 million and climbing as companies scrambled to stake out the legal rights of brands. The arena in which firms fight for brand rights is trademark law. Dominated by expensive lawyers and specialists, the field is ever-changing, but a basic understanding is vital to anyone dealing with brands, whether inside or outside brand-owning companies, creatives, administrators or marketers.

A trademark is defined as a brand name that has some basis in law. In general, a brand is recognized as legally protected simply if it is used on the open market regularly and consistently by its owner. But much stronger rights attach to a brand that is formally registered as a trademark with government regulators in the countries in which the owner does business. The first registered trademark in the world was the red triangle mark used by UK-based Bass beer. It has been renewed regularly since 1876.[1]

In the USA, trademark law is grounded in the Trademark Act (1946), related state statutes and common law from the courts. In the UK, the Trade Marks Act (1994) codified older UK regulations and brought them more closely in line with European Union standards embodied in the Community Trade Marks system set up in 1993.

Other national governments in Europe, Asia and Latin America have their own trademark systems, which can differ markedly from country to country. An international trademark registration system is administered under the Madrid Arrangement dating back to 1891 and updated in 1989. But the USA, UK and Japan are not part of this system. So its usefulness is somewhat limited.

Registering a trademark under any of these systems means doing a preliminary search to guard against trademark duplication, making an application and then awaiting official approval, based on standards that vary in detail from system to system, but generally follow similar parameters.

The law recognizes three basic trademark types – coined or fanciful, arbitrary and suggestive – in descending order of protection granted. Coined or fanciful trademarks are given the strongest protection. These are usually words that were unknown or unused before being applied as brands to particular products, such as Jeep vehicles, Kodak film or Dacron fabric. Arbitrary trademarks existed as words before being used as brands, but bear no descriptive or other relation to the products that they represent. Examples might be Apple computers or Camel cigarettes.

Finally, suggestive trademarks carry the least amount of protection. They are existing words that refer to the product they represent as brands in one way or another. For instance, Kleenex tissues are suggestive because the brand name is derived from the word 'clean', which suggests what tissues do. Similarly, Eveready is a suggestive brand in that it implies the utility and endurance of batteries. Brands falling into these three categories can be registered. Brands that are merely descriptive or generic usually cannot, such as English breakfast tea or olive oil.

DISTINCT VERSUS DESCRIPTIVE

It should be clear from this discussion of the hierarchy of legal strength in branding that there is a fundamental conflict at the core of trademarks – that of distinctiveness versus descriptiveness – and it can be the source of tensions within a company.

The law favours distinctiveness in brands. So, a brand that is unusual and not referential to the product or service that it represents is easier to protect. But at the same time, such a brand is more costly to promote and establish because consumers will not easily recognize or understand it. As a result, marketers often favour descriptiveness in brands. One that is easily comprehended and informative about its product or service can be a more effective and affordable selling tool, even though its long-term strength and ability to rise above the sea of brand clutter may be reduced.

> 66 A fundamental conflict at the core of trademarks – distinctiveness versus descriptiveness – can be the source of tensions within a company. 99

Balancing these imperatives can be difficult. Branding experts advise taking into account both sides when designing a new brand name. Many new brands walk a fine line between distinctiveness and descriptiveness, such as Post-it. Yet many memorable brands are fanciful creations, such as Xerox. Key to protecting any sort of brand, once established, is using it constantly and consistently. Trademark experts offer checklists for brand handling that include the following rules:

- Register it formally with trademark regulators.
- Capitalize the first letter and use italics, boldface type, colours or quotation marks.
- Only use the brand name as an adjective, not as a noun or a verb.
- Pair the brand name with a generic name, perhaps even inserting the word 'brand' between them, such as Post-it brand notes or Scotch brand tape.
- Apply registration or trademark notations, such as Xerox® or Shredded Wheat™.
- Maintain consistent spellings, visual formats and colour schemes.
- Train and educate people who might use the brand to treat it properly.
- Challenge promptly and forcefully any misuse of the brand.
- Keep records of correct treatment of the brand to defend your actions later if needed.

Defending an established trademark has been complicated recently by the internet. Oceans of unregulated and hard-to-trace information surge across the web, presenting difficult questions about monitoring and control. Unauthorized and improper use of brand names is endemic. In addition, the emergence of a new breed of low-cost, low-accountability manufacturers in China and Russia has made trademark counterfeiting more common and costly to businesses.

Finally, trademarks are also facing attack from a new class of social and environmental activists who target well-known brands to promote causes ranging from animal rights to family values. Often these efforts involve the misappropriation and satirical or farcical alteration of trade-marked brands. Much of this activity occurs on the internet and filters out on to street posters and handbills.

'To maintain the value of your brand, it is vital to ensure that you pro-tect its name, visual identity and other differentiating features of its getup as trademarks', advised UK trademark attorney Janet Fogg. 'The rights afforded to trademark owners are substantial and it is important to protect your intellectual property as carefully as your tangible prop-erty; both are valuable assets.'[2]

WAKING UP TO BRANDS

3M only started to recognize its corporate brand and product brands – like Scotch and Post-it – as corporate assets about six to seven years ago, said Powell, an Indiana native with a low Midwestern drawl. He explained:

'This was a change. The strength of those brands was developed over the years as a result of the ingenuity of the products. When Scotch tape was invented, it was the first transparent, pressure-sensitive tape ever invented … These were really unique and different products and that's how the brand names developed over the years.'

Managing the household-word status of Scotch and Post-it involves rig-orous adherence to rules along the lines of those sketched above, constant education both inside and outside the company, much cajolery and occasional legal action, Powell said. He went on:

'It is difficult for us to force other people … to use the brands properly and keep them from becoming generic. But we can control and manage how we use them. If the Scotch brand becomes the common way for people to ask for pressure-sensitive tape, there's not much we can do about that and it's not all bad. We have to make sure that when we promote the product, or advertise it, or use it in any form of written or verbal communication, that we do it properly. That we refer to it as Scotch brand tape, or Post-it brand repositionable notes.

'It was very clumsy to get people, even within our own organization, to start doing this going back about five to seven years ago. But now, it's amazing that people have become very comfortable with it. When they talk about Scotch, they talk about Scotch brand, or when they talk about Post-it or Scotchgard, or even 3M ... they refer to it as the brand. So if somebody ever challenged us and said Scotch has now become generic, we believe and our experience has proven our strongest defence against that would be that we could show documentation that reflects proper usage of the brand name in everything that we've done.'

> 66 We could show documentation that reflects proper usage of the brand name in everything that we've done. 99

3M operates a programme to remind the press, distributors and others who have occasion to handle or write about the brands that they are brands, and not generic terms. Powell said:

'We have policy manuals for the Scotch brand that we give to dealers. The manuals say how you can use the 3M brand, the Scotch brand or any of our other brands, and how you cannot use them. That form of education has really helped. We still get examples, probably weekly, where somebody has misused one of our brand names. We send them a nice letter, saying we appreciate their support in promoting our products, but we would appreciate it if you would refer to the brand name in this way. Generally, they're very receptive. In cases where they just spent a lot of money publishing a new brochure or something, they're not that excited. But at least we get them to change it for the next time.'

Competitors have not often gone so far as to steal the Scotch or Post-it brands outright and slap them on non-3M goods. According to Powell:

'Where we have the biggest problem with that is with the 3M brand itself. We get a lot of people that try to utilize that brand. We get dealers that are not authorized distributors of 3M products that use the 3M brand in their advertising ... We had one company that called itself 2M, but did it with the same colour red and the same typeface that we use for 3M. Many people looked at it and thought it was 3M. We obviously contacted them and made them stop doing that.'

Like other brand owners, 3M is confronting the new challenges to trademark management posed by the web. 'The internet has opened up a whole new area here', Powell said. The company has had to go around the world registering web domain names using its brands in various permutations – such as mmm.com, 3m.com, mmm-co.com, threem.com, etc. – to prevent them from being registered and used by people completely unconnected to the company. 'Now we have a whole new area of monitoring and action', Powell said. 'The law is still fairly unclear in this whole area.'

The household-word status of the Post-it and Scotch brands influences brand promotion and positioning strategy at 3M. As Powell said:

'Part of our strategy is to develop and focus on what we refer to as the specialness of these brands … We look at Post-it brand as being fast, friendly, colourful communication. So when we promote and advertise the product, that's the focus that we try to take. Scotch we look at as a friendly product that's reliable, that's solid, that will always do the job. So it has a personality. All of these come under the 3M brand umbrella, which we look at as being our authority brand. We've positioned 3M as being an innovative company that you can trust. You can trust the company so you can trust the products. So these brands definitely have personalities.'

NOTES

1 *Accountants' Digest*, March 1999.
2 Janet Fogg, 'Brands as Intellectual Property', in Susannah Hart and John Murphy (eds), *Brands: The New Wealth Creators*, London: Macmillan, 1998, p. 81.

14

DEBITS AND CREDITS: RANKS HOVIS AND BRAND VALUATION

'A cynic is a man who knows the price of everything, and the value of nothing'

Oscar Wilde

WHEN TWO MID-SIZED BREAD BAKERS, one Australian and one British, tangled in the takeover arena in 1988, no one could have guessed that their otherwise unmemorable fight would help launch one of marketing's most vexing struggles – the brand valuation debate.

Goodman Fielder Wattie, today known as Goodman Fielder and Australia's largest food group, was a company on the move in the 1980s, just coming off a big merger and hungry for more. Ranks Hovis McDougall (RHM) was a British baker in possession of the leading UK bread brand Hovis, but with a weakened balance sheet due to a recent acquisition-related goodwill write-off of its own.

In 1988 Goodman Fielder made a hostile takeover bid for RHM valued at £1.78 billion. At the time it looked like just another attempted buyout amid a junk-bond fuelled explosion of mergers and acquisitions worldwide. RHM, however, was in no mood to be gobbled up. Aware that its brands were the focus of Goodman Fielder's attention, and that brands were driving many big deals, RHM rebuffed Goodman Fielder and stated in its defence document:

'RHM owns a number of strong brands, many of which are market leaders, which are valuable in their own right, but which the stock market tends consistently to undervalue. These valuable assets are not included in the balance sheet, but they have helped RHM to build profits in the past and will continue to provide a sound basis for growth.'

Further manoeuvring followed and Goodman Fielder ended by abandoning its bid. But RHM was not finished. The company hired the London-based consulting firm Interbrand to estimate, in co-operation with the London Business School, the monetary values of all the brands in the RHM portfolio. It was the first 'whole portfolio' brand valuation. RHM then published a 1988 financial report that included the sum of Interbrand's estimates on the balance sheet as intangible assets. By adding in the brand valuations, RHM boosted its net assets to £979 million from £265 million just a year before, making it a much bigger fish in the corporate pond. RHM went on to leverage its expanded asset base to pay for acquisitions of its own. Ironically, it was bought out in 1992 by the Tomkins conglomerate for less than the Goodman Fielder offer, and RHM is reportedly now on the sale block again, as the mergers and acquisitions carousel spins on and on.

But the bread maker had a lasting impact on the world of brands. RHM's innovation in 1988 – to boost its balance sheet by adding in the estimated value of its brands – might have seemed just a bit of clever accounting on the surface, but it caused a stir that is still being felt. Grand Metropolitan, a large UK drinks group now part of Diageo, and Rupert Murdoch's News Corp. in Australia, had pioneered the capitalization of acquired brands as intangible assets separate from goodwill, but no one had yet capitalized brands developed in-house and no one had used the brand valuation concept in quite the way RHM did.

The asset-boosting tactic, observed marketing professor David Arnold in *The Handbook of Brand Management*, was 'the event that brought the issue of brand valuation into the public arena … This pioneering move by RHM drew attention to the off-balance sheet valuation of brands that was continuing in the mergers and acquisitions field on both sides of the Atlantic.'[1] Two decades later, the brand valuation issue remains unsettled.

PUTTING A PRICE ON IT

Business people are tantalized by the idea that a brand could be measured and analyzed; that a definite financial value could be assigned to a very indefinite symbolic entity; and that such a value could be recognized in financial accounts just like inventory or securities or cash.

If this could happen, the possibilities for improving business would be many. For instance, the worth of brands to a company could be better understood and recorded in the assets column of the balance sheet, no matter what the brand's origin. That way, brands could boost a company's total value. If the company was in an acquiring mood, brand-boosted assets could allow it to borrow more money; if it was on the defensive, they could raise the potential buyout price. Accurate brand valuations could give financial markets a clearer idea of the true worth of a company and influence stock price performance. Brand valuations could provide managers with vital information useful in brand portfolio management, licensing negotiations, setting marketing department budgets and advertising strategies. Reliable brand value data could help connect two often sorrowfully disconnected parts of the business – short-term financial assessment and long-term strategic analysis.

> 66 Accurate brand valuations could give financial markets a clearer idea of the true worth of a company. 99

The trouble is that, ever since the RHM episode, no one has been able to devise a way to value brands that is generally accepted, even though people have tried for more than a decade. RHM piqued the interest of many, but it did not establish a durable precedent. As a result, brand valuation remains disputed territory on marketing's frontier between the bean-counters and the creative types. Most in branding accept the concept, but there remain sceptics. 'Brand valuation and the "brands-on-the-balance-sheet" debate are controversial subjects ... Many marketing experts feel it is impossible to reduce the richness of a brand to a single, meaningful number, and that any formula is too much of an abstraction and too arbitrary', commented marketing professor Kevin Lane Keller.[2]

As a result of such scepticism, the UK has tightened its accounting standards in line with more conservative US guidelines by saying that companies can only count a brand as an asset if it has been acquired from someone else, and then only if it is depreciated over a span of time as part of goodwill, or the premium paid in an acquisition over the net asset value of the acquired firm. That ruling has subsequently been amended to limit depreciation and allow capitalization of some brands in some instances. Moreover, national standards continue to vary on the treatment of brands.

The ultimate result is a fudge. Some brands today are recognized as assets, and are not. Some brands are depreciated over 20 years, and some are not. The consequences are strange indeed. For instance, UK beverages giant Diageo capitalizes acquired brands such as Smirnoff and puts them on its balance sheet. But Guinness, the famous stout beer brand developed in-house by a Diageo predecessor company, is absent from the Diageo balance sheet.

Similarly, US soft-drinks leader Coca-Cola Co. at the end of 1999 reported total assets of $21.6 billion on its balance sheet, which was devoid of any specific reference to the immensely powerful Coca-Cola brand. Yet the stock market was giving Coca-Cola a market capitalization of more than $142 billion in mid-2000. Clearly, investors recognized some value in the company that accounting standards did not.

In addition, a study by Interbrand and Citibank showed that balance sheet assets in early 1998 failed to account for almost 71 per cent of the weighted average market value of the companies included in the UK's leading market index, the FTSE 100.[3] Whether contradictions like these will ever be reconciled is unknown and, as some increasingly see it after 20 years of argument, perhaps unimportant.

At Interbrand, which has grown since its pioneering work for RHM into the world's top brand consultancy, the focus now is on moving brand valuation beyond its initial, balance-sheet oriented scope to a broader agenda of providing managers with useful information. 'The brand on the balance sheet debate, in my view, was a technical debate that hijacked the principle', said Rita Clifton, chief executive of Interbrand, in an interview in the firm's London office. She went on:

'We do some work with clients that talk about brands on the balance sheet, but actually it's ironic just how far the accountancy professionals have changed their point of view about this. In the future, will it be important for companies to understand the value of their brands? Absolutely and increasingly important. In the future, it will give them a very objective base by which to evaluate what they're doing and the effects of what they're doing and so on.

'Will that mean brands on the balance sheet? I don't know because we talk to the accountancy profession all the time and views change. The accountancy profession is becoming just as aware of branding and the power of brands to generate long-term sustainable value as anybody else. It then comes down to the use of brand valuation. In my view, there is no excuse not to understand the value of your brand and what drives that value. How you then use that information is really up to the company. We have used brand valuations across an extraordinary range of management information purposes. Whether it's internal practice issues, or licensing issues, or understanding portfolio management, or market segmentation, these are very important pieces of management information.'

DEBITS AND CREDITS

Understanding the brand valuation debate, and how it came to exist in a kind of financial purgatory, not really accepted but not damned either, requires a bit of remedial accounting. Companies regularly issue two primary reports on their financial condition. One is the income (or profit-and-loss) statement, which deals with the revenues, costs and expenses of a business incurred over a set period, usually a year. The income statement is like an annual movie about a company's financial life. The other report is the balance sheet (or statement of financial position), which is more like a snap-shot in that it gives a profile of a company's financial worth and obligations at a given moment, usually the last day of the year. The balance sheet weighs assets against liabilities and equity.

Assets are items owned by a business that have value; liabilities are claims against those assets; equity is ownership interest. For instance, assets include buildings, accounts receivable, inventories, cash and short-term investments. Liabilities include accounts payable, accrued wages, salaries and debt. Equity includes common stock. Taken altogether, assets should balance out against liabilities and equity. Assets come in two varieties important to this discussion: tangible and intangible. The former are assets with physical form, such as a warehouse or cash; the latter are generally assets without physical form, such as copyrights, patents, permits and computer programs. So, where do brands fit in this picture? The answer is complicated, but typical of the sort of accounting quandaries that many companies face in a post-industrial, information age in which intellectual property is assuming growing importance in the business world.

It is clear that brands have value, but they do not really have physical form because they are composed of ideas and words and colours and symbols and sounds. That makes them intangible assets, and that is where they are normally classified, but only when they are allowed on to the balance sheet at all. The problem with brands is that their value is notoriously hard to pin down. So accountants, always conservative about their neat columns of figures, shy away from recognizing them. Accountants traditionally value assets based on their historical costs of acquisition. If a brand has been bought, then the price paid is an established fact, and established facts make for sound bookkeeping.

> **❝The problem with brands is that their value is notoriously hard to pin down. ❞**

Thus a brand that has been acquired from another company has some cost-based worth. If the value of tangible assets is subtracted from the total acquisition price in a deal, the remainder is 'goodwill' or the premium paid by the acquirer over and above the value of the sheer nuts and bolts of a company. Within goodwill are many intangible items, including brands, and an estimate of their worth can be made.

But how does one make a reasonable estimation of the cost-based value of a brand that has been built up in-house by a company, often over many years, through advertising, promotion, management time, word of mouth, distribution, product quality and uncounted other factors that go into shaping the feelings and opinions of consumers? The task is impractical, if only because of the hard fact that high levels of brand-building expense do not necessarily translate into high levels of brand value. 'There are many brands on which a fortune has been spent and whose value is effectively nil', observed marketing consultant Alex Batchelor.[4]

The difficulties of cost-based valuation, then, force accountants on to the less stable ground of estimating brand values based on other measures such as market standards or income potential. But here too, the challenges are difficult, as alternative methods show:

■ **Market approach**. One way of discovering the value of a brand could be to measure its worth on the open market, or what someone might be willing to pay for the brand. This method is used to revalue real estate, for example. But there is no open, efficient market for brands. So market-based valuation is of limited use.

- **Brand strength approach.** Another way might be to assess a brand's market share, awareness levels and consumer preference scores through surveys and interviews, and then extrapolate some financial value from those results. But market-research data is always shifting and subjective and inherently vulnerable to question.

- **Brand incremental value approach.** Yet another way could be to gauge the price premium that consumers will pay for a brand over and above the prices of unbranded goods in the same category, then to derive a value from the differential. But profit margin is transient and can be misleading as it is prone to undervaluing high-volume mass-market brands and overvaluing high-margin speciality brands. So it is not a reliable indicator, on its own, of underlying value.

- **Royalty relief approach.** The value of a brand could conceivably be fixed by judging what the company that owns it would have to pay in royalty fees to license a similar brand from someone else to maintain the existing level of consumer demand. But the problem here is that royalty rate information is not generally available. Where it is, rates are often tied up with other transactions and influenced by individual markets, limiting this method's usefulness.

- **Future earnings approach.** Finally, it is possible to find a brand's value based on its future earnings or cash-flow potential by projecting an income stream from products represented by the brand, then discounting it to net present value. While this method has become the most popular, its shortcoming is that it fails to account for unforeseeable market shifts brought about by technology or management mistakes or other surprise changes in market conditions.

THE INTERBRAND WAY

Interbrand, the London consulting firm that guided RHM through its portfolio valuation in 1988, has since conducted similar exercises for many companies and developed a proprietary brand-valuation method that attempts to combine the best of approaches such as those above and others.

'Our model is not a black box where you feed in data and something pops out', said Jan Lindemann, a director at Interbrand, in an interview. He went on:

'It's a very straightforward, very clear process that we have. It's a transparent process. We go through all the steps and actually it's a very good education. People learn a lot. In most cases, CEOs walk out and say, wow, it's great to learn that.'

The Interbrand process involves six main steps:

1 **Identify branded forecast revenues and earnings.** To begin with, the firm determines historic and five-year forecast sales and earnings for segments of the business having to do with the brand in question.

2 **Taxation.** The brand earnings figure is adjusted for taxes based on the prevailing corporate tax rate in the country in which the earnings are generated.

3 **Charge for capital employed.** An amount is then subtracted from the forecast branded earnings to strip out the fair return that could be expected on the tangible assets employed in the business. This procedure is increasingly used by many businesses to derive an economic profit figure similar to that espoused in the Economic Value Added, or EVA, concept marketed by the New York consulting firm Stern Stewart & Co. Backing out the charge leaves a figure for forecast earnings from intangibles only.

4 **Derive brand earnings.** Interbrand then must determine what portion of earnings from intangibles actually comes from the brand. It does this by calculating a 'role of branding index' that is compiled based on issues such as pricing, product quality, availability, customer service, etc. By applying the resulting index to the earnings from intangibles, a figure for brand earnings is found.

5 **Assessing brand risk.** A calculation must then be made to assess the likelihood that the forecast post-tax brand earnings will be achieved. Interbrand does this by compiling a 'brand strength' score that looks at the following aspects of the brand:

   ■ Leadership. Brand power as shown by ability to set price points, fight off competition and influence distribution patterns. Powerful brands are more valuable.

   ■ Stability. Brand durability and resilience as shown by consumer loyalty and historic strength. Established brands with faithful followings score more highly.

- Market. Stability, size and growth of brand competitive environment. Stable food and drink markets are more desirable than changeable technology or fashion markets.

- Geographic spread. Ability of the brand to transcend geographic and cultural boundaries. Global brands are worth more than regional or national brands.

- Trend. Brand talent to remain contemporary and relevant to consumers over time.

- Support. Marketing, advertising and promotional activity devoted to the brand. Consistent, generous, high-quality support around the brand improves the score.

- Protection. Legal standing of the brand in terms of trademark rights. Registered trademark is more valuable than rights established under common law.

6 **Capitalization of future brand cash flows**. The 'brand strength' score compiled from these factors is then used to set a discount rate. That rate is applied to the brand earnings figure. The result is Interbrand's version of brand value.[5]

Using this method, Interbrand annually ranks the world's most valuable brands. Its 2000 edition listed 75 brands and was most notable for a 13 per-cent slide in value for Coca-Cola and surging values for technology brands. The top dozen in 2000, in descending order, were: Coca-Cola, with a brand value of $72.5 billion; Microsoft, $70.2 billion; IBM, $53.2 billion; Intel, $39.0 billion; Nokia, $38.5 billion; General Electric, $38.1 billion; Ford, $36.4 billion; Disney, $33.5 billion; McDonald's, $27.8 billion; AT&T, $25.5 billion; Marlboro, $22.1 billion; and Mercedes, $21.1 billion (*see* Fig. 14.1).

When Interbrand is hired by a company to analyze its brands' values, the process itself is often as revealing as the result, although surprise endings have been known to happen, said Lindemann. He went on:

'Does it happen that sometimes somebody says, oh, I didn't expect that type of result? Yes, that can happen. But that is because sometimes people don't have an idea about their brands. Either people are completely fixated on the brand and therefore think all the value of the business must be in the brand, or people, especially in technically focused firms, may be surprised that the brand is worth anything at all ... For some it works as a damper, for others it opens their eyes.'

1	Coca-Cola	26	Budweiser	51	Wrigley's
2	Microsoft	27	Xerox	52	Chanel
3	IBM	28	Dell	53	adidas
4	Intel	29	Gap	54	Panasonic
5	Nokia	30	Nike	55	Rolex
6	General Electric	31	Volkswagen	56	Hertz
7	Ford	32	Ericsson	57	Bacardi
8	Disney	33	Kelloggs	58	BP
9	McDonald's	34	Louis Vuitton	59	Moët & Chandon
10	AT&T	35	Pepsi-Cola	60	Shell
11	Marlboro	36	Apple	61	Burger King
12	Mercedes	37	MTV	62	Smirnoff
13	Hewlett-Packard	38	Yahoo!	63	Barbie
14	Cisco Systems	39	SAP	64	Heineken
15	Toyota	40	IKEA	65	Wall Street Journal
16	Citibank	41	Duracell	66	Ralph Lauren/Polo
17	Gillette	42	Philips	67	Johnnie Walker
18	Sony	43	Samsung	68	Hilton
19	Amex	44	Gucci	69	Jack Daniels
20	Honda	45	Kleenex	70	Armani
21	Compaq	46	Reuters	71	Pampers
22	Nescafe	47	AOL	72	Starbucks
23	BMW	48	Amazon.com	73	Guinness
24	Kodak	49	Motorola	74	FT
25	Heinz	50	Colgate	75	Benetton

Sources: Interbrand Group and Citibank

FIGURE 14.1 World's most valuable brands league table 2000

BEYOND THE BALANCE SHEET

Despite continued debate about brand valuation, Interbrand and other firms such as Brand Finance are succeeding at selling their services by pitching them as more than a preliminary to reforming the balance sheet along the lines of RHM. As Lindemann said:

'The topic of brand valuation is focused now much more on its utility as a management tool. People are becoming more aware of this and it is becoming much more a common part of business education. We believe that probably in five or ten years, brand valuation, like economic value or cash flow, will be part of the curriculum in business schools.'

Interbrand and others in the brand valuation field anticipate that a 'brand value statement' may some day become an adjunct to traditional financial reports such as the income statement and the balance sheet, much as the cash-flow statement and economic-profit analysis have done. Lindemann concluded:

'Why not have a valuation of intangibles? That may be something that will develop. Traditionally, brand owners have been very cautious about this because they fear they would give away competitive information ... But I think they're increasingly forced by analysts and investors to show more about brand value. So I think we will see more of that. But the starting point will be the internal effort to understand brands better, to manage brands properly.'

NOTES

1 David Arnold, *The Handbook of Brand Management*, New York: Economist Books, 1992, pp. 213–14.

2 Kevin Lane Keller, *Strategic Brand Management: Building, Measuring and Managing Brand Equity*, Upper Saddle River, New Jersey: Prentice Hall, 1998, pp. 364–5.

3 *Accountants' Digest*, March 1999.

4 Alex Batchelor, 'Brands as Financial Assets', in Susannah Hart and John Murphy (eds), *Brands: The New Wealth Creators*, London: Macmillan, 1998, p. 100.

5 *Accountants' Digest*, March 1999.

15

BACK FROM THE BRINK: GUCCI AND BRAND RESCUE

'I would rather cry in a Rolls Royce than be happy on a bicycle'

Patrizia Reggiani Martinelli, ex-wife of Maurizio Gucci

MY WIFE WANTED A NEW HANDBAG for Christmas. She had not asked for a Gucci, but I knew she would like one, if I could afford it. So one day I introduced myself to Harrod's, the legendary London temple to shopping. Inside the vast department store, hundreds of black leather handbags, all pretty much identical to me, were laid out in shiny glass cases. When I saw the price tags, I reached back instinctively for my wallet. Still there, thank goodness.

I approached a sleek saleswoman, explained my situation and warily asked, 'Is there another handbag that's just as good as a Gucci, but maybe not quite so expensive?' She looked me up and down, tilted her head back, narrowed her eyes at me and said, 'Of course there is, sir, but if it isn't a Gucci, it isn't a Gucci'. Well … of course not.

Needless to say, I left Harrod's that day empty-handed, but amazed. What is it, I wondered, that makes otherwise rational people spend $1,000 for a piece of softened cowhide with a bamboo handle whose basic function could be performed equally well by a brown-paper bag? The answer, I knew, was the power of the brand.

Luxury and fashion brands, especially those with the status-symbol appeal of Gucci or Chanel or Louis Vuitton, can motivate people to spend ridiculous sums of cash on things they don't really need. But this special power must be used with great care and tact. For when a good brand heads south, it can fall fast and hard, and bringing it back may be next to impossible.

Gucci – the fabled Florentine maker of expensive handbags and loafers – once made this descent. It rose to fame in the 1950s and 1960s accessorizing celebrities like Jacqueline Kennedy and Queen Elizabeth. But by the 1970s and 1980s, its glamour squandered by mismanagement, the brand was showing up on all manner of junk, much of it unauthorized, even Gucci toilet paper. Then, in what is possibly the greatest brand rescue story of all time, Gucci clawed its way back to trendiness and respectability. Today, it is once again a totem of status among the smart set.

'It was not that difficult. You just had to be rational', said Domenico De Sole, the Harvard-educated lawyer from Italy who saved Gucci, along with the Texas-born fashion designer Tom Ford. He went on:

'We are an exclusive brand. We view ourselves as brand managers, which is very important. We have to give the brand a lot of thought. The retailer tries to sell as much as he can. We want to sell as much as we can, but the guiding principle is ... how we can enhance and strengthen the brand.'

As chief executive of Gucci Group and architect of its resurgence, De Sole and his story offer an ideal case study in managing a brand by providing it with effective discipline and control – keys to successful branding in any business, not just $1,000 handbags. But there is much more to Gucci. In fact, there is a tale so melodramatic that if Giuseppe Verdi were still around, he would have bought the rights and staged it at La Scala.

TWO TALES TO TELL

Gucci's London office is in Mayfair, just around the corner from the Ritz Hotel. De Sole has a small office decorated with a photo of a sailboat. Friendly and funny, he looked more like a bookish professor than a fashion world power-broker. In an interview, he talked with his hands and arched his owlish eyebrows to emphasize points.

He had two tales to tell. One was about the Gucci family that he had come to know and how their poor judgement had driven a great brand into the ground. The other was about what happened after 1994, when he and Ford took over a company that by then was a thorough mess. He recalled:

'People were fighting all the time. The designers were fighting. It was just a disaster. They couldn't produce anything. They couldn't ship anything. They couldn't make decisions. I remember my first meeting with the production people in Florence. It was insane.'

The once-proud brand was being so over-exploited, due to excessive licensing and inadequate quality control, that it was being slapped on ball caps and cheap warm-up suits. To attack this crisis, De Sole said he imposed a basic principle applicable to any high-margin, aspirational brand. He called it managing for 'exclusivity'. It involves exercising strict control over not only marketing's traditional four Ps – product, price, promotion and placement – but public and press relations, production quality, positioning and, ultimately, perceptions. As De Sole said:

'Exclusivity is what drives profitability. Sales alone are meaningless. If I want to sell more it's very simple. We have hundreds of requests from people who want to sell Gucci. I could open another 2,000 doors in one hour and sales next year will double. But then I will have no profits. If you look at the better brands that really understand exclusivity – Louis Vuitton, Chanel, Prada to a certain extent, and so on and so forth – something that distinguishes them and makes them so successful is great unity of style … quality of product and design, a consistent pricing policy.'

> 66 Exclusivity is what drives profitability. Sales alone are meaningless. 99

These were the ideas guiding De Sole when he took the helm at Gucci six years ago, having worked closely with the company since 1980 through its worst years. 'I was a man on a mission. I had a great sense of what needed to be done. I spent a lot of time with Tom just talking. We talked about everything for an endless time … The implementation was very quick', he said.

The first job was to repair a business that had virtually ceased functioning. Beyond that, it was a question of rebuilding, repositioning and restoring corporate control over the brand by:

- regaining a fashion edge through sleek and cosmopolitan design;
- killing off bad licensing deals that were putting the brand on shoddy products;

- keeping production in Tuscany to preserve actual and perceived high quality;

- repricing every product in the line, usually downward, to be more competitive;

- buying out retail franchisees and closing poorly selected distribution points;

- expanding, upgrading and standardizing Gucci-owned stores around the world;

- heavily boosting promotion in prestige and opinion-making media channels.

By forcing through these actions and others, De Sole and Ford brought order out of Gucci's chaos. The brand is again a symbol of international chic and rivalled in its rarefied market only by such prestige names as Louis Vuitton, Prada and Hermes. Gucci's revenues have exploded over the past decade and were projected to exceed $2 billion in fiscal 2001. Its stock, traded in New York and Amsterdam, tripled in price in 1999, gave up ground in 2000, but was rallying again in late summer.

Gucci Group ranks as the third-largest luxury goods group in the world today and recently bought the valuable Yves Saint Laurent, Sergio Rossi and Boucheron brands. Moreover, De Sole plans to add more prestige names to the Gucci stable with a sizable acquisition war-chest.

Gucci's is a classic back-from-the-brink business tale. But beyond that, it is a real-life comic opera fit to share a billing with *Rigolleto*. Money, sex, glamour, jealousy, revenge, murder – all the elements are there, thanks to the quarrelsome family that founded and then nearly destroyed the firm that bears their name. The story of the Gucci clan would simply be unbelievable, if it were not true.

UP AND DOWN THE SAVOY

Born in 1881 in Florence, Guccio Gucci left an impoverished Italy and made his way to London, where he found work as an elevator attendant in the up-market Savoy Hotel. In his vertical travels he caught glimpses of the turn-of-the-century high life and developed a fondness for it. He returned to Florence, cashed in his pounds sterling for a truckload of Italian lire and in 1921 started a leather-making business on the Via della Vigna Nuova.

Luggage, handbags and saddlery items were handcrafted in the back and sold in the front. The shop grew steadily on the strength of its high quality. Gucci, perhaps sensing already that his simple products would gain from a bit of upscale image-making, concocted a family history making the Guccis out to have been saddle makers to the Florentine aristocracy. Larger quarters were taken up along the Arno River in 1937, by which time Gucci had begun using an equine bit-and-stirrups logo on his wares. The following year he opened a shop on Rome's famed Via Condotti, beginning a pattern of putting the brand on display in prestigious locations.

With Mussolini in power and Italy wracked by war, leather was in short supply and Gucci began using hemp, linen, jute and bamboo in his designs. He also brought his sons – Aldo, Vasco, Ugo and Rodolfo – into the company. The post-war years saw the rise of Italian style around the world and produced a string of classic Gucci designs, such as the bamboo-handled purse, the renowned loafer shoe and scarves specially made for the likes of Grace Kelly.

After the war Rodolfo opened a shop in Milan. Another followed in Manhattan in 1953, the year Guccio died. During this period the company adopted an interlocking Gs logo and a distinctive green-and-red striped webbing in its designs. The webbing played off the colours of the Italian flag, beginning a conscious effort at reinforcing 'Italian-ness' as a key secondary association for the brand. Further expansion throughout the jet-set 1960s saw the opening of stores in London, Palm Beach, Paris, Beverly Hills, Chicago, Tokyo and Hong Kong. Elizabeth Taylor joined the growing list of celebrity Gucci clients. So did Maria Callas and Audrey Hepburn.

In the turbulent 1970s strains within the Gucci family worsened into open feuds. Rodolfo and Aldo fought for control of the business. The brand suffered in the process due to neglect. Ill-advised licensing agreements and brand extensions began to take the Gucci name into mass markets and down the slippery slope that would lead to the street vendor's stall.

The turmoil worsened when Rodolfo's 20-year-old playboy son Maurizio met 24-year-old Patrizia Reggiani Martinelli at a party in swinging Milan. The shy and bespectacled young man, whose mother died when he was five, was bewitched by the beautiful, dark-haired daughter of a laundry woman. Patrizia's life-long goal had been to marry a rich man, said her school friends. She was later famous for the following quip: 'I would rather cry in a Rolls-Royce than be happy on a bicycle.' Maurizio's father tried to stop the wedding, but the two were married in 1972. Soon Patrizia was living in a luxury flat in Milan, wearing dazzling jewels and throwing champagne parties.[1]

By this time the Gucci brand was beginning to circulate in less exalted circles. Sweatshirts and warm-up suits began carrying the logo. Necklaces with the word 'Gucci' spelled out in chunky gold-look plastic were sported by break-dancers and disco divas. The once exclusive brand was becoming a ghetto-look icon. The low point came in 1975, when New York merchandiser and future Hollywood studio chief Dawn Steel started a company called Oh Dawn selling toilet paper with the Gucci emblem on it. Gucci sued and Steel closed down in 1978, but the descent of the Gucci brand was complete.

> **"Luxury brands must be desired by all, but consumed only by the lucky few. "**

Through their constant internecine battles, the Gucci family had lost sight of a cardinal rule of luxury goods branding, explained by HEC's Kapferer: 'Paradoxically, luxury brands must be desired by all, but consumed only by the lucky few'.[2]

Back in Florence, with the brand running itself into the ground, the family was in a state of all-out war. The struggle between Aldo and Rodolfo had worsened and was dragged into the courts. In 1980 Rodolfo hired De Sole, an American lawyer born in Rome in 1944 but educated at Harvard University and practising in Washington at the legal firm of Patton Boggs & Blow. Brother Aldo was pushed aside. Rodolfo consolidated his control of the business and incorporated it in 1982 as a public limited company, Guccio Gucci SpA. A reorganization put control of the sadly declined brand in Rodolfo's hands, but he never got a chance to show what he could do with it. He died in 1983.

His half of the company passed to his son Maurizio, who suddenly underwent a transformation out from under the shadow of his domineering father. 'Maurizio changed overnight', the high-living Patrizia said in an interview afterwards. 'He stopped listening to me.'[3]

Aldo, uncle to Maurizio, became entangled in a tax-evasion scandal probed by the US Internal Revenue Service (IRS). Maurizio pounced on the opportunity and kicked Aldo off the Gucci board. De Sole was called in to manage the affair. In the process he became a close adviser to Maurizio. Aldo and his family were elbowed aside and management of the company came under Maurizio's control. De Sole arranged a $21-million tax settlement with the IRS. 'I still remember signing that cheque for $21 million … It was something because we were still a small company', he recalled.

Then one day Maurizio boarded his private jet in Milan, took off and never returned to Patrizia. He became involved with a young, blonde, interior designer and filed for divorce. Abandoned and angry, Patrizia lashed out in public, saying her husband had gone mad, that he was impotent, that her divorce settlement – reportedly worth about $1.3 million – was 'little more than a plate of lentils'. She started telling anyone who would listen that she wanted her ex-husband dead.

Distracted by his new life and happily ensconced with his girlfriend in a Milan palazzo, Maurizio recruited De Sole to come aboard as an executive and largely run the company in his stead. De Sole was named chief executive of the Gucci America Inc. subsidiary in 1984 and worked out of New York. 'I took over the company and it was a disaster. It was a joke', he said.

RESTORING ORDER IN AMERICA

Over the next three years, with Maurizio preoccupied elsewhere, De Sole re-established order in Gucci's US operations and elsewhere. The worst licensing deals were ended. The never-ending battle against counterfeiters was escalated. Sales and profits recovered, helped by an emerging boom in Japan and the Pacific Rim, whose nouveau riche were ravenous for European luxury goods. Not only Gucci, but Prada, Versace, Louis Vuitton, Hermes and others reaped an Asian bonanza.

De Sole's success, while still modest compared to what would come later, attracted the interest of private investors on the hunt for under-valued brands. In 1987 the enigmatic Arab-backed Investcorp bought out the 50 per cent of Gucci still owned by Aldo and his family. The power and financial clout of a respected and deep-pocketed backer was to be a big help to De Sole.

Maurizio, once again enmeshed in family quarrels, returned to the company intending to reassert his authority. Investcorp and De Sole took him in and were initially pleased. Maurizio and De Sole became close at this time and reportedly bought and sold a New York department store together at a profit of $25 million.[4]

With such successes reviving his reputation, it looked as if Maurizio's return meant the Gucci brand could safely be remanded to the stewardship of its founding family. De Sole explained:

'The company was really doing well. Then in 1990 Maurizio Gucci and his family … came back to the company, together with Investcorp as a partner. Everything seemed to be peaceful. Maurizio was in power. Investcorp was a financial partner. Actually, I was thinking about leaving the business and going back to Washington to my law firm. But I had a lot of pressure to stay.'

Which was a good thing. For, although he had convinced Investcorp and De Sole that he was capable of concentrating on the business and managing it effectively, Maurizio disappointed again. Shortly after his return, his angry ex-wife Patrizia developed a brain tumour and went into hospital for a risky operation. She made it through and during recovery was visited by Maurizio. He leaned over her bed and whispered in her ear, 'Just checking to see if you'd died', she alleged later.

She was further enraged afterwards when Maurizio made it known he was planning to marry his girlfriend. At about the same time he spent an estimated $12 million redecorating his office in Milan. Meanwhile, operations at Gucci under Maurizio's leadership quickly degenerated. In the fiscal year 1993 (ended 31 January), the company lost $32.3 million on estimated revenues of $198.6 million. The losses continued the following year. Creditors were pounding on Gucci's door. Payrolls were not being met. As De Sole said:

'Maurizio, who was really a nice guy, turned out to be a disaster as a manager of the company almost overnight. It was basically broke again by 1993. So Investcorp was getting pretty desperate by that time and they had no choice. They had to buy Maurizio out … The company was losing a lot of money.'

Investcorp made its move, doubling up on its earlier bet by buying out the half of the company it did not already own. Maurizio walked away with an estimated $150 million. Never one to conserve his resources, he purchased luxury homes in Milan, New York and Saint Moritz, as well as a black sailing yacht called the Creole in which he cruised the Mediterranean.

With Maurizio gone for good, De Sole was persuaded by Investcorp to move from New York to headquarters in Florence in 1994 to become chief operating officer. He said:

'They called me up and said ... you're an American citizen but you were born in Italy. So why don't you go back and see what you can do? So I went back there and the company was a mess. Everybody was fighting. But they had a great name. I knew that, and I knew the company very well because I'd been working with it for a long time. So I had a pretty good idea what needed to be done.'

He set about executing virtually the same reassertion of brand control that he had overseen years earlier in the USA, only this time on a global scale. He was soon named chief executive. Ford, the Texan designer who had been working with Gucci since 1990, became creative director and began the design revolution that would do so much to reinvigorate the brand and shape its future.

MURDER IN MILAN

For the Guccis, the Investcorp purchase of Maurizio's 50-per-cent stake and his surrender of management control to De Sole marked the end of family involvement with the brand and the company founded by grandfather Guccio. But it was not the end of the lurid story of Maurizio and Patrizia.

On 27 March 1995 Maurizio was climbing the front stairs into the building where he kept a personal office at 20 Via Palestro in Milan – a stylish and business-like city of clattering trolleys and designer boutiques – when an out-of-work car mechanic started shooting at him from the pavement. Two bullets hit the 46-year-old millionaire in the hip and shoulder. He spun around and looked at the gunman, who fired a third shot that grazed his arm. Maurizio collapsed in a puddle of blood on the grey-carpeted steps. A fourth shot execution-style to the right temple killed him. A groundsman who witnessed the attack was shot twice in the arm but survived. The well-groomed assassin jumped into a green Renault Clio and escaped.[5]

De Sole was at headquarters in Florence when he got the news.

'We were really fixing the company by then. Tom had become creative director and things were moving along. I remember very well that day. I was very depressed and upset. I liked Maurizio a lot, although at the end we were not on speaking terms because I had to be counsellor to him over what happened with the company in the early 1990s. Then I took this phone call that he had been shot. That really shocked me, I couldn't believe it. He was a decent person. I heard all these rumours about his wife ... We had some common friends who told me she did it, but I never believed it. It sounded like a soap opera.'

Police initially focused their enquiry on Maurizio's investments in a Swiss casino. But attention soon shifted to Patrizia, who allegedly hurried to Maurizio's home after his murder to order his girlfriend off the premises. She also responded to reporters' questions about the murder by saying, 'On a human level I'm sorry, but from a personal point of view I can't really say the same thing'.[6]

The police investigation took two years. Finally, in January 1997, police woke up Patrizia at 4.30 am and arrested her. Also apprehended were four accomplices. One was the gunman. Another was the get-away car driver. The third was the porter of a seedy hotel in Milan's red-light district who had acted as a go-between. And the fourth was Giuseppina Auriemma, former owner of the Gucci store in Naples and Patrizia's long-time psychic adviser and friend.

Investigators charged them with premeditated murder and said Patrizia had paid them about $350,000 to have Maurizio killed. Auriemma said Patrizia had nagged her about finding a hit-man to knock off Maurizio. Patrizia claimed the four took it upon themselves, without consulting her, to carry out a deed she had spoken of only hypothetically. Her lawyers argued Patrizia's brain-tumour surgery had left her mentally unstable. They claimed that Auriemma handed Patrizia a bill for the killing after it took place and held it over her head as blackmail, even threatening harm to Patrizia's daughters.

'I was naïve to the point of stupidity ... Never let the friendly fox into your chicken coop. Sooner or later, it could get hungry', Patrizia said in her final plea to the court.[7] In November 1998, Patrizia – known by that time across Italy as the Black Widow – was convicted after a sensational five-month trial that captivated Italians. She was sentenced to 29 years in prison. At the time of this writing, she was appealing against her conviction to a higher court. Auriemma was sentenced to 25 years. The get-away car driver got 29; the go-between, 26; and the gunman, a life sentence.

For the Gucci family, the murder and its aftermath was the culmination of a sad history of strife over money and power. But for the Gucci company, some observers have said, the tragedy may actually have enhanced the glamour of the brand, winning it global headlines and a sheen of romance and danger.

GAMBLE ON THE CATWALKS

Born in Rome, Domenico De Sole grew up moving around Italy because of his father's career in the army. He studied law at the University of Rome and won a scholarship in 1969 to Harvard Law School. After Harvard he took a job in Washington, married and was made a partner by 1979. In all that time he had no experience whatever managing brands. Not even trained as a businessman, he had made his career as a lawyer in Washington, arguably America's least commercial city. But through the 1980s he had come to know the players and the problems at Gucci.

The initial phases of rescuing the company in early 1994, he said, largely involved knocking heads together at headquarters and putting back into motion a business that had ground to a virtual halt:

'They were writing memos all the time. I said, forget the memos. I don't want memos. People were fighting all the time. The designers were fighting … Everybody was complaining. I said, *basta*, enough. I don't care about all this, just tell me the problems and we'll work things out.'

As an example of the company's state of paralysis, De Sole said no purchasing was being done. A production manager came to him and said he needed to buy some leather for the Florence production units. 'I said, what kind of leather do you need? He told me and I said, what are you waiting for, go buy it. He said, who gives me authorization? I said, I give you authorization, just go do it.'

Another time, there was a proposal to make 3,000 backpacks that had been in discussion for weeks, but managers were afraid to proceed. 'I said, okay let's just make a bet that they will sell. So we made 3,000 backpacks and we sold them in a week in Japan', he said. De Sole made the business function again so Ford could go to work on the troubled design profile. 'It was just a matter of getting it going', De Sole said. 'Tom was concentrating on the collection and I made the company work.'

Ford was born in the college town of Austin, Texas, but spent most of his early years in Santa Fe, New Mexico. He was educated at New York University and the Parsons School of Design in New York and Paris and worked with Perry Ellis before joining Gucci to give it a new look. As De Sole said:

> 66 The company is managed in a very informal way. We want to avoid these big bureaucracies. 99

'I don't get involved in design. My career as a designer ended when I was six. Tom and I talk about products, obviously, what do we want to do with handbags from season to season … But the company is managed in a very informal way. We want to avoid these big bureaucracies.'

In early 1994, faced with repositioning the Gucci brand on a very tight budget, Ford and De Sole decided their slim resources would not allow a big advertising push. So they settled on a high-risk public-relations strategy seeking maximum exposure in the fashion press from the much publicized Milan fashion shows. If it backfired, they would have gambled all for nothing. But if it worked?

Ford went into the studio, knowing that much was riding on his style judgement and how it was received by the fickle writers and photographers of fashion's travelling media circus. He produced autumn/winter 1995–6 men's and women's collections that were a smash hit, producing a torrent of gushy news stories and photo spreads.

Almost overnight Gucci was hot again, without the expense of a fortune in advertising. De Sole took full advantage. He moved quickly to stamp out counterfeiting and production of Gucci kitsch for mass sale. He steered through a reincorporation of the company as Gucci Group NV, and a flotation of 48.2 per cent of Investcorp's equity on the Amsterdam Stock Exchange. The remainder of Investcorp's stake was sold off later at considerable profit. In De Sole's debut year the red ink stopped flowing and Gucci made a modest profit, its first in a long time, of $17.4 million on revenues of $263.6 million, up 30 per cent over the previous year.

Soon fashion-forward consumers were seeking out Gucci stores in search of Ford's clothes and, while there, taking a second look at the shoes and handbags at the historic core of the business, which in itself posed challenges for De Sole. In dealing with them, he demonstrated a typically firm understanding of the Gucci brand and one of its hallmarks – its perceived quality.

Much ink has been spilled in recent years in business publishing on the subject of quality. Theories about total quality management, or TQM, and quality function deployment, or QFD, have rippled through boardrooms with mixed effect. Keller of Dartmouth College, has identified 'perceived quality' as a key attribute in designing marketing programmes to build brand equity.[8]

De Sole showed his awareness of this in 1994 as he toured the hills of Tuscany, rallying the dispirited Gucci workforce. This conservative community of leather craftsmen had been ill-used by Maurizio. Many had not been paid for work performed and goods supplied. Some were worried that De Sole, seen as a hard-nosed American, would move Gucci production overseas to cut costs, following the textile industry's recent exodus from Europe and the USA to Asia and Latin America. But De Sole's answer to these anxieties revealed much about his grasp of the Gucci image, its perceptions among customers and its unique selling points.

'People were afraid that I would take the stuff to China or Timbuktu, but I said no, that's nuts, it would kill the brand', he said, explaining that an essential secondary association of the Gucci brand is its Italian origin and related perceptions of high-quality Italian craftsmanship. To jeopardize that, De Sole knew, might have won short-term efficiencies, but would have meant long-term folly:

'One of the reasons all production of leather goods is done in Tuscany, all our ready-to-wear is done in Italy, and why we will never take this stuff to Hong Kong – not because things in Hong Kong aren't great because they're very good people and hard workers – is because there is a great association with Italy and the quality of certain luxury products. That's a fact. In Tuscany there is this great tradition of quality for leather goods and people are very aware of it. A lot of clients that buy Gucci, they want to see "Made in Italy". They wouldn't buy it otherwise, I'm convinced.'

Brand monitoring at Gucci tends towards the intuitive, but some empirical research is done and consumer surveys have revealed two major strengths of the brand, De Sole said. First, styling, and second, he said:

'The brand has a personality. It is what people expect from the brand. Our consumers are convinced, to an overwhelming number, like 60 to 70 per cent, that we produce a product of a better quality than our competitor. Now, I think that is true. But this goes beyond whether it is true or not because in the end perception is critical ... We really do go to great pains to deliver a very high-quality product. Don't get me wrong. The point is there are other brands in which the quality is not that important. I'm not being negative, I'm sure their quality is fine. But in the minds of consumers, which we know because we study our own brand and other brands as well, there are brands that people buy because they're super-trendy. In our case, there is this balance.

'People who buy Gucci products buy for two reasons: the design and they really are convinced that we deliver better quality … It's not that I think we owe it to people to give them high quality. I do think that, but in the end, we have no choice because that's what they expect. That's who we are. There's a tradition that Gucci would sell great leather. So that's what people expect from us.'

To protect the tradition of Tuscan craftsmanship, De Sole improved wage scales for workers. He instituted partnering programmes for Gucci's best and most dedicated artisans and extended them credit for plant upgrades. In 1993 Gucci produced 250,000 handbags. Four years later it was producing upwards of 2 million a year. Higher output and increased foot traffic in the stores, thanks to Ford's fashion success, increased cash flow and started giving Gucci the traction it needed for long-term growth. De Sole pulled in more business by repricing the Gucci product line. For instance, the price of the medium-sized, bamboo-handled leather handbag was dropped to $1,190 from $1,300.

Sales boomed, nearly doubling to $500.1 million in 1995, with net income rising more than fourfold to $81.4 million. The following year sales grew by 76 per cent to $881 million and profits more than doubled to $168 million (*see* Fig. 15.1).

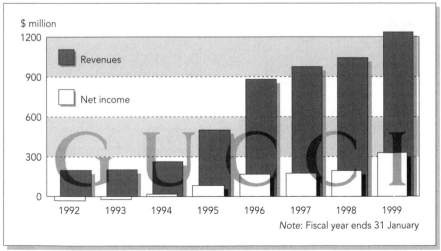

Note: Fiscal year ends 31 January

Sources: Company reports, Hoover's Company Profiles, Lehman Brothers

FIGURE 15.1 Gucci annual figures

REPOSITIONING TO LAST

As income grew, the methodical De Sole began moving to fortify the high ground that Ford had won for the brand on the catwalks. Several steps were involved in upgrading and standardizing presentation of the brand through carefully managed communication channels.

At the media level, De Sole cranked up the volume on advertising. Provocative and sexy ads, echoing the look of Ford's collections, were splashed across the pages of top fashion magazines. Ad-spending shot up to $70 million by 1997 from just $6 million in 1993. The target market was the same affluent woman that most luxury brands chase. De Sole said:

'Our customer base is mostly female, young, doesn't have to be a fashion freak, but interested in fashion, and urban, quite sophisticated. But by the same token, the brand has appeal beyond that. The image is driven very much by the ready-to-wear, but there are plenty of people who just buy our accessories.'

At street level, De Sole began jetting around on 'terminator tours'. Sometimes arriving unannounced, he swooped into Gucci stores and took action. He required display windows to be identical worldwide. Franchisees not up to standard were bought out. In 1996 he closed the Gucci duty-free shop in Hong Kong and a franchised boutique in Taiwan. In 1997 he closed 31 stores chiefly for branding reasons. He recalled:

'People said, are you crazy? No, because we manage the brand and we felt these stores were negative visibility for the company. We decided we needed to close them. If a point of sale is poor and does not enhance the image of the brand, you need to close it ... We want to increase sales, but the number-one issue is the management of the brand. Every time I see a location for a store, my question is, does it enhance the brand or not? The fact that a site could make a lot of money is great because we want to make a lot of money. But I'm convinced that long term, the biggest money-maker for us is the enhancement of the name.'

> 66 Every time I see a location for a store, my question is, does it enhance the brand or not? 99

Gucci, like competitors such as LVMH and Hermes, suffered on the stock market in 1997 and 1998, when the bottom fell out of the crucial Japanese tourist business due to that nation's economic crisis. Nearly half of Gucci's operating profits were coming from Asia at the time. But the business continued to grow, with profits and sales up again both years, albeit more slowly than before. Taking advantage of the Asian slump, De Sole bought out some important franchisees in Taiwan, Guam and South Korea, and renegotiated pricey leases in Hong Kong and elsewhere. He also bought out long-time licensee watchmaker Severin Montres and created a Gucci Timepieces division.

Seeing opportunity in Gucci's depressed stock price and confident that the brand was in no real trouble, the acquisitive French billionaire Bernard Arnault started buying Gucci shares in late 1998. By early 1999 the chief of Parisian luxury goods giant LVMH had built a large Gucci stake, including a 9.5-per-cent interest bought from Patrizio Bertelli, chief executive of Gucci arch-rival Prada.

De Sole resented Arnault's purchases and feared what he called a 'creeping takeover'. The two went to war. Arnault declared he had no intention of taking over Gucci, but also demanded board representation and increased his holdings to 34.4 per cent of the stock. De Sole manoeuvred to avoid the embrace of Arnault, one of Europe's most feared corporate raiders. After weeks of controversy, De Sole cut a deal with another rich Frenchman, François Pinault, who controls distributing and retailing giant Pinault-Printemps-Redoute (PPR). Acting as white knight, Pinault's group bought 40 per cent of Gucci for $3 billion and promises of further help. Arnault was furious and sued in the Dutch courts. The case was still pending at the time of this writing.

Using proceeds from the PPR sale, De Sole purchased the Yves Saint Laurent, Sergio Rossi and Boucheron brands. YSL especially was in need of attention. The turnaround process for YSL so far has closely resembled the one followed for Gucci. Re-establishment of control over licensing, production and distribution have been the keys. 'That's the way you really manage luxury brands ... We think that's the way to do it', De Sole said.

Gucci ranked as the 44th most valuable brand in the world, worth an estimated $5.2 billion, in the 2000 edition of an annual survey of top brands by consulting firm Interbrand.[9] Looking ahead, De Sole said he has plans for Gucci to become a third power in the luxury goods business to rival LVMH and Swiss-controlled Richemont. The business is becoming more compartmentalized as it grows. 'We have somebody now who works specifically on Gucci full-time ... I don't get as involved in the day-to-day as I used to', he said.

But responsibility for the brand remains a team effort. There is no such thing as an office of brand management at Gucci. No single individual is responsible for nurturing or protecting the brand because everyone is. Understanding of the exclusivity principle is paramount. According to De Sole: 'Everybody shares the same philosophy. Everybody understands what needs to be done to promote the brand ... If we decide we want to close the DFS store in Hawaii because we want to enhance the brand, everybody understands it'.

NOTES

1 The story of the Gucci dynasty is documented in reports from Reuters, the Associated Press, *Women's Wear Daily* and Italian newspapers. It is treated in further detail by Sara Gay Forden in her book, *The House of Gucci: A Sensational Story of Murder, Madness, Glamour and Greed*, William Morrow, 2000.

2 Jean-Noël Kapferer, *Strategic Brand Management: Creating and Sustaining Brand Equity Long Term*, London: Kogan Page, 1997, p. 82.

3 Reuters, 7 May 1998.

4 *Sunday Telegraph*, 12 July 1998.

5 Reuters, 7 May 1998, and Forden, *House of Gucci*, pp. 3–5.

6 Reuters, 7 May 1998.

7 Associated Press, 4 November 1998.

8 Kevin Lane Keller, *Strategic Brand Management: Building, Measuring and Managing Brand Equity*, Upper Saddle River, New Jersey: Prentice Hall, 1998, p. 176.

9 Interbrand, *The World's Most Valuable Brands Survey*, 18 July 2000.

16

IN THE BEGINNING:
L'ORÉAL AND BRAND CREATION

'When you ask people what they want, they'll tell you what they know'

Dimitri Katsachnias, head of Parfums Cacharel, L'Oréal

PARFUMS CACHAREL WAS A FADING STAR in an otherwise bright galaxy of fragrance master brands owned by cosmetics world leader L'Oréal when CEO Lindsay Owen-Jones put Dimitri Katsachnias in charge of the unit in 1997. The intense, young chemical engineer, transferred from the Lancôme business, was charged with the difficult task of restoring Cacharel's lustre by creating new perfume brands.

The global perfume industry sees as many as 150 launches a year, an astounding rate of brand creation that annually produces just two or three winners and scores of also-rans. Standing out from the crowd is tough, especially with a master brand like Cacharel lacking the panache of a fashion designer's name, but Owen-Jones had confidence that Katsachnias and his team could handle the job.

The Cacharel team scorned the usual industry tactic of copying a successful perfume and wrapping it in a brand designed around surveys and focus groups. Instead, they took the almost quaint approach of trying to judge the mood of young women and capturing it in a scent, a bottle, a package and a brand.

'Our business has to do with emotions, with signs of the times really from a sociological point of view', Katsachnias said in an interview in his Paris office. 'I don't believe in surveys because when you ask people what they want, they'll tell you what they know. A survey will not make you create something. A survey will only make you understand if they get the message or not.'

The result of Cacharel's efforts was Noa, launched in October 1998 and one of the biggest-selling fragrances to appear in years. The tale of Noa's creation offers a fascinating look into the myriad considerations involved in the high-stakes process of creating a new brand – a challenge that most people in the marketing world avoid these days because extending existing brands is easier, cheaper and less risky.

Brand creation is sometimes necessary, however, and few companies have as much experience with this as L'Oréal, the French giant whose stable of master brands includes Maybelline, Giorgio Armani, Garnier, Lancôme, Ralph Lauren, Helena Rubinstein, Redken, Biotherm, L'Oréal-Paris and Vichy.

L'Oréal manages its business – ranging from shampoo and hair colour to skin cream and lipstick – from an increasingly global perspective. Market leadership demands constant innovation and experimentation with new technologies and products. Owen-Jones has moulded a company known on the stock markets as a solid and steady performer in an industry not lately noted for such qualities. Growth has been driven recently by cosmetics, which accounts for the bulk of the company's sales, but L'Oréal remains one of the world's largest perfume manufacturers, along with Chanel and LVMH. In fragrances, L'Oréal hedges its marketing bets by sheltering new brand launches under master brands that command loyal clientele in targeted segments, such as Armani.

Cacharel, however, had lost much of its authority by the mid-1990s. Notable for older and still popular perfumes such as Loulou and Anaïs Anaïs (launched in 1978), the house of Cacharel had not scored with a major new scent in many years. Moreover, it had been bypassed by a market trend toward endorsement of new scents by designers. Creating a new brand like Noa was really the only option open to a division like Cacharel.

ROLLING THE DICE

Brand creation, at first glance, would seem to be the most basic task in branding. But, in actuality, it is one that many brand marketers try desperately to avoid. The reason? 'Only one in five commercialized new products lasts longer than one year on the market', observed John Quelch and David Kenny in a 1994 *Harvard Business Review* article.[1]

As a result, many brand marketers no longer follow the traditional Procter & Gamble model of putting a wholly new brand on every new product, whether it is Tide detergent or Pringles potato chips. Instead, most new products today are rolled out as extensions of existing brands or, at the very least, as new sub-brands endorsed or associated in some respect with a master (or umbrella or family) brand. 'Most managers will extend a line before they will invest the time or assume the career risk to launch a new brand', Quelch and Kenny commented.

> **Most new products today are rolled out as extensions of exisiting brands or as new sub-brands.**

After all, why spend the money and time on a risky new brand introduction if you already have a strong brand that can be stretched into new markets? Most leading brands today are ones that have been around for decades, and the cost of a brand launch in the USA can run to $40 million, while an extension costs as little as $5 million.

One of the risks of brand extension, however, is missing out on the potentially greater rewards that can be had by starting an all-new brand. The point is made by General Motors' Saturn cars or Gap's retailing chains Banana Republic and Old Navy. All three brands were put on the market as all-new and unrelated to their parents, and for good reasons. Saturn represented a new way of doing business for GM; Banana Republic and Old Navy took Gap up-market and down-market, respectively, without diluting the core Gap image. These three brands were tremendous successes for their owners.

In the case of Noa, the master brand was Cacharel. But it was a master brand that had been diluted by extension into shirt shops in malls and ladies lingerie sold in supermarkets. Cacharel regained some of its power with the fragrance Eden launched in 1995. But with Eden, as with Noa, the new product brand was seen by observers as bringing as much help to Cacharel as vice versa. 'Cacharel in itself still lacks autonomous substance', commented HEC's Jean-Noël Kapferer.[2] With this as a backdrop, the Katsachnias team went to work in 1997, surely aware that their house needed a new brand like Noa perhaps even more than Noa needed a master brand like Cacharel.

SCHUELLER'S HAIR DYE

L'Oréal was formed in 1907 by the French chemist Eugene Schueller in a two-bedroom apartment in Paris to market his invention, the world's first synthetic hair dye. Schueller enjoyed enormous success and his company expanded quickly into shampoos and soaps. L'Oréal began advertising on the radio in the 1920s well before rivals. In 1934 it launched the first soap-free shampoo.

The business continued to grow in the 1950s as post-war demand for beauty products surged. L'Oréal in 1953 created a licensee, Cosmair, to sell goods in the USA. Expansion into other overseas markets followed rapidly under the direction of François Dalle, who took over after Schueller died in 1957. When the company went public in 1963 on the Paris Bourse, Schueller's daughter Liliane Bettencourt retained a majority interest. She later swapped half her stock for a 3-per-cent interest in Swiss food giant Nestlé, which today remains a major L'Oréal holder, along with Bettencourt.

L'Oréal acquired up-market cosmetics house Lancôme in 1964. In the following year the company entered the perfume market with the creation of Guy Laroche Perfumes. Later key purchases included Biotherm in 1970; Gemey in 1973; Vichy in 1980; the cosmetics businesses of Warner Communications, including the Ralph Lauren and Gloria Vanderbilt brands, in 1984; US beauty group Helena Rubinstein and Laboratoires Pharmaeutiques Goupil both in 1988; and 47.5 per cent of Lanvin the following year.

By the time Owen-Jones, a Briton, took over in 1988, L'Oréal was the world's largest cosmetics company. It took major steps in the USA by acquiring Maybelline in 1995, a deal that made L'Oréal the world leader in mass-market make-up and number two in that sector in the USA behind consumer goods titan Procter & Gamble, maker of Cover Girl and Max Factor. L'Oréal most recently has continued to scoop up smaller brands, such as Soft Sheen, Matrix Essentials, Miss Ylang and Carson, while also taking steps to streamline and globalize its portfolio. In 1999, 88 per cent of total L'Oréal sales (*see* Fig. 16.1) came from ten global master brands, among which Cacharel was not counted.

Source: Hoover's Company Reports

FIGURE 16.1 L'Oréal annual figures

COFFEE AND FLOWERS

Development of a new perfume can take up to three years. Noa emerged in 18 months, an unusually short gestation period reflecting the limited use of time-consuming survey work. The Cacharel team came at the project with a sense that young women wanted a brand that was 'hopeful ... pure, very strong and very calm and determined at the same time', Katsachnias said. Whether this hunch would be enough to be a hit was unknown, but the team, including marketing wiz Tho Van Tran, packaging designer Annegret Beier and perfumier Olivier Cresp, were well aware of the potential pay-off.

Attrition rates are brutal in the fragrance business. L'Oréal and its rivals – Chanel, Coty, Estée Lauder, Unilever, Procter & Gamble, Revlon and LVMH – crank out brand after brand in search of a classic. When they find one, such as Chanel No. 5 or Arpege, profit margins of more than

20 per cent can roll in for decades. Not only that, but a big fragrance can move into shower gels, body lotions, soaps, men's fragrance, and then a ladies' follow-up. Truly unique aromas may end their days profitably, but anonymously, scenting laundry detergents and air fresheners.

Getting to that lucrative level, however, first requires success with a perfume, usually at the so-called prestige level – and there is no sure-fire formula for doing it. 'When you have 150 new fragrance launches per year, if you don't manage to get very quickly in the top brands, you disappear', said Patricia Turck-Paquelier, director general international at Giorgio Armani Perfumes, another L'Oréal unit.

> 66 When you have 150 new fragrance launches per year, if you don't manage to get very quickly in the top brands, you disappear. 99

Cresp, one of only about 300 professional 'noses' worldwide, was commissioned to design a scent for Noa. After much trial using a standard perfumiers' palette of about 3,000 basic ingredients, he settled on a 'juice', as the perfume itself is known in the industry, that mixed peony flowers, white musk, blackcurrant and 12 other ingredients, including coffee.

Beier, the packaging designer, developed an unusual spherical glass bottle, an innovative spray nozzle and an origami-style box. In the bottle, she insisted on placing a marble-sized white bead for allure. Finally, an edgy advertising campaign came from Tho Van Tran. In one television commercial, a self-assured young model carrying a bottle of Noa strides confidently forward through a vaguely threatening urban streetscape while things around her move in reverse. With the creative process complete, Katsachnias tackled supervising plastic-mould and assembly-line construction, production budgets and roll-out schedules.

Launches began in late 1998 and were quickly successful. Noa was priced low for a 'prestige' scent at $37.64 per 50-ml bottle. With Europe and Latin America blanketed by the end of 1999, Noa was out-performing expectations. Much remained to be determined in 2000 in the all-important US and Asian markets, but the new brand was being hailed as a success within the industry and by L'Oréal.

The company's 1999 annual report stated: 'Noa's Europe-wide success shows how successfully this brand [Cacharel] has been rejuvenated. Leading the way in sales terms, it helped Cacharel to consolidate its market position and develop a new core product alongside Anaïs Anaïs.'

NOTES

1 John Quelch and David Kenny, 'Extend Profits, Not Product Lines', in *Harvard Business Review on Brand Management*, Boston: Harvard Business School Press, 1999, p. 109.

2 Jean-Noël Kapferer, *Strategic Brand Management: Creating and Sustaining Brand Equity Long Term*, London: Kogan Page, 1997, p. 175.

PART 3

BRANDS ON THE INTERNET

'We're getting into a stage where people don't care if Yahoo! or AOL or Microsoft is the leader, they just want what's best for them'

Karen Edwards, vice-president, Yahoo!

A YOUNG MAN IN A WHITE NEHRU JACKET and jeans stood before a hushed audience of several hundred terribly British suits in a chandeliered hotel conference room and declared that the internet was changing the world. He had just sold his small web start-up firm for several million pounds. Everyone listened.

Disarmingly confident, the brash young entrepreneur said not only branding, but retailing, advertising, information, media, distribution, procurement – all would be utterly remade (like his net worth) by this powerful new technology. Businesses that understood it would survive; those that did not would die.

Just days later, in a similar room before a similar audience, another business-man – this one in sober pinstripes and neatly knotted silk tie – said that actually nothing much was changing because of the internet. He was the CEO of a legendary West-End retail establishment. Again everyone listened.

In magisterial tones, the sleek executive assured that retailing would stay roughly the same (like his salary), as would business patterns known well by everyone in the room. The internet would go on, of course, but the hoopla around it would die away in time. No need going off half-cocked, he implied.

Both these predictions will ring a bell with anyone who was in business in London, New York, San Francisco or just about anywhere else in late 1999 and early 2000. The truth, as usual, lay somewhere in between.

The internet is a powerful force for change in business and society, but it is still quite young. A profound shake-out and consolidation cycle is under way among the legions of e-brands that have popped up almost overnight. The likeliest survivors of this winnowing process come easily to mind – Yahoo!, Dell, Amazon, AOL. As a group, these names have revolutionized branding by accelerating dramatically the speed at which

brands can gain public awareness. But even among these e-elite, profitability remains elusive for some, and the long-term staying power of all
has only barely been tested.

Consulting firm Interbrand in the 2000 edition of its annual listing of
the world's top brands ranked the financial values of web brands such as
those just mentioned on a par with much older and more established
brands such as Pepsi, Wrigley's, Colgate, Volkswagen, Xerox and
Kellogg's. Yet, older brands have survived macro-economic ups and
downs that are still uncharted territory to the web leaders.

As the internet matures, the dot-com stars will face tough tests of their ability not only to maintain the high levels of consumer awareness they have
quickly achieved, but to differentiate themselves from each other and off-
line competitors by developing deeper consumer understanding and
relationships. At the same time, established brands are fast making their
presence felt on the web. Gap, Barnes & Noble, Tesco, Disney, Schwab and
others prove it is possible for traditional brands to make the jump to the net.

The internet doubtless holds great opportunity for branding. Whether
the new breed of e-brands are around for the long haul to take advantage
of it remains to be seen. Aside from speeding things up, consumer-ori-
ented web brands – and their counterparts in the related web hardware,
business-to-business and infrastructure sectors, like Cisco Systems, Oracle
and Ariba – have changed little else about branding.

The long-term keys to success remain the same: identification of market
segments based on basic consumer needs and wants, targeting of those
segments with appealing brands, and reasoned positioning with consistent product and service value equal to or better than rival offers. These
rules apply to any brand, online or otherwise. This has been shown since
the mid-2000 market correction in dot-com stocks amid troubles at
numerous e-ventures that failed to meet these stern standards.

'What's really interesting about e-brands is that, when we all started talking about the power of the internet and stuff like that, people got
incredibly carried away and seduced by the new technology', observed
Interbrand's Rita Clifton. She went on:

'What happens sometimes in these cases is that people forget some old
truths. A lot of people who start up internet-based companies somehow
funnily imagine that setting up a web-based business means people will

stroll past your site every day or somehow find you ... on the internet, and then say, ooh, I must spend time ploughing through this person's literature to find out what's going on.

'All that really has happened is that e-brands are competing in exactly the same marketplace as any brand – to get noticed, to get famous, to get people to try their product, which might well be their service on the web, and then to come back. But it's the product and the service and the reputation that make people come back. We're all fighting for people's attention and to create a certain belief and point of view and set of values in people's minds. That's no different for an e-brand than it is for any other brand.'

> ❝E-brands are competing in exactly the same marketplace as any brand.❞

Of the thousands of internet brands that have flooded the market in recent years, odds are that most will be worthless or nearly so a few years from now, according to investment bankers. Some of these brands, such as the once-vaunted boo.com fashion retailing website in Britain, look like casualties already.

BOO HOO

Ernst Malmsten and Kajsa Leander, both photogenic Swedes responsible for an earlier successful online bookstore, raised an estimated $120 million in 1998 and 1999 from numerous US and European investors for boo.com. The site was pitched as 'a gateway to world cool' that would sell fashionable sportswear over the web. Leander was a former model, Malmsten a one-time poetry critic.

Their venture illustrated vividly the folly of some e-tailers in believing, and indeed perpetrating, the most extreme business hyperbole in recent memory. The basic need defining boo's market was clothing – stylish clothing to be more precise. The consumer 'want' that boo had to target, presumably, was a desire to obtain stylish clothing via the net. If boo ever had these basics in mind, it evidently soon forgot them.

The company spent its generous start-up capital with stunning panache, lavishing millions of pounds on trendy Carnaby Street offices, more than 400 staff and, crucially, a highly sophisticated website plagued by repeated delays, with each setback preceded by media hype ramp-ups that turned into major let-downs. The end came in May 2000, when boo failed to procure a needed injection of $30 million in cash, forcing it to shut down and liquidate. Development of the site was estimated to have cost $50 million. When the liquidator from KPMG managed to sell it off, the entire back-office kit went for $375,000. The brand was sold later for an undisclosed sum to help chip away at boo's estimated $25-million debt load. The buyer of the brand relaunched boo.com in late 2000 as a much simpler clothes shopping site.

By the time its cash and its luck ran out, boo had become the poster child for e-commerce excess. A brand, however trendy and well-known it may be, must have a viable underlying business proposition and keep it upper-most in mind. Understanding of this had grown tenuous at some e-commerce firms at the height of the tech bubble that burst shortly after boo's collapse, wiping out billions in paper stock-market profits in the USA, the UK, France, Germany and throughout the developed world.

Peapod, an online grocer based in Chicago, was among e-brands that perhaps lost sight of the basics. Co-founder Andrew Parkinson in 1999 said the company was creating 'a research learning vehicle' for packaged goods companies by selling them information about Peapod's customers.[1] Shouldn't the head of money-losing Peapod have been talk-ing instead about creating ways to sell food more conveniently and profitably to customers via the internet?

TRUE TALES

Part 3 of *Brands in the Balance* presents two case studies of e-brands that have survived, and in one case thrived, in part by keeping branding basics in plain view, while also discovering some new twists:

- Karen Edwards, vice-president of marketing at US web legend Yahoo!, talks about the blinding speed with which she helped to create what is now ranked as one of the world's most valuable brands, showing a talent for imaginative brand building.

- Daniel Gestetner, CEO of UK-based internet shopping portal ShopSmart, talks about the challenges of branding on the web, displaying how a small start-up can make itself known quickly by following a very Yahoo!-like branding strategy.

ShopSmart and Yahoo!, while vastly different in size and scope, share two important qualities. First, they are run by sensible business managers who understand the meaning of branding. That helps to explain why they have, so far, survived the e-brand shake-out. Second, ShopSmart and Yahoo! have a common challenge, which is perhaps the most critical facing many e-brands today.

As early movers in their respective markets, both brands won high levels of awareness and established distinct brand personalities. Through clever public relations and pioneering television work, ShopSmart and Yahoo! made names for themselves quickly and at minimal expense compared to some late-comers who had to buy advertising exposure at greatly inflated rates.

However, both ShopSmart and Yahoo! won early fame without clearly delineating in consumers' minds a definite brand positioning. ShopSmart staked out the narrower image of the two. It was about buying things on the web. Yahoo! sought to own a much broader perception, as a friendly entry point to the internet for a multitude of purposes, including navigation, searching, shopping, e-mail and chat.

Neither brand explicitly promoted its specific service attributes or its value versus competitors or its capable staff or its international reach. This was deliberate, as neither wanted to be boxed in. The web changes so fast that it is difficult to predict what a brand might have to do next to remain competitive. So, branding in the early days for both companies was about winning awareness while keeping options open.

> **The web changes so fast that it is difficult to predict what a brand might have to do next to remain competitive.**

Today, tens of thousands of web sites are competing for the attention of more than 155 million internet users worldwide. ShopSmart and Yahoo! both realize that they must do more to explain themselves to consumers and to differentiate themselves from the ever-expanding competition.

If early e-branding was about grabbing consumers' attention, it is now about holding that attention by carving out positions in the market that offer real value superior to off-line alternatives and to hordes of online competitors. Over the long haul, that will be much trickier than being the best at getting noticed.

NOTES

1 Evan Schwartz, *Digital Darwinism*, New York: Penguin Books, 1999.

17

TO THE WEB BORN: YAHOO! AND THE E-BRAND

'Good businesses will do well on the internet. It's all about how well you manage, what's the value of your offering to customers'

Karen Edwards, vice-president, Yahoo!

NO COMPANY HAS HAD AS MUCH INFLUENCE on the development of the e-brand as Yahoo!, the hugely successful, all-purpose web portal from Santa Clara, California, that is the model for legions of start-ups when it comes to establishing a commercial identity on the internet.

The irreverent attitude, the quirky TV commercials, the fanciful name, the flouting of branding conventions like targeting market segments, positioning against competition, emphasizing service features – the whole style is so familiar by now that it is easy to forget Yahoo! invented it. From its early publicity stunts to its trend-setting television commercials to its present status as the world's most valuable internet-services brand worth an estimated $6.3 billion, according to Interbrand, Yahoo! has set the standards for a dynamic, young industry that continues to test branding's boundaries.[1]

The Yahoo! story can be deceiving. On the surface it seems to be about ignoring the rules, about cocking a snook at marketing traditions, about helping the little guy get a handle on the big, confusing internet. And in some ways it is. But make no mistake. Yahoo! is not a bunch of amateurish, shoot-from-the-hip branding, uh … yahoos.

David Filo and Jerry Yang, founders of the company, were a pair of Stanford University students who turned their list of favourite web sites into a thing called Jerry and David's Guide to the Web. Today, they may be portrayed as the original geeky computer guys who viewed the net as a cool hobby and didn't know or didn't care much about making money. But they had a public relations firm under contract as far back as 1995. Just a year later they hired an accomplished brand manager in Karen Edwards, a Harvard MBA who previously had worked in brand marketing and public affairs for Clorox, Chevron USA, Apple Computer and Twentieth Century Fox.

Yahoo! is all business when it comes to its brand, and it's a good thing. While it has succeeded perhaps beyond all expectations, it is entering a testing period, along with the rest of the dot-com world. School days are over for e-brands. No more swanning around, trying to get noticed by venture capitalists and an adventurous few consumers, while living off generous sponsors and great expectations. The real world has arrived – as of the new millennium – and that means serious competition.

E-brands pride themselves on their hit rates and click throughs. But eyeballs don't pay the bills. Customers do, and that means differentiation – finding effective market positions on the web that set off one brand from the next and deliver consistent value in goods and services to millions of consumers, whose needs and wants quite easily could continue to be met by off-line rivals or other online competitors.

Yahoo! is streets ahead on this front, with more than 150 million daily users worldwide – its presence on the web in Japan and Korea is actually more dominant than in the USA. Moreover, it is one of precious few internet ventures consistently in the black, with profits of $203 million on sales of $855 million in the 12 months ended 30 June 2000. Still, in an interview, Karen Edwards said differentiation is the next big hurdle:

'Differentiation becomes more and more important as the category matures. In the early days, people just wanted to know the safe choice. Where can I go first? Where can I just get started? People tried Yahoo! because it was the brand they knew. Awareness was really key. Then the next phase was people wanted to know what was best. What's the service that most people like? What's the leading company? I want to go with the leader. I want to make a relatively educated decision. So, we were able to then get people who switched from some of the other services that were of lesser quality. They came over to Yahoo!

'We're getting into a stage where people don't care if Yahoo! or AOL or Microsoft is the leader, they just want what's best for them. People now are looking for more differentiation. They really want to understand how Yahoo! is different ... Product and service attributes become more important. But community and critical mass are also key.'

As in any business, bigger and better will spell long-term success on the internet. But, of course, not everyone can be the biggest and the best, as the shake-out now under way is proving. Chances are good that Yahoo! will be one of the e-brands that survives the industry's transition to adulthood because the company is already so big and diverse, offering a search engine, auctions, shopping, messaging, e-mail, news, stock quotes, personal home pages, clubs, games, chat, bill paying, book-marking and on and on. But when Yahoo! started out, it was far from clear just what it would become.

> **“People now are looking for more differentiation. They really want to understand how Yahoo! is different. ”**

THE JERRY AND DAVID SHOW

Filo and Yang were doctoral candidates in electrical engineering at Stanford when they discovered the internet in the early 1990s. The web was then a temperamental techie network used mostly by academics and scientists. Its future as a new frontier for business brands was unimagined.

In early 1994 the two put their personal list of favourite web sites out on the net for public use. Jerry and David's Guide to the Web at the time was just one of hundreds of hobbyist guides, but it attracted a following among early netizens who saw it as friendly and easy to use. Many web sites then had acronym names beginning with 'YA' for 'yet another ...', as in YACC, or Yet Another Compiler Compiler. Filo and Yang decided to rename their guide YA-something. They opened the dictionary at the Ys and picked 'yahoo' because they felt like yahoos, or so the story goes. They added an exclamation mark and later a formal title – Yet Another Hierarchical Officious Oracle.

As Yahoo! grew, Filo and Yang developed custom software to locate, identify and edit material on the internet. Their system grew rapidly until their personal computers and Stanford's were overburdened. In early 1995 Marc Andreessen, co-founder of Netscape Communications, invited Filo and Yang to house their files on larger computers at Netscape headquarters in nearby Mountain View, California.

The Netscape deal was a signal that Filo and Yang were ambitious to expand their presence on the web – not as conquerors like Microsoft in Seattle, but as diplomats. Yahoo!'s ability to work with other companies has served it in good stead over the years. Instead of doing everything in-house, many of its services are provided by other firms through partnership arrangements. This out-sourcing strategy has minimized overhead and made Yahoo! a lot of friends, rather than enemies.

The founders realized in 1995 that Yahoo! had evolved into a full-time business from an all-consuming hobby. They wrote up a formal business plan, hired additional staff and brought in a PR firm. They also made decisions that were crucial to the subsequent development of the company. First, Filo and Yang decided they wanted Yahoo! to continue to be a free internet service, rather than a paid service like the early web pioneers America Online, Delphi, Compuserve and Prodigy. 'We were betting on the internet, as opposed to betting on an online service', Edwards said. From a brand perspective, she added, that meant 'we then needed to own and embrace the good and the bad of the internet, which back then had almost more negatives than it had positives'.

Second, Yahoo! opted to fashion itself as a media, not a technology, company. That meant focusing on categorizing web sites to make the internet more comprehensible – a time-consuming task requiring a lot of thoughtful human intervention, unlike the automated hunt-and-find systems run by early web search engines, such as WebCrawler, Excite or Infoseek. As Edwards said:

'We're about aggregating content. We present a variety of different viewpoints and content. Technology is something that we've always believed we could either license or acquire. Our philosophy was that this human piece was the part that was difficult and hard to replicate and actually a very strong point of differentiation.'

Later, Yahoo! added a search engine to its services that it licensed first from OpenText, then later successively from Altavista, Inktomi and now Google.

By opting not to be a technology leader, Yahoo! was forgoing the chance to position itself as technically superior in a particular niche. Instead, it chose to be good at a variety of services, but that meant it needed to stand out in some other way. That choice made the brand all-important. 'When you're not a technology company ... Then what else is going to differentiate you? So we view the brand as being a very important differentiation for Yahoo! versus other businesses', Edwards said.

Finally, the company went global quite early on, when many other e-brands were concentrating solely on the US market. Yahoo! entered Japan in January 1996, long before competitors. Today it has a commanding market share in Japan and Korea, where close to 90 per cent of web users use Yahoo!

A FEW CLICKS DOWN THE ROAD

By 1996, when Edwards took over brand management, Yahoo! was on the brink of making web history. Over the next two years Yahoo! would make a series of key branding moves, propelling it and the internet beyond the world of the online digerati and into the public eye like never before.

Edwards hired a second PR firm. Yahoo! stepped up its vigorous pursuit of public relations, a low-cost form of brand promotion. It gave internet demonstrations at festivals, sponsored rock concerts and sporting events. It pitched news stories to journalists on the lifestyle pages instead of the business section. It published a general-audience magazine about the internet. The approach was fun and friendly, positioning Yahoo! as an accessible place to learn about the web. It helped the firm win early converts to the net and gained greater awareness for the brand.

Yahoo! got a bit more serious – pitching stories to the business press and emphasizing the professionalism of management – in the run-up to its spectacularly successful April 1996 initial public offering of shares on the stock market. Edwards supervised the communications. Around this time she also started shopping for an advertising agency. She contacted several large shops, but they turned her away, saying they did not do technology advertising. 'I would tell them, I don't want to do technology advertising, I want to make Yahoo! a household name. That's what I told Jerry and David, too. And people were kind of laughing … They were, like, yeah great. Well, good luck.'

Edwards hired a small San Francisco firm called Block Rocket. The principals had no computers and little familiarity with the internet. She said:

'My philosophy there was that I wanted people who really understood consumer brands and had worked on consumer brands, like cars and beer and snacks, as opposed to people who understood technology. I already had the religion and I wanted somebody who could temper that.'

A key moment arrived when Yahoo! became the first internet company to advertise on mass-market television, at great cost, with its now well-known 'pond commercial'. It features an elderly man fishing and having no luck. He heads home, logs on to the net and types in a search for the word 'bait'. In the next scene, he is back at the pond and hauling in a 250-lb bluefin tuna. The spot then fades to black and the company slogan appears, 'Do You Yahoo!?'

The campaign was followed up on television and radio. It grabbed the attention of the general public, but it did not say much about Yahoo!'s target market, its service features or its competitive positioning. The 'Do You Yahoo!?' slogan suggested giving people the power to find things on the web, but without explicitly explaining the company and its services. This was by design, Edwards said. She recalled:

'It was a risky thing to do because you haven't told me what Yahoo! is. And, why aren't you telling me why Yahoo! is better? We wanted it to be an invitation and we wanted it to be as broad as possible. Our philosophy is that a broad brand allows us to be in whatever business we want to be in …

We were trying to achieve that early. Otherwise, our first advertising could have said: "Our pages load faster. You'll get more accurate results when you search on Yahoo! Ours is a directory made by real people as opposed to an automated search engine." There's so many things we could have said. But then, what happens when we launch mail, or shopping? What happens when we're global and all that? We knew all that was possible on the internet. So we didn't want to put ourselves in a little box.'

> 66 Our philosophy is that a broad brand allows us to be in whatever business we want to be in. 99

After the pond commercial Yahoo! did some further television and radio spots, but also charted further new territory for web brands with clever non-advertising communications. The 'Do You Yahoo!?' slogan started showing up on T-shirts and backpacks, on the Zamboni machine that smooths the ice at the San Jose Sharks' hockey rink, on stickers and postcards distributed by direct mail and at restaurants and bars. Yahoo! mugs and posters appeared on popular evening television shows, such as *Ally McBeal*. Yahoo! does not disclose the percentage of revenues that it spends on marketing. But Edwards said it has been stable since the beginning. That level was once estimated at 45 per cent by *Forbes* magazine.

Meanwhile, other web brands stampeded after Yahoo! on to the small screen. AOL, Lycos, Auto-By-Tel, Excite and Dell Computer all had network commercials airing by mid-1997, and many more were to come. Job recruitment website HotJobs.com spent half its 1998 revenues buying a single, 30-second commercial during the 1999 Super Bowl football game. Its business subsequently soared. The rush was on in the web world to build brands and Yahoo! was at the front of the pack.

Yahoo!'s stock price soared to dizzying heights as it gained fame and rode the late 1990s bull market in web stocks. The share price rose tenfold between January 1997 and October 1999 with three splits. The tech rally peaked at ridiculous levels around Christmas 1999. Ever since, Yahoo! has levelled off and e-fever has cooled. Looking ahead, Edwards said Yahoo! is confident it will be one of the e-brands that survives the shake-out that has followed.

Yahoo!'s size and brand strength give it the power to erect barriers to entry for smaller competitors. Back in 1996, she said, a variety of rivals could conceivably have caught and surpassed Yahoo! with better technology.

'But it's kind of tough now. A brand is a really distinct advantage. The internet is certainly not going away. It's not a fad ... But this recent rationalization has made it clear that half-baked ideas aren't going to go very far, and that consumers don't have a lot of time to waste on things that don't make sense and aren't of good value. What's happening is that the strong are going to get stronger and it's going to be harder and harder for the weaker ones to survive. And a lot of hare-brained things just aren't even going to get off the ground.'

Consumers are also less likely now to experiment with web ventures that feel like they may not be around in six months, she added. 'So it's getting even more brand sensitive. Consumers are more prone to do business with brands that they perceive as leaders ... That's a strong advantage that Yahoo! has.'

NOTES

1 Interbrand, *The World's Most Valuable Brands Survey*, 18 July 2000.

18

TO THE WEB BORN 2: SHOPSMART AND THE E-BRAND

'The critical thing with the internet is giving people a call to action'

Daniel Gestetner, CEO, ShopSmart

IF YOU COULD DISTILL A BRAND TO ITS ESSENCE by boiling off the components that are not strictly brand matter – like the product it stands for, its price, sales reps, ownership, retailers, store displays, etc. – you would end up with something pure, something free of outside variables ... something like ShopSmart.com.

ShopSmart is the leading internet shopping portal in Britain, Germany and Sweden. It spent £10 million on brand-building advertising in 2000. Its brand logo – a wiggling, giggling cartoon shopping bag – gets a lot of exposure as sponsor of the Channel 5 movie, an evening UK television staple. It cut a crucial marketing deal in August 2000 with AOL Europe and Wal-Mart Europe that looked certain to make ShopSmart one of the long-term survivors of the present e-commerce shake-out.

The company neither makes nor handles any physical products. It has no field reps, no delivery vans, no imposing office building or plant. It is not listed on the stock market. It charges consumers nothing. Its packaging and display are limited to its web site, as well as promotions in UK Asda stores and German Wal-Marts and its status as the price-comparison service on AOL UK and AOL Germany, under the deal in which AOL and Wal-Mart (parent of Asda) bought a 22.5-per-cent stake in ShopSmart.

Run by a typically young and laid-back bunch of web-heads out of modest quarters in an unfashionable part of London, ShopSmart is about as close as a business can get to being a pure brand enterprise. Yet, even in this rarefied state, ShopSmart is a brand like any other brand. It must compete for the attention of consumers. It must be simple, concise, accessible and visible. It must represent something meaningful that delivers consistent value to consumers or they will reject it. 'What this is all about is a consumer brand', said CEO Daniel Gestetner, just eight years out of university. 'The only way this proposition works is if we instil in consumers' minds the vision of ShopSmart as a brand.'

This truism, which Gestetner said he has respected from the beginning, is only now hitting home with some e-brand owners and investors, one year after the cresting of a 'New Economy' mania in late 1999 and early 2000 that, for an instant in time, looked set to rewrite the fundamentals of brand marketing. Web-based business-to-consumer (B-to-C) retailing exploded on to the scene in the late 1990s with the emergence of overnight branding sensations such as boo.com, Amazon.com, Priceline.com, Value America, Webvan and thousands of others across the USA and Europe.

The e-brand phenomenon bred a hubris that questioned old assumptions about brands – that building them takes years of effort, millions in advertising, careful research and planning and a viable underlying business proposition. Some e-brands seemed to take an incredible 'Field of Dreams' approach to branding – build it and they will come, whether a ball game has actually started or not. By Christmas 1999 the talk in marketing was of 'speed branding' and the death of traditional brands. People were quitting their jobs to start or join web start-ups. Venture capitalists were investing in ideas alone. The stock market was on an internet-fuelled rampage, setting record highs on a weekly basis.

> **❝Far from enjoying some special immunity to branding's basic rules, e-brands may be even more subject to them than traditional brands. ❞**

Then the inevitable happened. The market's e-darlings started cutting financial projections. Servers crashed. Delivery mix-ups spread. Hackers struck. Losses mounted. In the spring of 2000 web stocks took a nose dive and people started waking up to the realization that it takes more than a bright idea to build a brand and a business.

In fact, it could be argued that, far from enjoying some special immunity to branding's basic rules, e-brands may be even more subject to them than traditional brands precisely because, like ShopSmart, many are such purely brand-based businesses. Moreover, the marketplace they compete in is one in which the customer is always only a mouse-click away from walking out of the shop door.

SILICON CRICKLEWOOD

ShopSmart's office is in a high-security building down a gated alleyway in Cricklewood, London. In the lobby is a pool table and it is not just there for show. Employees were shooting some stick before lunch on a recent afternoon. No neckties were in evidence. Everyone looked 20-something, like the boss.

Youthful and low-key, ShopSmart is a typical web start-up in many ways. But it is not technically an e-tailer like Amazon.com or Peapod.com or Tesco.co.uk, the British online supermarket service. ShopSmart is a shopping portal that lists, reviews and links to hundreds of e-tailers. It has a nifty price comparison service that can shop for a specified item among the merchants in its database and produce a ranking of prices and information on delivery, stock availability, etc.

Clothing leads the shopping list of users, followed by CDs, books, videos, electronics – the usual line-up of net-worthy items. Other than that, Gestetner has no clear profile of his customers. They need not register to use the site. So ShopSmart has little data on them. 'We know where consumers are going, what shops they're going into, what categories. But we don't know the demographics', Gestetner said.

Despite this lack of target-market knowledge, ShopSmart has the fourth highest brand-awareness level among UK dot-com advertisers, a recent study showed, and Gestetner is spending millions building that up. He said his conservative business plan puts ShopSmart less than two years away from profitability.

'The internet is going to be huge ... It's going to be part of our lives. We're going to do so many things over the internet', said the 29-year-old entrepreneur who, along with 80 staff, is betting that ShopSmart can be the Which? Guide or Consumer Reports magazine of the web by imposing itself as a useful and impartial intermediary between consumers and e-tailers. He went on:

'We give you a lot more added value. We're your friend. We're not going to try to rip you off. That's the whole consumer proposition. We try to put that into our brand, which is about safety and security and being the place you want to go first to go shopping online.

'The challenge for us is to ensure that we get the message across about what we do. Channel 5 was an amazing deal we did, the sponsorship … That's great for building up the brand. What it doesn't do is tell consumers what we do … The critical thing with the internet is giving people a call to action, giving people a reason to go to your web site. Just 18 months ago, if you said ShopSmart.com to someone, they might have gone to check it out because it was new and it was trendy and it was the thing to do – to check out these new web sites. Nowadays, with thousands of new web sites coming online all the time, you need to differentiate yourself a lot more to give consumers a reason to come. That's what we're achieving quite well, although it's an uphill struggle to try to get people to really understand what we do.'

Even with the AOL-Wal-Mart deal, ShopSmart will have to work hard to explain itself to consumers as the novelty of the internet wears off. Already, the top question in web consumers' minds has stopped being 'What's this all about anyway?' and started being 'What's in it for me?'

'The proposition is about giving the consumer added value. The day we stop giving the consumer added value is the day they start going straight to the e-tailer', Gestetner said.

ShopSmart has four revenue streams: advertising on the site through buttons and banners; sales commissions from a small portion of its listed retailers; category sponsorships; and referral fees charged to retailers selected by ShopSmart customers through the price-comparison system. The company has a stupendous advertising budget. The *Financial Times* newspaper in London estimated ShopSmart spent £10 million on ads in 2000, including £3 million for the Channel 5 movie deal.[1]

One of the chief criticisms of B-to-C e-tailers in late 2000 among market analysts was that many were pouring buckets of money down the advertising drain with little or no result. 'It's absolutely true', Gestetner said. 'There are a lot of dot-coms that have thrown money away … that have spent millions on advertising without having a proposition.' But this is not the case at ShopSmart, he said. He added:

'We are generating a significant revenue … We're making our branding pay. But a lot of other dot-coms that have spent £3 million, £5 million, £10 million haven't had a proposition to back it up. They've just raised the VC [venture capital] money because it was easy to raise VC money, then spent it on TV or billboards or whatever, and then they just fizzled away.'

Some, like ShopSmart, have survived because they have a solid business model, he said. 'If you've got a strong proposition and you can deliver on it, then it's fine … Amazon.com is the classic. People like Yahoo! and Freeserve and lastminute.com show it can be done. There are a lot of people that have done it, but it's not easy.'

Although barely two years old, ShopSmart was one of the earliest major UK e-commerce sites. By the time e-fever reached its crescendo in the UK around Christmas 1999, ShopSmart was already well-established. A flood of new ventures followed and jacked up advertising rates. Gestetner said:

> **❝It's all about building a brand, which requires spending on advertising. ❞**

'Now that some of these companies have folded or been acquired, we can spend less to get the same share of voice, It's all about building a brand, which requires spending on advertising. I could stop advertising tomorrow and break even. The reason I don't … is because I need to build a brand and we need to do that now. The internet, because it's growing so rapidly, offers huge potential if you can get in there early, before the growth really starts occurring, and we're still in early days now. That's what makes it different and exciting. You can create a brand from nothing.'

FROM CAKES TO CLICKS

Gestetner is the great-grandson of David Gestetner, inventor of the first commercially successful stencil duplicating machine in 1881. The elder Gestetner founded Gestetner Co., which went on to market a line of top-selling office equipment, including the Cyclostyle. The company is still in business. Daniel graduated from university in 1992. He went to work for UK supermarket group Tesco as a cake buyer, then spent four years at the New York-based cosmetics group Revlon as a marketing manager. In 1997, as part of a Revlon internet strategy group, he came down with the web bug. He quit Revlon in early 1998 and returned home to Britain with ideas about an internet shopping site. He and brother Leo Gestetner started working on a business plan.

At about the same time, and quite separately, young computer consultant Martin Reeves launched ShopGuide, a web-based directory of UK online shopping sites. The well-financed Gestetner brothers saw ShopGuide and recognized that Reeves had technical know-how that they lacked. 'We decided we could be partners with him', Gestetner said. 'He had a whole new skill set that we didn't have. He had three years' internet knowledge and all the technical skills, and he was a great visionary in terms of the whole product.'

They joined forces and in February 1999 relaunched ShopGuide, only to discover quickly that the brand name was too limiting. They envisioned being more than a guide to shops, but did not get a good grasp on their brand personality until hiring Steve Chippington as marketing director in summer 1999. Gestetner said:

'He's a very strong branding guy, and the first thing he did was say, well, let's look at your proposition as a brand and what we're trying to achieve. We did some research and some focus groups. We looked at what our consumers wanted, having realized that the name ShopGuide was far too restrictive. We weren't just a guide. ShopGuide implies that you are just a guide to shopping. We're not. We're trying to fulfil all the consumer's needs to go shopping online … We started brainstorming about names. We had an absolute nightmare trying to think of good names. So we brought in an agency.'

The agency, following textbook guidelines for brand-name development, advised taking one of two options. First, invent a completely fanciful name – like Yahoo! – which would have no overt reference to the service provided, but be more easily defensible as a trademark. Or, come up with a descriptive or associative name that would be catchy, but also tell consumers about the web site.

'We could have gone down the route of a fun name that means nothing, but to create a brand like that you have to spend a huge amount more money. We reckoned you'd have to spend £5 million to establish a name like that … If we could find a more descriptive name, then obviously the marketing costs were much lower. So, we got to ShopSmart.'

As is often the case on the internet, someone already owned the ShopSmart domain name. 'We spent a huge sum of money buying it … from somebody in New York who owns domain names, a very smart guy who wanted $1 million for it. We managed to get it for $100,000', Gestetner said. At the time of writing, ShopSmart was seeking trademark registration for its brand name and had already established ownership of variants, such as shopsmart.net, shopsmart.org and shopsmart.eu.

The announcement of the AOL-Wal-Mart agreement marked a huge turning point by linking ShopSmart to both the world's largest retailer and the world's largest internet service provider.

NO E-EXCEPTION

While the business grows, Gestetner said it faces branding challenges, some of which are unique to the internet. In spite of the excited publicity surrounding them, e-brands actually suffer from a competitive disadvantage versus traditional brands. Namely, they are not very visible to consumers who are not active on the web. E-brands by nature are not in the shop windows on the street. They are not in kitchen cabinets or refrigerators or in other places where traditional brands are able to project themselves.

ShopSmart has addressed this problem by tying up with Wal-Mart and Asda. 'We're trying to make (the brand) three-dimensional', Gestetner said. 'You've got the internet, but there are also other outlets, whether it's print, or walking into a high-street store, or your local bank. We want to be in consumers' minds and consumers' eyes.'

A coming together of traditional brands and e-brands can already be seen in some industries and more is ahead. 'There's going to be lots of consolidation over the next few months and years in the internet space, in general, with lots of high-street brands aligning themselves with online brands and vice versa', Gestetner said. 'We need to keep ourselves in consumers' eyes.'

Despite recent setbacks for the industry, Gestetner said his faith in the promise of the web is unshaken, although tempered by the knowledge that a web brand is in many ways like any other.

❝The brands that have worked on the web are the ones where there are real people running real businesses. ❞

'The brands that have worked on the web are the ones where there are real people running real businesses. At ShopSmart we've got a strong team of directors and managers and employees that know what they're doing ... A CEO can't just sit back and let it happen, but there are companies out there that have done that. Boo.com is an example, but there are plenty of others, as well, where the CEO and the senior management team have lived in a euphoria ...

They thought they were riding a wave, they were on top of a cloud, they were untouchable, without realizing – hang on a second guys, we've got to run a business.'

NOTES

1   *Financial Times*, 2 February 2000.

PART 4

BRANDS IN SOCIETY

Oh Lord, won't you buy me a Mercedes-Benz?

Janis Joplin

BRANDS CAN DRIVE PEOPLE to all sorts of extremes. Motorcycle gang members tattoo themselves with Harley-Davidson logos. Corporate executives splash out wads of cash for a Rolex watch to display their status. Anti-capitalist rioters smash McDonald's restaurant signs to strike a blow against the system. A teenager strangles a basketball buddy in the woods behind school to steal his Nike Air Jordans.

All these behaviours, while different in many ways, are alike in at least one – they represent people trying to define themselves as individuals by relating to a commercial identity. Brands help people to tell the world – and themselves – who they are and where they belong, whether it's in the Hell's Angels, or the ranks of the conventionally successful, or a fringe-left activist movement, or the cool-shoe crowd.

The same goal of self-realization might be achieved by joining a church, a club or a political party, by embracing an ideology, a nation or a workplace, by being involved in a community, a sport, a hobby or a family. For many people, these traditional avenues to social belonging and fulfilment are still open. But for a growing number, they are closing. Traditional institutions take time, effort and stability to maintain. Sadly these qualities are in short supply. As a result, in some lives, the bulwarks of non-market-based culture are eroding. In their place, more people are seeking meaning in the ideas and symbols that the market economy makes so very prominent and so effortlessly attainable – commercial brands.

The promises made by brands are alluring: prestige, power, sex appeal, fun, sophistication, friendship, wisdom, adventure – all supposedly achievable by simply purchasing a product or service. Buy a Land Rover 4 × 4 and be adventurous … buy Marlboro cigarettes and be rugged … buy an Apple laptop and be brilliant … buy a Ralph Lauren blouse and be beautiful … buy a Coca-Cola and enjoy life.

'Relationships with mass brands can soothe the "empty selves" left behind by society's abandonment of tradition and community and provide stable anchors in an otherwise changing world', wrote Susan Fournier, Harvard Business School marketing professor.[1]

Is this modern phenomenon something to worry about? What are its implications for brands? The answers to these questions are being debated in marketing and social and environmental activist circles. For some people the rise of brands is a cause for fear, anxiety, even violence; for others it is not.

While the dogged pursuit of a new 7-Series BMW or an Armani suit might seem to be a hollow and crass ambition, perhaps it is preferable to the pursuit of class warfare, or racial purity, or some of the other fanaticisms that traditional institutions have foisted on civilization over the past century or so. In any case, questions such as these are probably best left to the philosophers and the poets, while business faces the more pressing issue of what the social power of brands means to brands themselves. And it means a lot.

CUTS BOTH WAYS

In a world where communication is instantaneous and style is just as important as substance, the strong brand is a double-edged sword. It accomplishes its original aim of helping a business to sell more goods and services, but today it also exposes that business to the attentions and agendas of a wider public.

This is the fascinating paradox behind the recent controversies surrounding some of the world's biggest brands, such as Nike, pilloried in recent years for paying Asian workers low wages; Shell, attacked for its political dealings in Nigeria; Nestlé, mired in an endless battle over infant formula; McDonald's, targeted by a wide array of activists; and Microsoft, challenged at every turn for its market dominance. In each of these cases a strong brand name, while conferring obvious competitive advantages in the marketplace, has also helped to transform its parent into a target for attack by activists and governments.

> **❝People are making big companies into villains these days. ❞**

'It's a very interesting thing; since the Russians gave up and there's no major terrifying war scenario, people are making big companies into villains these days', said Lee Clow, CEO of top advertising agency TBWA Worldwide. He went on:

'When you're small and feisty and have attitude and edge, when you're just doing it, you're cool. When you become so ubiquitous that you can put your logo on every jersey on every football team on the planet, all of a sudden people react and say, "I don't want anybody to be that big and that powerful". That's the problem with Bill Gates and Microsoft – "I don't like the richest man in the world". That's the weird dynamic that's going to have to be managed by successful brands.'[2]

How should this social paradox of successful branding be handled? One answer might be to lay low and dodge any controversy that comes along. This is often the knee-jerk reaction of business executives – hush it up and it will go away. But it doesn't go away any more, precisely because the brand keeps it in the headlines. Another strategy might be to hide the company itself behind a wall of seemingly unconnected product brands. But consumers are not so easily thrown off the trail today. Giving up entirely on branding is clearly not an option. The economic power of brands is too great. So, what is the solution?

It is to change business. To change the way companies go about their daily affairs. To put social and environmental responsibility on the agenda of the board of directors. To bring political and ethical factors into the decision-making process. To get into the habit of rejecting the occasional project that, while possibly profitable, risks damaging the brand in the eyes of an increasingly watchful world. According to Susannah Hart, director of consulting firm Interbrand UK Ltd:

'It is the responsibility of brand owners to begin to ask themselves more wide-ranging and searching questions: rather than ask a straightforward question such as "Will it sell?" they must ask a series of more complex questions: "Will it make a contribution to our customer's success?" "Will it improve the customer's and society's well-being?" "Does it add to our country's cultural stock or bring pride to our nation?" ... Brands are not just about making money for their owners or their shareholders, not just about fulfilling basic consumer needs. Brands possess great power and the truly great brands will be those that learn to balance this power with responsibility.'[3]

By seeking and winning unprecedented consumer attention in the fast-moving information age, owners of major brands have garnered for themselves the power to sell more goods and services. But, like any power, brand power brings with it certain risks and obligations. A few of the world's largest corporations are coming to grips with this idea, which unsurprisingly often sits more comfortably with small and mid-sized businesses than it does with giant multinationals.

Part 4 of *Brands in the Balance* presents case studies of two large companies, based on lengthy interviews with top executives who are well versed in dealing with the social ramifications of branding:

- Raoul Pinnell, global head of brands and communications, and Tom Henderson, manager of reputation support, at Anglo-Dutch energy group Royal Dutch/Shell, discuss managing a major brand through crisis, shedding light on an unprecedented test of constructive engagement with brand critics.

- Michael Eisner, CEO of US media and entertainment giant Walt Disney Co., discusses the challenges of keeping a modern mega-brand dynamic and contemporary while respecting its traditions, showing resilience in the face of an unavoidably precarious balancing act.

As Shell and Disney can testify, people relate to brands in different and sometimes surprising ways. At their best, brands are helpful and convenient signposts on the increasingly confusing consumption landscape; at their worst, they are annoying and offensive intruders into public space and private lives.

To some people the mounting influence of brands is pernicious and threatening. Young people, especially, may see brands as part of an unjust economic system. Thirty years ago, Dow Chemical and United Fruit were reviled by hippies and socialists; today animal rights and labour activists attack McDonald's and Nike. As the outward faces of capitalism, brands make ready targets for the eternal disenchantment and rebellion of youth, and never more so than today.

> 66 Brands make ready targets for the eternal disenchantment and rebellion of youth. 99

On the street, some young people are rejecting major brands as emblematic of established power. Elite brands are becoming targets for rebellion and violence. McDonald's have been bombed by terrorists in Athens, and attacked by farmers in France and animal activists in Belgium. Rioters in London and Seattle smashed up Nike, Gap, Starbucks and Mercedes-Benz locations. On the web, activists organize anti-brand

actions with lightning speed after passing snap judgements that con-
demn or exonerate a brand – and its corporate parent – in mere hours.

A stinging manifesto of the latest version of left-wing brand backlash was
recently offered up by Naomi Klein, a young Canadian journalist, in her
fascinating book *No Logo*. Activists have fastened on commercial brands
as the enemy in recent years for two reasons, she explained. First, they
subvert more meaningful value and belief systems by reducing culture to
a business transaction. Second, brands present a handy platform for promoting other social and environmental causes. According to Klein:

'By attempting to enclose our shared culture in sanitized and controlled
brand cocoons ... corporations have themselves created the surge of
opposition described. By thirstily absorbing social critiques and political
movements as sources of "brand meaning", they have radicalized that
opposition still further. By abandoning their traditional role as direct, secure
employers to pursue their branding dreams, they have lost the loyalty that
once protected them from citizen rage. And by pounding the message of
self-sufficiency into a generation of workers, they have inadvertently
empowered their critics to express that rage without fear.'

In conclusion, Klein called vaguely for 'a truly globally minded society,
one that would include not just economics and capital, but global citizens, global rights and global responsibilities', as well as 'a citizen-centred
alternative to the international rule of brands'.[4]

BEATING BRANDS INTO PLOUGHSHARES

Like many social critics on the left and right, Klein has offered some
penetrating analysis and insight, but come up short on alternatives. This
would be a negligible aspect of her valuable commentary if it were not
for the fact that it is precisely the point. What is the alternative to a
world without brands? Interbrand's Rita Clifton has said:

'It's tempting among a particular tribe of people around the world to knock the
capitalist world and to knock the marketplace economy. Brands need advertising,
so they're often the most prominent part of the market society ... But what I
would say is this – companies that don't provide what people want go out of
business. The *reductio ad absurdum* of the premise of a no-brand world is a world
of grey communism. I mean, there is a temptation to say, let's all forget it and go
back to the land ... But the problem is that you have to stop and think about
why people stopped living that way in the first place.'

Indeed, no matter how much anyone wishes, brands are not going away. Nor are they necessarily an evil that must be tolerated as an unavoidable component of the market economy. Brands actually offer a potentially powerful force for social and environmental progress when viewed realistically for what they are – extraordinarily effective two-way conduits between consumers and business. As Clifton observed, 'You can create a very convincing case for business being the most powerful force for good'.

By holding the private sector more accountable for its actions, brands can be put to good use as tools for social, ethical and environmental progress.

NOTES

1   Susan Fournier, 'Understand consumer-brand relationships', working paper 96-018, Harvard Business School, Harvard University, Cambridge, Massachusetts.

2   Rita Clifton and Esther Maughan (eds), *The Future of Brands: Twenty-five Visions*, London: Macmillan, 2000, p. 71.

3   Susannah Hart, 'The Future for Brands', in Susannah Hart and John Murphy (eds), *Brands: The New Wealth Creators*, London: Macmillan, 1998, pp. 213–14.

4   Naomi Klein, *No Logo: Taking Aim at the Brand Bullies*, New York: Picador, 1999, pp. 441–6.

19

UNDER FIRE:
SHELL AND THE BRAND IN CRISIS

'It can take 100 years to build up a good brand and 30 days to knock it down'

David D'Alessandro, president, John Hancock Mutual Life Insurance Co.

BRANDING AS USUAL ENDED AT Royal Dutch/Shell Group in 1995, when the world's second largest oil and gas firm reeled under a double dose of controversy from which it is still recovering. The execution of Nigerian human rights activist Ken Saro-Wiwa, and an environmental furore over disposal of the Brent Spar oil storage buoy seized Shell by its marketing throat and shook it hard.

'Brent Spar and Saro-Wiwa were a wake-up call for the people in charge of this overall business', said Tom Henderson, manager of reputation support for the Anglo-Dutch energy giant, which over the past five years has responded broadly on two fronts, offering a good look at how to handle a brand in serious crisis in the dynamic age of information.

In an interview at Shell's grim London headquarters building on the south bank of the River Thames, Henderson and Raoul Pinnell, global head of brands and communications, described the 'journey' that Shell is embarked on. It has two paths. One is external and involves engaging critics in open dialogue. The other is internal and focused on reassessing Shell's brand approach from the bottom up. The overarching conviction behind these efforts is that brands today hold their owners accountable to more than the bottom line and that this reality cannot be ignored.

'There is a new world order emerging', said Pinnell, an outspoken new-comer at Shell hired three years ago after working in marketing at Nestlé, Heinz, Prudential and NatWest. He continued:

'People have legitimate concerns in relation to that new world order. I personally don't think the new world order is negative. But again, what are the consequences of our actions? We are not prepared to allow any institution, any company, any individual to behave in a certain type of way any more. I think that's a force for good.'

These carefully worded comments by Shell's chief brand manager reflect the depth of concern at Shell about the aftermath of the events of 1995. Whether this concern means Shell is actually changing the way it does business on the ground remains an open question, according to its many critics among environmental, human rights and other activists. But one thing is clear. Shell is helping to chart the course for brand management in the future by undertaking what is certainly the business world's most ambitious experiment to date in 'constructive engagement' with its activist opponents, and by reassessing the meaning of the Shell brand.

'There are people out there who are not customers of Shell, but who are important to our business', Henderson said. 'These people are helping to turn this company from a large, lethargic entity into something that really wants to go out and explore these wider stake-holding publics.' Shell's corporate journey from being one of the oil industry's early inno-vators to being a 21st-century branding pioneer has been a long one with somewhat unlikely beginnings.

FROM SEA SHELLS AND TANKERS TO HOT DOGS AND TOILETS

Shell got its start in 1833 when Marcus Samuel opened a shop in London selling sea shells to Victorian naturalists. The business expanded gradually into a general import–export company. After a tour of Russia's Baku penin-sula, where oil was first commercially drilled in the Old World, Marcus's son Marcus Jr started adding kerosene fuel to Shell Transport & Trading Co.'s cargo lists. In 1892 he commissioned the construction of the world's first purpose-built oil tanker, allowing Shell to transport large volumes of Baku kerosene to the Far East via the Suez Canal, and to challenge the strangle-hold on lucrative Asian markets then enjoyed by US giant Standard Oil.

Marcus Jr and his brother Samuel adopted early on the familiar scallop-shell logo for their brand. But at first they struggled to compete with Standard. The US firm sold kerosene to the Chinese, Japanese and other Asians in blue tin cans. After being emptied, the cans could be beaten flat and used to make all sorts of handy household objects. So even though Standard's kerosene was more expensive than Shell's, people paid up for it to get the cans. The Samuels realized their problem and started making their own cans, painted red and yellow to contrast sharply with Standard's blue. A memorable colour scheme was born, as was a bitter rivalry between two oil giants that continues even now.

Quite separately in the Netherlands, a company called Royal Dutch Petroleum had been formed in 1890 to develop an oilfield on the remote tropical island of Sumatra. It had also built a fleet of tankers to compete with the British and the Americans. But stiff resistance from Standard led Royal Dutch to merge with Shell in 1907, creating the Royal Dutch/Shell Group. Sixty per cent of the equity went to the Dutch and 40 per cent to the British. The arrangement continues today and Shell still has dual headquarters in The Hague and London. Royal Dutch dropped its crown logo and adopted the red-and-yellow colours and scallop-shell logo for all products, including something called 'motor spirit'.

> 66 By the 1980s Shell had worked its way deep into the fabric of everyday life across most of the world. 99

The rise of the car and two world wars fought with petroleum-fuelled machines led to explosive growth for Shell, as for the entire oil industry. The 1950s, 1960s and 1970s were boom years as Shell brought in vast new reserves in North Africa, Iraq, Canada, Colombia, Nigeria and the North Sea. Larger tankers were constructed. Filling stations sprouted around the world, and the bright yellow Shell logo became one of the world's most widely recognized brand symbols.

The OPEC crisis of 1974–5 saw oil prices skyrocket and Shell prospered, aggressively expanding in chemicals and lubricants. Through its hugely successful Select convenience retailing unit, it became the world's largest seller of hot dogs, the world's second largest retailer of soft drinks after McDonald's, and the owner of more public toilets than any other private business on the planet. By the 1980s Shell had worked its way deep into the fabric of everyday life across most of the world.

The Shell brand had also been stretched well beyond its original identity. But at headquarters in London and The Hague, managerial appreciation of this was sorely lacking, resulting in a stunning absence of commitment to uphold the brand image or develop its personality more fully. To top managers, the scallop shell, or pecten, remained a simple stamp of ownership, and it was clear why.

Inside Shell, as in other oil companies, top management had long been dominated by a technical caste of petroleum engineers and chemists. Their careers had been built on finding oil, getting it out of the ground, and refining it into useful products. The mundane job of selling these products on to the public had been left to marketing people well down the totem pole. As a result, ideas about branding and marketing were poorly developed within the company, especially compared to consumer-goods firms where brands were seen as vital components of business. As Pinnell said:

'In many fast-moving consumer-goods companies there is an emotional tie between management and the brand. They just believe in the brand at their very core. They believe in it. In a company like Shell, this is not believed at an emotional level. This is a rational company, an engineering and chemical company.'

Institutional neglect of marketing and branding for most of the oil industry's history had few repercussions. Apart from the occasional public relations embarrassment over a tanker spill or a refinery explosion, companies such as Exxon, Mobil and Shell continued to rake in profits as gasoline prices and demand rose inexorably. These conditions held for a century, until the 1990s.

After the Persian Gulf War, a powerful economic expansion took hold in the USA. Oil prices around the world started to fall. A long period of retrenchment seized the industry. Shell, burdened by a cumbersome organization of more than 100,000 employees across 130 countries, struggled to keep pace with rivals on measures of overall profitability. Return on average capital employed, a common profit yardstick, was middling at best at Shell through most of the decade (*see* Fig. 19.1). In 1995 Shell's sluggish ways and chronic brand blindness were to have dire consequences.

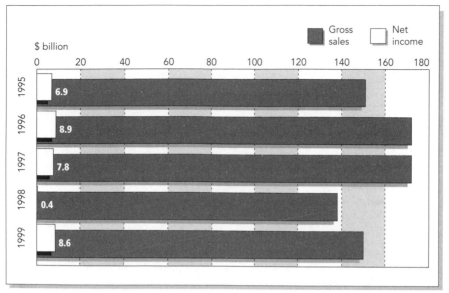

FIGURE 19.1 Shell annual figures

Source: Company reports

FROM NIGERIA TO NORWAY

Shell started drilling for oil in the Niger Delta of West Africa shortly after the Second World War. The heavily populated region, then still under the sway of the British Empire, held a rich reserve of hydrocarbons. The company swiftly became the largest firm working the field and a local power. Throughout the years of independence for Nigeria and a civil war in 1967–9, Shell pumped huge volumes of crude out of the Delta and made substantial profits. But unrest grew among the local Ogoni people as they, like many others in oil-producing regions, grew resentful and envious of Shell's gains.

By the early 1990s a vocal Ogoni opposition movement was openly criticizing Shell's activities. The company was blamed for polluting the Delta and for cozying up to the repressive military regime of General Sani Abacha in power in the capital of Lagos. In the face of press reports linking it closely to Abacha, Shell repeatedly denied any wrongdoing in Nigeria.

The Ogoni opposition movement's best-known leader was Ken Saro-Wiwa, a poet, author and activist who had gained fame across West Africa for his 1985 novel *Sozaboy* about the civil war, and for writing a popular 1980s television soap opera that examined the lawlessness of life in Lagos. In late 1995 Saro-Wiwa was arrested in connection with the murder of four Ogoni chiefs. The trial that followed drew intense international attention and was widely criticized as a sham court. At the end of the proceeding Saro-Wiwa made a statement that included the following passage:

'I and my colleagues are not the only ones on trial. Shell is here on trial, and it is as well that it is represented by counsel said to be holding a watching brief. The company has, indeed, ducked this particular trial, but its day will surely come and the lessons learnt here may prove useful to it, for there is no doubt in my mind that the ecological war that the company has waged in the Delta will be called to question sooner than later, and the crimes of that war be duly punished. The crime of the company's dirty wars against the Ogoni people will also be punished.'[1]

Despite pleas from activist groups and several governments, Saro-Wiwa and eight co-defendants were executed by hanging on 10 November 1995. A storm of controversy followed, with Shell being widely criticized for failing to intervene to save Saro-Wiwa's life. Bills were introduced in the US Congress calling for sanctions against Nigeria. Pressure groups called for boycotts of Shell products. A purge of senior executives at Shell Nigeria followed weeks later, but the Saro-Wiwa affair was only half of Shell's *annus horribilis*.

In the 1970s and 1980s the company was a lead developer of the North Sea oil fields and invested millions of dollars in custom-built marine equipment such as Brent Spar, a floating storage buoy that had been used for 15 years as a tank to hold crude oil pumped from beneath the ocean floor. Shell decommissioned the huge steel hulk in 1991 and announced it planned to sink the facility on to the deep sea-bed of the North Atlantic. Greenpeace, the environmental activist group, opposed the plan and claimed Brent Spar held 5,000 tons of oil that could spill into the ocean. Activists sailed out to Brent Spar and occupied it in 1995, demanding Shell change its plans.

The Greenpeace campaign gained wide support across Europe. Senior figures, including ministers in several EU governments, called for a boycott of Shell products. In Germany, Shell filling stations were fire-bombed and one was raked with gunfire. The European Parliament and several governments condemned Shell's plan, despite having raised no objections during an earlier opportunity to review the plan that the UK and Norway still backed as safe. On 20 June Shell announced it was abandoning the plan to sink the 14,500-ton buoy, citing the shifting of policy goalposts in Europe and concern for the safety of its employees following the German bombings.

Greenpeace later admitted that its estimate of 5,000 tons of oil stored in the buoy was wrong. In fact, Brent Spar contained only about 50 tons of oil. The group was forced to issue a public apology in September, but added that it still opposed dumping of any kind of industrial waste at sea. Shell invited proposals for alternative disposal methods for Brent Spar and hundreds of ideas poured in. It finally decided to cut the buoy into pieces to use as the foundations of a new quay in a Norwegian fjord. The three cut and cleaned sections were placed on the sea floor in July 1999 to be filled with ballast and covered in concrete, bringing an end to the episode.

BACK TO BASIC MARKETING

Shell emerged from the nightmare of 1995 a badly bruised company with a damaged brand name. The mishandling of events in Nigeria and the North Sea had cost it decades of consumer trust and confidence, and had revealed the depth of Shell's failure to comprehend brand value. 'One of the things about Brent Spar was that it just wasn't thought to be important' in upper management, Pinnell said. 'Whether we were right or wrong, the issue was we needed to have dialogue with our customers, who did think it was important. But that idea just wasn't really accepted.'

The company fumbled on for several months, then made changes after 1995 financial results proved disappointing. One of the changes was the hiring of Pinnell. Immediately upon arrival, the consumer goods marketer retained brand consulting firm Interbrand to do a study on the value of the Shell brand. The study showed – in hard data that Shell's technical leadership could grasp – that the brand had been badly damaged and ranked far below the value of comparable world brands, such as Coca-Cola. 'That was a wake-up call. It was actually an insult and persuaded [upper management] to take more care and attention to understand this. So the brand valuation exercise was extremely useful', Pinnell said.

From that point on, Pinnell campaigned within Shell to make the brand a priority. He launched a massive brand-tracking survey programme, one of the largest in the world, that is teaching Shell management some basic marketing lessons. The survey involved 22,000 consumer interviews in 1999 using a questionnaire and assistance from a research firm (*see* Fig. 19.2). Some results surprised the company. One finding was that physical location, while important for a filling station, is a less crucial driver of consumer preference than other factors, such as clean toilets, good coffee and smiling cashiers.

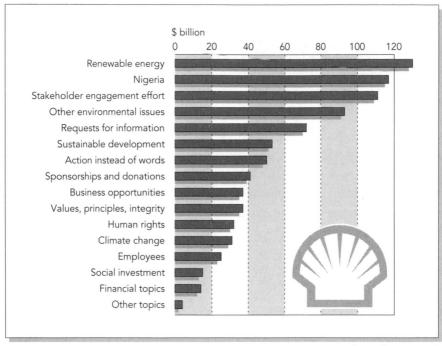

FIGURE 19.2 Responses by topic to 'Tell Shell' public communication programme, 1999

While such insights may seem obvious to some companies more experienced with consumer research, they were eye-openers for Shell. 'We haven't yet adopted a full understanding of what marketing can really do ... There are basic marketing questions that this industry hasn't really approached', Pinnell said.

The survey also found that Shell's target market, typical for oil companies, was male, middle-aged and middle-class. As Pinnell said:

'It is very similar to the profile of drivers in general ... Now this may sound, again, simple. But it's terribly important for the business because otherwise you get all sorts of intelligent people thinking about who they'd like our market to be ... The fact is these consumers are men in suits, these are reps on the road and let's understand that.'

Twenty-three per cent of the customers who drive into Shell's forecourt give the company 77 per cent of its business, Pinnell's research showed. 'These may be basic pieces of information', he said, but he added that they were largely unknown to Shell until very recently.

To begin developing a more complete brand image for Shell, Pinnell instituted more brand consistency and started a globally standardized campaign to enhance the brand's image, striving to promote secondary associations of prowess in technical innovation and caring. The innovation message leaned heavily on a relationship with the Ferrari racing team, while the caring angle emphasized customer relations over gushy corporate image ads, Pinnell said.

OUT FROM BEHIND THE CURTAIN

Another change that followed the débâcle of 1995 was the adoption by Shell of an innovative policy of 'constructive engagement', or holding an open dialogue with its critics, as well as a renewed drive to look beyond its core hydrocarbons business towards alternative energy sources.

Shell adopted nine business principles expressing its responsibilities to shareholders, customers, employees, business partners and society at large, and committing itself to sustainable development, business integrity, employee political rights, and other basic principles. New social and environmental initiatives were tackled, including an assistance programme for young entrepreneurs called LiveWIRE, a sustainable energy research grants programme, and an aggressive push against doing business with firms that use child labour in Brazil and elsewhere.

In Nigeria the company spent $50 million on community development projects, although violence in the Niger Delta continued in 1999. Strict conservation techniques were followed in the construction of the controversial Cuibaba gas pipeline in South America. Finally, and perhaps most significantly, a $500-million renewable energy research programme was launched with mixed results. Shell was building wind power turbines, working on wood fuel alternatives and manufacturing photovoltaic panels for solar power. 'My colleagues and I are totally committed to a business strategy that generates profits while contributing to the well-being of the planet and its people. We see no alternative', said Mark Moody-Stuart, Shell chairman, in a recent company promotional booklet.[2]

Few of Shell's promises or projects appear to be revolutionary. But the debate that has accompanied them in official company material has been ground-breaking, so much so that Shell has come in for criticism in the oil-industry for letting the programme go too far. Still, it is carrying on with it. 'We may not like what these people have to say, but we've got to hear it', Pinnell said.

> **❝We may not like what these people have to say, but we've got to hear it. ❞**

Shell is publishing reports and posting items on its internet web site that address head-on some of the issues about human rights and the environment that have dogged it since 1995. The pieces contain some scathing comments from opponents. An early 2000 report called *How Do We Stand*, part of a People, Planet and Profits programme, contained the following unattributed statement: 'I'm sorry, but if you expect any self-respecting activist to believe a word you say about your commitment to human rights, then you are as arrogant as the PR firm that came up with the strategy'. Another critic was quoted in the report saying: 'Every facet of the industry from exploration to consumption is at odds with environmental conservation. Is that fact lost to you people? I think not.'

The programme has also elicited praise, often of the cautious sort reflected in another comment: 'Are you being truthful? Are you different? Time will tell by the actions you take. If you are sincere, I applaud your efforts and wish you the best of luck.'

A typical attitude towards the Shell brand was expressed by Marieke van der Werf, the Dutch co-founder of the communications agency New Moon. She said Shell should be in a position to lead the world into better transportation and energy use:

'But it's terribly difficult for a company like that to adapt … If these companies were to pay more attention to their social responsibility, they would have my loyalty. But they have to understand what kind of responsibility is involved, and they have to act quickly before they lose me, and others like me, forever.'[3]

Shell's efforts, both internal and external, to repair the damage done to its brand by 1995 are having measurably favourable results. But the company has some way to go, Pinnell said, in convincing itself and consumers of its high principles. 'After all, we are our actions, aren't we?' he said.

NOTES

1 Remarks sourced from Greenpeace website, www.greenpeace.org, and widely available.

2 Mark Moody-Stuart, 'Message from the Chairman', in *How Do We Stand*: *People, Planet and Profits*, London: Dutch/Shell Group, 2000, p. 2.

3 Rita Clifton and Esther Maughan (eds), *The Future of Brands*: *Twwnty-five Visions*, London: Macmillan, 2000, p. 20.

20

PUSHING THE LIMITS:
DISNEY AND THE MEGA-BRAND

'A brand is a living entity, and it is enriched or undermined cumulatively over time, the product of a thousand small gestures'

Michael Eisner, CEO, Walt Disney Co.

THE FINAL SCENE OF *Who Framed Roger Rabbit* flickered to black, the lights in the screening room came up and Michael Eisner, chairman of Walt Disney Co., announced: 'It's a Touchstone movie'. Roy Disney, nephew of the founder and head of the animated films business, said, 'I agree'.[1]

That sealed it – the innovative, sexy and occasionally vulgar *Roger Rabbit* would be released under the label of Disney Co.'s adult *alter ego* Touchstone Pictures to shield the family-oriented Disney brand, even though *Rabbit* was a Disney project with the might of the Disney marketing machine behind it.

That moment in the screening room in 1988 was just one of thousands of branding judgement calls made along Disney's 16-year journey under Eisner's leadership to unparalleled economic success and unaccustomed controversy. Since 1984, when the hard-driving New Yorker took over, Disney has transcended brand boundaries to become a colossus of entertainment and media. No other brand in the world today can match it for size and versatility across a cartoon rainbow of brand categories.

Movies, music, cruise ships, sports teams, theme parks, radio, television, books, games, hotels, clothes, toys, land, Broadway shows, internet sites – all these goods and services reside in the house the Mouse built. The Disney brand's value was pegged by consulting firm Interbrand in 2000 at $33.5 billion, eighth worldwide behind only Coca-Cola, Microsoft, IBM, Intel, Nokia, General Electric and Ford.[2]

Yet success for Disney has come at the price of controversy. Eisner has pushed to the limits the brand and the tolerance of consumers who know it through Mickey Mouse, Snow White, family vacations to the theme parks and the endearing founder, Uncle Walt. Besides *Roger Rabbit*, Eisner tested the limits of the brand's image by clearing production of *Down and Out in Beverley Hills*, the first over-18 only rated film by a Disney-owned unit; buying Miramax Films, producers of the ultra-violent *Pulp Fiction*; jacking up ticket prices at the parks and encountering big problems with Disneyland Paris and the failed Disney's America project in Virginia. Between 1984 and 2000, he personally hauled in an estimated $680 million in pay, bonuses and stock gains, while paying friends and colleagues hundreds of millions more.[3]

Eisner's Disney has deviated sharply from the wholesome, family-friendly, regular-folks image developed by his predecessors, Walt and brother Roy Disney. As a result Eisner has earned the scorn of critics as varied as rival movie moguls and thrifty shareholder activists to conservative Southern Baptists, Civil War historians and Caribbean labour organizers.

However, he has won the admiration and applause of investors and others who see his reign over the Magic Kingdom as a triumph. Under his leadership Disney returned from steep decline in the 1970s to renewed vitality. It revolutionized the home video industry and revived a great animated features tradition with beloved classics such as *The Lion King* and *The Little Mermaid*, while also backing award-winning live-action films such as *The English Patient* and *Shakespeare in Love*. Eisner's Disney has made many people, including Eisner, very rich. That is the ultimate goal of brands and of show business. After all, as Woody Allen once said, 'If show business weren't a business, it would have been called "show show".'

> 66 The story of Disney is replete with branding lessons. 99

The story of Disney is replete with branding lessons. Before Eisner's arrival, it was a case study in the danger of letting a brand stand so still that it fossilizes. After Eisner took over, Disney showed how finding ways to expand

and elaborate a venerable brand without alienating some consumers is next to impossible. The talent that Eisner has displayed over the years, and from which others can learn, is in maximizing the value of the brand by striving to balance preservation of its heritage against the imperative to keep growing and exploring new markets. Most of the time he has managed this adroitly; occasionally he has stumbled.

'Disney is different', said Eisner in an interview that ranged from his views on brand building and the limits of market research, to the irascibility of Donald Duck. 'We're not Alka-Seltzer, you know', he said. 'We just have to try to continue to make product – movies, television shows, with these characters. That's the most important thing to do.'

Eisner, whose formal business education consisted of a single course in accounting, was largely dismissive of grand theories about brands and brand management. In the interview, he returned again and again to the concept of enhancing the brand by focusing on product:

'I figure if I like it and it goes to my bright side, rather than my dark side, then it's probably okay for Disney. I am actually the brand manager of the Disney brand. I do adjudicate all conflict as it relates to whether we should do something or not. I am really the one who's the final editor of what we can do and what we can't do. To that extent, I'm very conscious of the brand.

'But, do I spend my time ensuring that the brand is strong, or do I spend my time trying to create entertainment? When I sit down in Phantasmic at Disneyland … or on Main Street in Disneyland Paris, or at the opening of *Tarzan* or *Dinosaur*, I say to myself, this is what makes our brand great.

'What I don't want is for Disney to be a museum, an archive of the way great family programmes used to be. That's what it was from the time Walt died for 10 or 20 years. I'd rather take some risks and create a symphony that may be great or may not be great, create another event, build a park in Hong Kong, do things that are first-rate. Then the brand's enhanced. The fact of the matter is, having made *Beauty and the Beast* and *Aladdin* and *Mulan* and on and on, that is what has made our brand stronger than ever.'

UNCLE WALT

Walter Elias Disney was born in Chicago in 1901. He studied art, shipped out with the ambulance corps in the First World War, then launched a commercial art career in Kansas City. By the early 1920s he was making short animated films called Laugh-O-Grams, with older brother Roy as his business manager.

Laugh-O-Grams ended in bankruptcy after Roy moved to California. Walt followed him out to Hollywood and together they set up a new shop. They put food on the table for a few years thanks to a contract for a series of simple, silent cartoons known as the Alice Comedies. After 56 productions, Alice lost her market appeal, forcing Disney Brothers Studio to develop a new lead character, Oswald the Lucky Rabbit. He was also a modest commercial success, but the Disneys were out-foxed by their distributor and lost the rights to Oswald at a fateful meeting in New York.

Immediately afterwards, on the long and depressing train journey back to Hollywood, Walt thought up Mickey Mouse. Some historians contend others had a hand in Mickey's creation. Whatever the case, the lovable rodent made his debut in 1928 in *Steamboat Willie* – a history-making cartoon that merged movement and sound for the first time. Mickey mania exploded across America and the Disneys for the first time showed a talent for cross-branding.

Before *Steamboat* opened, the brothers trademarked their main character. After the debut, they moved swiftly to extend the brand. They took a flat fee of $300 for the licence to put Mickey on writing pads, their first merchandising deal. Throughout the 1930s Mickey appeared in more cartoons, as well as comic strips and books. Breakfast cereals maker General Foods paid $1.5 million for the rights to put Mickey on boxes of Post Toasties, making him the first licensed character on a cereal box. Goodyear Tire & Rubber Co. made a 50-foot high Mickey balloon to lead the Macy's Thanksgiving Day parade. The Disneys hired a full-time merchandising manager. The first Mickey Mouse watch was sold, followed by toy trains and ice-cream cone wrappers. By the late 1930s the Disneys were in branding in a big way.

Another landmark came in 1937 with the release of Walt's dream project – *Snow White and the Seven Dwarfs*, the world's first full-length animated feature film. It was a box-office smash and again the Disneys showed themselves to be ground-breaking brand managers by orchestrating a masterfully comprehensive merchandise campaign in tandem with the movie. Royalties on toy models for the dwarf Dopey alone reputedly brought in more than $100,000.

Pinocchio and *Fantasia* followed in 1940. During the Second World War, *Dumbo* and *Bambi* appeared, along with another innovative brand extension – an RCA Victor record album of the songs from *Snow White*, the first soundtrack album from a feature film. *Cinderella* appeared in 1950, which was also the year of the first Disney TV special, *One Hour in Wonderland*. Shown on NBC and sponsored by Coca-Cola, it was watched by 20 million viewers and opened the doors to a long and profitable life on the small screen for the Disney brand and its characters. In 1954 Disney deepened its involvement in television and branched into theme parks. The company made a deal with the TV network ABC, allowing it to show Disney films weekly in exchange for financing assistance to develop an amusement park in Anaheim, California. In the following year Disneyland opened at a cost of $17 million. In less than two months 1 million people had visited. Disney stretched the brand further that year with *The Mickey Mouse Club*, a daily ABC TV series with cartoons and child-actor hosts, the Mouseketeers.

Sleeping Beauty, *101 Dalmatians*, *Mary Poppins* and *The Jungle Book* appeared in the late 1950s and 1960s. But as plans were being laid for a second theme park in central Florida, Walt died of lung cancer in 1966 at age 65. His brother Roy took over as chairman for five years, overseeing production of films such as *The Love Bug* and *The Aristocats*, as well as the opening of Disney World near Orlando in 1971. When Roy died in that year, it was the end of act one of the Disney story. The first 50 years had been driven by the unique pairing of Walt's relentless creativity with Roy's business acumen for exploiting the wonderful brand identities generated by his brother. Act two was to be very different.

BARBARIANS AT WONDERLAND'S GATE

After the deaths of the Disney brothers, the company they founded began to lose its way. The twin dynamic of Walt's creative flair and Roy's practicality collapsed. In its place emerged a stalemate between two warring corporate camps – the 'Walt men' in production and the 'Roy men' in administration. From 1971 until 1976 Disney released only one full-length animated feature, the mediocre *Robin Hood*, and just a handful of shorts and forgettable live-action films. In 1977 several top animators resigned, complaining that Disney had lost Walt's spirit. The studio slid into Hollywood's minor leagues. Disney managers were stifled by debate over the ever-present question – 'What would Walt have done?'

> 66 Disney managers were stifled by debate over the ever-present question – 'What would Walt have done?' 99

Kim Masters, in her book *Keys to the Kingdom: How Michael Eisner Lost His Grip*, observed that in the 1970s, 'Disney was a quirky place that shunned innovation. Its managers seemed to be so conscious of the value of the Disney brand name that they actually were afraid to exploit it.'[4]

The theme parks continued to operate and Epcot Center opened in Florida. But attendance and profits waned. Ron Miller, son-in-law of Walt and company president, started the Touchstone Pictures venture. Tokyo Disneyland opened with mixed success. The cable-TV Disney Channel began operating, but Disney unwisely withdrew from network TV, thinking that it would compete with the Disney Channel. Boardroom bickering worsened in the early 1980s and the Disney stock price slumped.

Throughout this period, on the other side of the country in New York City, Eisner had been building a career in show business. Son of a well-to-do Manhattan family, he spent boyhood weekends on an estate in Westchester County and attended exclusive private schools. He graduated from Denison University, a liberal arts college in Ohio, with an English degree and no particularly clear ambitions. After landing a job as a clerk at NBC, he was hired at rival ABC as a junior TV programmer. His first big production was a special called *Feelin' Groovy at Marine World* featuring a water-skiing elephant and Bing Crosby. Over the years he gained a reputation for spotting commercially saleable projects. Working with Barry Diller at ABC, he was involved in TV hits such as *Happy Days* and *Laverne and Shirley*.

Eisner and Diller moved to Paramount Pictures in 1976. There they formed the nucleus of a high-powered team of executives who turned around the movie studio with a string of successes including *Saturday Night Fever, Grease, The Elephant Man, Raiders of the Lost Ark* and *Beverly Hills Cop*. By 1983, just as Disney was reaching the bottom of a long downhill slide, Eisner was coming into his own as a hot Hollywood property. The two would be brought together by the unlikely figure of Roy E. Disney, son of co-founder Roy O. Disney and nephew of Walt.[5]

Throughout 1983 and 1984 Disney's stock price fell precipitously as talk spread that the company was in deep trouble. Frustrated with management, Roy E. resigned from the Disney board of directors. His secret plan was to disentangle himself from the business so that he could buy more Disney stock and increase his holdings, then move to reassert Disney family control over the listless company. Rumours of his intentions leaked out and soon the takeover sharks of 1980s Wall Street were circling.

In April 1984 feared corporate raider Saul Steinberg revealed he was building an equity stake in Disney. The stunned Disney board, fearful of a hostile takeover and break-up sale, agreed to buy off Steinberg with a greenmail payment of $328 million. He went away, but the show of weakness only attracted more trouble. Soon another hostile takeover threat surfaced in the person of financier Irwin Jacobs. Alarmed yet again and unable to pay another ransom, the board turned to Roy E. for help. The heir to the Disney family's mantle of leadership managed to force out Disney's top executives.

Then, after weeks of tense manoeuvring and negotiation, he brought aboard Eisner as chairman and CEO, along with Frank Wells, another studio executive, as president and chief operating officer. The two asserted quick and firm control over the company, which was by then in considerable disarray. More than 1,000 employees were quickly let go. The takeover threat receded and Eisner and Wells promptly took Disney in new directions that effectively transformed it from a family business into a modern corporation, with all that that entailed.

MAGIC KINGDOM INC.

A father and occasional visitor to Disneyland, Eisner certainly had a feel for the Disney brand and its image when he took charge of it, even if he had no experience in brand management as such. In his autobiography he wrote:

'I'd never heard anyone talk much about "the brand" before Frank [Wells] and I arrived at Disney. To me, a brand was a marking that you put on horses and cattle. Brand management sounded very austere and serious – something that people did at Procter & Gamble, perhaps, but not in a creative business ... But Disney was different. The name plainly stood for something.'

Eisner was also well aware that the Disney brand badly needed an injection of new life:

'The name "Disney" promised a certain kind of experience: wholesome family fun appropriate for kids of any ages, a high level of excellence in its products, and a predictable set of values. By the time Frank and I took over, nearly two decades after Walt's death, Disney had begun to seem awkward, old-fashioned, even a bit directionless ... Our job wasn't to create something new, but to bring back the magic, to dress Disney up in more stylish clothes and expand its reach.'[6]

The new management duo, assisted by the younger Jeffrey Katzenberg, started their reign over the Magic Kingdom with a run of hugely success- ful, adult-oriented live-action films like none Disney had ever seen. Hits like *Down and Out in Beverly Hills*, *Three Men and a Baby*, *Good Morning Vietnam*, *Dead Poets Society* and *Pretty Woman* made Disney a Hollywood force again by involving major stars and showing Disney could succeed at the box office, but they risked changing perceptions of the Disney brand. According to Eisner:

'By producing projects like *Down and Out in Beverly Hills*, we also ran the risk of alienating our core audience. It wasn't easy sitting next to Patty [Roy E.'s wife] and Roy Disney during the first public screening ... after each increasingly vivid expletive, I felt a drop or two of sweat forming somewhere.'

But, he added, the movie was a success and 'prompted no backlash'.[7]

The core Disney brand was seen by the company as unharmed because the new films were purposely released under the Touchstone Pictures label as a way of protecting the parent Disney brand from controversy. The same approach was followed with a new unit called Hollywood Pictures and with the acquisition of Miramax, the independent studio responsible for risky films such as *Pulp Fiction*, *The Crying Game* and *sex, lies and videotape*, as well as *The English Patient* and *Shakespeare in Love*.

Disney's film branding tactic was grounded in a belief that consumers would not connect its *alter-ego* studio brands with the parent brand, as cited by the business commentator Kapferer:

'A multi-brand policy is necessary to protect the main brand image. This partly explains why the Disney Corporation uses a number of brands in film production, for example Buena Vista and Touchstone. This enables them to produce films of every type without endangering the revered Disney name.'[8]

Addressing this topic, Eisner remarked:

'We've had voices that criticize us for various things that aren't done in the Disney brand, but that may be done in some other part of the company. There are a lot of things written in the business press about Disney. You would think that would start to tarnish the brand possibly, but the fact of the matter is that the people who read the business press, and the people who might read a specific complaint about an ABC television programme or whatever, don't really have a conscious separation between ABC or Touchstone Pictures or Hyperion Books or Miramax Films and Disney. By and large, when people think of Disney around the world, they think of the theme parks, they think of the animated movies, they think of Mickey Mouse or Winnie the Pooh or whatever.

'Our research shows that 99 per cent of the world didn't even know that we owned anything other than Disney until we bought ABC [in 1995]. That was such a public moment that I think the knowledge of our multiple ownership of things is probably up. Maybe now 90 per cent think we only own Disney. That's a guess. That wouldn't be true in New York and London and Los Angeles. But it is true everywhere else.'

Regardless of whether or not consumers knew who was backing them, 27 of Disney's first 33 live-action films under new management were profitable. More than six earned profits exceeding $50 million, according to Eisner. Moreover, a year after being bought by Disney, Miramax's profits were up tenfold.

Assured by their success in live-action, Eisner, Wells and Katzenberg moved to bolster the core brand by bringing renewed life and energy to Disney's animation studios. After the off-beat Touchstone release *Roger Rabbit*, the animation shops cranked out a run of smash cartoon feature films that brought children and parents back to Disney by the millions, including *The Little Mermaid, Beauty and the Beast, Aladdin, The Lion King, Pocahontas, Toy Story, A Bug's Life, Mulan, Tarzan* and *Hercules*.

These movies were positioned as the hubs of massive cross-branding campaigns that eclipsed all prior Disney merchandising efforts. Pre-release anticipation of the new films was fed by media previews and advertising. Debuts became press spectacles. Cross-market revenues were gathered with sales of toys, books, magazines, records, clothes, accessories, video tapes, fast-food packages and other items. Under Eisner and Wells, Disney and its characters became a cartoon-branding juggernaut.

> **❝Under Eisner and Wells, Disney and its characters became a cartoon-branding juggernaut. ❞**

The rebirth of animation was accompanied by a Disney-led revolution in home video. Where the tape industry had been focused on selling a few tapes at high prices to middle-men for rental to consumers, Disney began selling tapes of its old animated classics directly to consumers at cheaper prices through mass merchants. The strategy was to plunder Disney's vast film library to tap a previously unrecognized market of children who would watch the movies over and over. Videos became an enormous Disney profit centre.

Eisner and Wells put Disney back on network TV and steered it into publishing with Hyperion Books, music with Hollywood Records and professional sports with hockey's Mighty Ducks. At the same time, they moved Disney into retailing by opening the first Disney Store in 1987. It was followed by hundreds more worldwide as the branding and merchandising effort shifted into high gear.

TOO MUCH OF A GOOD THING

By the late 1980s the Disney brand was everywhere, from the shelves of discount merchandisers and video shops to the counters of fast-food restaurants and convenience stores. In his autobiography, Eisner wrote, 'If the company was in danger of being dismissed as irrelevant when we arrived, now we faced the opposite risk. Overexposure was threatening to dilute the integrity of the brand.'[9]

In response, the company launched its first brand inventory and consumer research studies. 'The results of the brand inventory were a revelation to senior management', reported Dartmouth College's Keller. The inventory study showed 'Disney characters were on so many products and marketed in so many ways that it was difficult to understand how or why many of the decisions had been made', while the consumer study uncovered perceptions that the Disney brand was being over-exploited.[10]

As a result, Disney set up a brand equity team to improve management of the brand, especially by focusing on the licensing programme, which was restructured to give Disney greater control. A brand caretaker was appointed reporting directly to Wells and Eisner and charged with ensuring that no business activities undermined public faith in Disney. In addition, Disney restructured its merchandising programmes into broad brand lines targeted at specific age groups and distribution channels. To support further the core brand, the Disney Channel was improved and Eisner and Wells moved some of the more successful animated features on to the live stage, starting with *Beauty and the Beast*.

The theme parks were reinvigorated with new attractions and higher ticket prices. Disney-MGM Studios, the Grand Floridian and other Disney hotels opened. The Euro Disney Resort in France, later renamed Disneyland Paris, opened to huge financial losses, but eventually recovered. A proposal to build a theme park called Disney's America in northern Virginia was withdrawn in 1994 in the face of embarrassing opposition from historians and local activists. But it stood out as one of few major setbacks. Even as Eisner and Wells pushed Disney into new territory, they discovered the brand had limits.

We've never gone so far that we've been in trouble', said Eisner, but Disney often has had to say no. Eisner recalled:

'Once somebody came to us with the idea of having Mickey involved with insurance to guarantee children's college education. Our research showed that that was not really a good use of the brand.

'Once I went to General Motors to try to convince them to make a safe car, a car that a parent would buy their kid … They were kind of interested in that and we did some research. But the audience did not want us involved with Disney-branded automobiles because of the obvious implication of accidents.

'Once we had a company that distributed the California state lottery on our television system and we got a lot of flak for being within a hundred yards of gambling and gaming, which we hardly were … We've made movies that are PG [parental guidance suggested], but we've never gone further than that under the Disney brand. We make these decisions every day. But, by and large, when we do projects like *Lion King* or *Dinosaur*, or *Aladdin* or Disneyland Paris or Walt Disney World or whatever, we tend to enhance the brand.'

MONEY MOUSE

After ten years of working with Eisner to re-establish Disney as one of the world's most dynamic and highly valued companies, Frank Wells died in a helicopter accident while on a skiing trip in Nevada in 1994, setting off events that would usher in a difficult period of uncertainty. Eisner was stunned by the death of Wells, a larger-than-life character who commanded great esteem and affection in Hollywood.

The hunt for a replacement initially centred on Katzenberg, head of Disney's resurgent movie studios. But some board members had reservations about him, as did Eisner, who eventually told Katzenberg he would not get the job. Katzenberg resigned to form a new company, DreamWorks SKG, with media moguls Steven Spielberg and David Geffen. He also sued Disney for $250 million in bonus money he claimed was owed to him for helping to make dozens of films. The case was settled out of court.

In the midst of this troubling episode Eisner underwent emergency quadruple-bypass heart surgery at the age of 52. He recovered quickly, but questions about Disney's managerial succession plan grew urgent, especially after Eisner was forced to pull the plug on the proposed Disney's America theme park project in northern Virginia.

Disney made headlines again in 1995 when it purchased Capital Cities/ABC for $19 billion, a steep price that some on Wall Street questioned while applauding the strategic sense of the combination. More than ever after the massive deal – which made Disney one of the world's largest corporations – the succession question was at the fore.

In mid-1995 Eisner finally announced his new partner in the head office would be Michael Ovitz, founder of the CAA talent agency and the consummate Hollywood insider. The selection was greeted enthusiastically in the media and on Wall Street, despite some worries about Ovitz's lack of experience in working in a large company. 'The two Michaels', as a watchful press tagged them, clashed right away. Within a year Ovitz was gone. To add to the big-bucks controversy surrounding Disney, Ovitz took a $100 million golden parachute with him, despite having contributed next to nothing to the company. Speculation flared again about succession, but was subsequently quietened by the appointment of the capable and respected Robert Iger, a veteran ABC executive brought in by the merger, as president and COO.

The Ovitz affair, however, put the fortunes of Disney executives under growing scrutiny, as did Eisner's own pay history. Eisner first made headlines for his extravagant compensation in 1988, when he ranked as the highest-paid US CEO with a pay packet of $40.1 million. From 1994 to 1998, he often topped the CEO pay list, raking in a total of $631 million over the five-year period, plus an estimated $50.7 million in 1999, reported *Forbes* magazine. Asked whether his pay and that of other executives had sullied the brand, Eisner said his success and compensation had created 'envy and jealousy and things like that'. He added:

'This stuff gets written about and, yes, I think some of the public that reads the entertainment press … has a different view of me than they do now of Uncle Walt. I don't know what Walt's image was when he was alive and kicking, but I think it wasn't all "Uncle Walt". Do I wish that the public was only interested in the products, rather than the people who make the products? Yes. But they aren't.'

Interest in Disney's financial results also increased after reported net income fell and revenues inched ahead only 2 per cent in 1998 and 1999 (*see* Fig. 20.1). In the first nine months of the fiscal year 2000, however, results improved sharply. Revenues rose 9 per cent to $19 billion; net income 27 per cent to $1.5 billion.

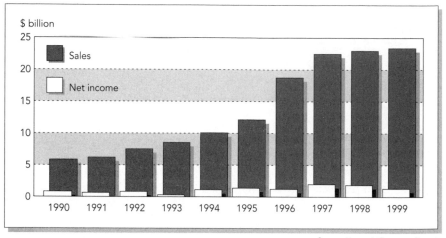

Source: Hoover's Company Reports

FIGURE 20.1 Disney annual figures

HAITIAN WAGES AND GAY DAYS

The new Disney as fashioned by Eisner and associates is a cultural force so powerful that even Walt, never short on imagination, would have trouble recognizing it. In moving beyond the founder's vision into markets he never approached, Disney has come in for its share of criticism. Like many large brand owners, Disney in recent years has been targeted by politicians and a new class of web-savvy activists intent on promoting various social, environmental and religious causes.

A group called the National Labour Committee, for instance, in the name of wage equality for workers in developing nations, produced a video called *Mickey Mouse Goes to Haiti* about poverty among Haitian workers said to be exploited in plants manufacturing Disney clothes for sale in the USA. Disney said every accusation in the video was wrong and that standards at its former Haitian facilities were monitored carefully. The company added that none of its licensees uses Haitian facilities anymore.

On the other end of the ideological spectrum, the Southern Baptist Convention, a US fundamentalist Protestant sect, called for a boycott of Disney, charging that it supported homosexuality by holding Gay Days at its parks, and that its movies spread anti-family and anti-Christian messages. Disney said the issue has died down and that the company recently met with Southern Baptist leaders.

Disney did not help itself on the public relations front when it took a hard line on its trademark rights and told a tiny Florida day-care centre to paint over Disney characters on its outside walls. The company said it wanted to ensure that the centre did not appear to be endorsed by The Walt Disney Co.

Despite the company's confidence that its core brand was safe inside a ring-fence of *alter-ego* brands, US vice-presidential candidate Senator Joseph Lieberman in August 2000 lashed out at Hollywood in general, and Disney in particular, for programming that he said 'hurts our country and our kids'. A long-time critic of Hollywood, the Democrat said on a television show broadcast by Disney-owned ABC: 'Look, I love the movies. I love music. But there is still too much violence, too much sex, too much incivility in entertainment, which makes it very difficult for parents, who are working so hard to give their kids values and discipline, to do so.' In 1999 Lieberman and others in Washington made a dramatic 'Appeal to Hollywood' armed with a petition urging executives – including Eisner, Time Warner CEO Gerald Levin and News Corp. CEO Rupert Murdoch – to change the 'toxic culture of violence and vulgarity surrounding our children'.

Asked about Disney's struggles with negative publicity since he took over and whether it has had any impact on the brand, Eisner said, 'All of our research shows that the brand is stronger than ever ... Even with some of the hiccups that we may have had, the brand has become stronger.'

Disney regularly does surveys of consumer attitudes towards the brand, 'but I'm not sure that any of it means anything', Eisner added dismissively. Throughout the interview, he returned over and over again to the theme of building the brand by focusing on product and quality. He stressed that he personally, as head manager of Disney's brand and characters, spends little time examining and evaluating the brand as such. 'Maybe we should, maybe we should sit around and just agonize endlessly over which way Pluto should bark. We'd probably ruin it that way though', he said.

He and senior staff do not evaluate ideas based on any sort of brand building system, he said, suggesting that it is more a gut-feel process.

> **"It's what you do that makes your brand stronger, not sitting around and talking. "**

'People try to say, well we should do this project because it will work well in Italy or something. I mean, forget it! I want to know whether I like it. It's that simple. It's just about doing great things ... It's what you do that makes your brand stronger, not sitting around and talking about, should we put commercials on Sunday morning in the US that talk about the number of scholarships we give out. We do give out a lot of scholarships, but that's not what we're about.'

More important, he said, is developing products that enhance, and sometimes reinterpret, the Disney brand personality and the personalities of the characters around it. He said:

'There are people surveying their brains out here. But I would rather sit in a room and try to figure out what we're going to do with the next *Fantasia*. I think the *Fantasia* we just put out, *Fantasia 2000*, with Donald on Noah's Ark, has more brand enhancement for Donald and Daisy than any 40 things you could find out in research.'

Defying a general trend in industry towards more quantitative brand research, Eisner said Disney does not calculate financial values for its various character/brands or other brands under its control. Nor has it calculated a value for its corporate brand 'because it's not for sale'. He said he does not view the Disney brand as over-extended, despite renewed efforts in early 2000 in the merchandising business to slash the numbers of licensees and gain greater control over Disney goods. He explained:

'I don't feel that our brand is over-extended. I think if you do things well and high-quality, the audience, the consumer, the customer loves it and respects it. The only time that there's a problem is if you do something in an inferior way. So it really doesn't relate to volume, it relates to quality.

'Our brand relates to how good an animated movie is, how good a live-action movie is, how good a theme-park ride is, how good a T-shirt or a sweatshirt is. Some of it's licensed; some of it's produced solely by ourselves; some of it's on television; some of it's in theatres; some of it's on Broadway or the West End. Every single piece that has the Disney brand, whether it's a piece of stationery or *Lion King* in London, has to be excellent. As long as it's excellent, it enhances the brand.

'The problem is when it fails in that area. Often it fails in that area because a licensee may not do a good job or we haven't watched him carefully enough, where it's out of sight, out of mind. It's usually that area that hurts because the big projects we can keep a pretty good eye on. But you may have a Disney store where there's a rude cast member or a piece of bad merchandise.'

PERFORMER BRANDS

Crucial to understanding the brand approach at Disney is getting a feel for how the company manages the Disney characters, each a unique hybrid of sub-brand and almost human personality. If more brand managers thought of their brands the way Eisner thinks of Mickey or Pluto or Donald Duck, brands would certainly be more interesting, and would arguably be more effective as marketing tools.

Eisner said he looks at the Disney stable of characters as a brand portfolio and as a cast of performers:

'First of all they're characters and we talk about them as though they're living, breathing characters who could be in the next room … Like Buzz Lightyear, he has a father in [*Toy Story* director] John Lasseter, who treats Woody and Buzz as though they were his children. He knows what his children should be doing. It's pretty funny when you talk to people like that. Certainly the characters in the *Lion King* are alive and real to us. When you get to some of the characters where the people who designed them are not still around, then you're interpreting what they should do and they become more of characters that are also brands.

'But I think of brands in the way that a celebrity is a brand. Michael Jordan is a brand, and probably thinks twice before he does everything he does. Maybe he doesn't, but still he's a brand. We have Disney brand management for the whole company. We don't really have, like, Pluto's brand manager who walks around with a leash. You have to reinvent these characters. You have to bring new vitality, new creativity, sometimes even slightly more modern design. Mickey has been redesigned 20 times over 75 years. Mickey changes. Mickey was the positive, upside of the personality of Walt. We try to have Mickey continue to be not such a goody-goody. If he gets too nasty, then that's not good either. You know, this is not brain surgery. It's instinct, common sense, things like that.'

NOTES

1 The screening room decision is described by journalist Kim Masters in her book *The Keys to the Kingdom: How Michael Eisner Lost His Grip*, New York: HarperCollins, 2000 p. 227.

2 Interbrand, *The World's Most Valuable Brands Survey*, 18 July 2000.

3 Eisner's pay history is well documented in numerous sources, including *Forbes*, 1 July 2000.

4 Masters, *The Keys to the Kingdom*, p. 139.

5 Eisner's career is entertainingly documented in his autobiography, Michael Eisner with Tony Schwartz, *Work in Progress*, New York: Penguin Books, 1998.

6 Eisner and Schwartz, *Work in Progress*, pp. 234–5.

7 Eisner and Schwartz, *Work in Progress*, p. 157.

8 Jean-Noël Kapferer, *Strategic Brand Management: Creating and Sustaining Brand Equity Long Term*, London: Kogan Page, 1997, p. 283.

9 Eisner and Schwartz, *Work in Progress*, p. 239.

10 Kevin Lane Keller, *Strategic Brand Management: Building, Measuring and Managing Brand Equity*, Upper Saddle River, New Jersey: Prentice Hall, 1998, pp. 375–6.

BRANDING FOR HUMANITY

'A brand has to feel like a friend'

Howard Schultz, CEO, Starbucks

AT THE BEGINNING OF *BRANDS IN THE BALANCE* I wrote about my frustration at arriving in southern Spain and discovering a landscape dotted with billboards for all-too-familiar brands. But on that same trip, after two weeks of enjoying the local cuisine, we all gobbled up some McDonald's burgers on the way to the airport.

They tasted just like McDonald's burgers in Chicago or London or Rome. I knew my family would be safe eating them. I knew roughly what they would cost. I knew we would be able to consume them quickly. I knew the restaurant would be plastic and characterless, but also clean and orderly – just the thing we needed on the mad dash to catch our flight.

Brands can work. By offering certainty in a chaotic world they can help people get through their daily lives. In the process they also play a key role in fuelling the engines of economic prosperity by connecting business with consumers in a rich mutual interchange of market information. Yet, as we have seen, there is a growing sense in the marketing field that brands have become much more than this – more than simple conduits of pricing data, product and service characteristics and consumption rates.

Commercial identities in the post-industrial age transmit whole tapestries of impression and experience to individuals who come in contact with them, focusing in a single symbol or word or sound a sea of feeling and opinion. Based on advertising, news, casual conversation, mood, chance encounters or deliberate study, consumers make judgements, not just on the goods and services represented by brands, but on the firms that own them, the people who manage them, their motives, decisions, actions and origins.

To succeed in a marketplace awash in information and perception, marketing managers are increasingly looking for ways to make brands transcend their history as symbolic proxies for goods and services. Brands are being called upon to convey to consumers some sense of their owners' values and responsibilities, their commitment to community, to the environment, to employees, to society at large.

Expanding the scope of the brand in the marketplace has also meant raising its profile within the company. From financial valuation and trademark defence to organizational structures and CEO involvement, brands are at the forefront of discussion in corporate management and strategy. Companies are transforming their brands from marketing tools into iconic standards of integrity and performance, transmitting to employees and others on the inside a clear idea of company goals and expectations.

The internet is becoming a vital test-bed of these sorts of raised ambitions for brands. As web-based ventures fight to differentiate themselves and to win a lasting role on the consumer horizon, they are accelerating the pace of branding and providing a unique laboratory for watching pure brands at work.

Finally, in a society in which some people are losing their hold on traditional institutions, many are grasping at commercial identities for permanence and meaning. As unfortunate as this may seem, it does not necessarily constitute a crisis. After all, civilization has not always been terribly well served by traditional institutions. In any case, no amount of sign-carrying or brick-throwing will change this reality. Brands are here to stay. They form an integral and valuable component of the existing economic system, for which no superior alternative is presently on offer. Rather than vaguely wishing they would disappear, the best way to deal with brands is to find ways to elevate and transform them into a force for progress.

> **"The best way to deal with brands is to find ways to elevate and transform them into a force for progress."**

BRANDING'S SOCIAL PARADOX

In a strange way, anti-brand activism is helping to do this. By contributing to an environment in which a powerful brand presents its handlers with as many risks as it does opportunities, the enemies of branding are doing business a favour. Brands function today in a social paradox that gives their owners a compelling incentive to be more circumspect about their activities than they might be in the absence of strong brands. In this way, brands are being made to hold their owners more accountable, and potentially to make them more aware of the impact of their activities on the broader public and the planet.

In the information society, brands are coming to be seen as guardians, not only of market share, but of the essential humanity of the goods, services and companies that they represent. This is a crucial expansion of the brand's role, and one with which a few leaders are just beginning to come to grips.

In the new world of branding, a company that lives and dies by the strength of its brand can ill afford to make mistakes. Skimping on the production line, misbehaving as a corporate citizen or employer, losing sight of a brand's core values or handling a brand in a way that turns off customers risks damaging its value, putting it in play or otherwise dulling its competitive edge. Damage of this sort can hit with blinding speed these days, thanks to the internet, consumers who are smarter than ever and an aggressive press that pounces on the slightest corporate miscues. Even a decade ago, these perils were much less extreme.

The potential dangers posed by the public exposure that strong brands bring to their owners could be greatly aggravated by the arrival of a serious economic downturn. Recessions are unkind to brands and, despite years of expansion throughout the 1990s and into the 2000s, a downturn is bound to come some day.

Facing up to these present and future challenges means not just talking the talk on brands, but walking the walk. It means putting brands in a central place in the company. It means keeping the brand in clear view when evaluating projects and decisions. It means implementing some of the valuable systems for brand management and brand building presented by experts who study brands closely.

On a very basic level, it means viewing brands as people, or employees, not as conceptual constructs. Brands in many ways are like people. They are born. They get started in life and begin their careers. They may soar to success; struggle in mediocrity; or fail utterly. Some live longer than others. A few may even seem immortal. But in time all brands age, fade away and die. Through their lives, brands can generate value or they can impose costs. They can make mistakes and have good luck and bad. Most importantly, they can build relationships with real people, who have opinions and feelings about them. Those opinions and feelings may be positive or negative, but most often they are a complicated mix that is difficult to understand.

In today's world a brand occupies a space on the consumer landscape much like that of a person. It may be a reassuring friend, a pompous hypocrite, a seductive flirt, an inspiring leader or an irritating nag. It may excite, anger, confuse, comfort, challenge, annoy. Often a brand is just another face in the crowd that no one notices much at all.

'People don't necessarily have relationships with corporations, but they do have relationships with brands that might symbolize corporations or what the corporation produces', observed Rita Clifton, CEO of consulting firm Interbrand. She went on:

'When you get into group discussions, consumers talk about brands like people. They can describe their personalities. They can say, if this brand came to life, it would be this colour, this age. People talk about brands as friends.'

That is the parting message of this book for business managers who deal with brands – try looking at your brands as people. Not as symbolic abstractions or communication packages or messages or cost centres or any of the dozens of other descriptions used by marketing experts.

❝Understanding a brand is as difficult as understanding a person. ❞

Yes, brands are all those things, of course. But brands are more complex than any of those things. They have personalities, problems, strengths and intangible characteristics that are impossible to capture in a simple balance-sheet entry or a handy textbook definition. Understanding a brand is as difficult as understanding a person.

In looking at brands as people, you should also look at them as employees – quite possibly the most sensitive and important employees a company can have. Unlike a salesperson whose handling and presentation of a brand filter through their individual personality, the brand's personality is your business's personality as outsiders see it. It may not seem that way to the business manager looking out at the rest of the world from inside a company. But that's how it looks to consumers. To them, your brand *is* your business. Make that brand into an interesting, capable and appealing person that can genuinely be trusted, respected and relied upon and it will make lasting friends of consumers.

BIBLIOGRAPHY

Aaker, David, *Managing Brand Equity: Capitalizing on the Value of a Brand Name*, New York: Free Press, 1991.

Aaker, David, *Building Strong Brands*, New York: Free Press, 1996.

Aaker, David, and Joachimsthaler, Erich, *Brand Leadership*, New York: Free Press, 2000.

Arnold, David, *The Handbook of Brand Management*, New York: Perseus, 1992.

Butterfield, Leslie, and Haigh, David, *Understanding the Financial Value of Brands*, London: Brand Finance, 1998.

Carpenter, Phil, *eBrands: Building an Internet Business at Breakneck Speed*, Boston: Harvard Business School, 2000.

Clifton, Rita, and Maughan, Esther (eds), *The Future of Brands: Twenty-five Visions*, London: Macmillan, 2000.

Dearlove, Des, and Crainer, Stuart, *The Ultimate Book of Business Brands: Insights from the World's 50 Greatest Brands*, Oxford: Capstone, 1999.

Eisner, Michael, and Schwartz, Tony, *Work in Progress*, New York: Penguin, 1998.

Forden, Sara Gay, *The House of Gucci: A Sensational Story of Murder, Madness, Glamour and Greed*, New York: William Morrow, 2000.

Hart, Susannah, and Murphy, John (eds), *Brands: The New Wealth Creators*, London: Macmillan, 1998.

Harvard Business Review, *Harvard Business Review on Brand Management*, Boston: Harvard Business School Press, 1999.

Interbrand, *The World's Most Valuable Brands 2000: Interbrand's Annual Survey*, London: Interbrand, July 2000 (www.interbrand.com/valuebrands.html).

Kapferer, Jean-Noël, *Strategic Brand Management: Creating and Sustaining Brand Equity Long Term*, 2nd ed., London: Kogan Page, 1997.

Keller, Kevin Lane, *Strategic Brand Management: Building, Measuring and Managing Brand Equity*, Upper Saddle River, New Jersey: Prentice Hall, 1998.

Klein, Naomi, *No Logo: Taking Aim at the Brand Bullies*, New York: Picador, 1999.

Lasn, Kalle, *Culture Jam: The Uncooling of America*, New York: William Morrow and Co., 1999.

Masters, Kim, *The Keys to the Kingdom: How Michael Eisner Lost His Grip*, New York: HarperCollins, 2000.

Ortega, Bob, *In Sam We Trust: The Untold Story of Sam Walton and How Wal-Mart is Devouring the World*, London: Kogan Page, 1999.

Peters, Tom, *The Circle of Innovation*, New York: Alfred A. Knopf, 1997.

Pugh, Peter, *The Magic of a Name: The Rolls-Royce Story, The First 40 Years*, Cambridge: Icon Books, 2000.

Schwartz, Evan, *Digital Darwinism, Seven Breakthrough Business Strategies for Surviving in the Cutthroat Web Economy*, New York: Penguin, 1999.

Strasser, J.B., and Becklund, Laurie, *Swoosh: The Unauthorized Story of Nike and the Men Who Played There*, New York: HarperCollins, 1991.

Swasy, Alecia, *Soap Opera: The Inside Story of Procter & Gamble, New York*: Touchstone, 1993.

Trevillion, Kylie, and Perrier, Raymond, 'Brand Valuation: A Practical Guide', *Accountants' Digest*, Issue 405, London: The Institute of Chartered Accountants, March 1999.

INDEX